THE
LITTLE GIRL
WHO FOUGHT
THE GREAT
DEPRESSION

JOHN F. KASSON

THE LITTLE GIRL WHO FOUGHT THE GREAT DEPRESSION

SHIRLEY TEMPLE

AND 1930S AMERICA

W. W. NORTON & COMPANY

New York • *London*

For information about permission to reproduce selections from this
book, write to Permissions, W. W. Norton & Company, Inc.,
500 Fifth Avenue, New York, NY 10110

For information about special discounts for bulk
purchases, please contact W. W. Norton Special Sales at
specialsales@wwnorton.com or 800-233-4830

Manufacturing by RR Donnelley, Harrisonburg
Production manager: Devon Zahn

Library of Congress Cataloging-in-Publication Data

Kasson, John F., 1944–
The little girl who fought the Great Depression : Shirley Temple and 1930s
America / John F. Kasson. — First edition.
     pages cm
  Includes bibliographical references and index.
  ISBN 978-0-393-24079-5 (hardcover)
  1. Temple, Shirley, 1928– 2. Motion picture actors and actresses—United
States—Biography. 3. Popular culture—United States—History—20th centu-
ry. 4. United States—Civilization—1918–1945. 5. United States—Intellectual
life—20th century. 6. Depressions—1929—United States. 7. United States—
History—1933–1945. 8. United States—History—1919–1933. I. Title.
  PN2287.T33K37 2014
  791.43'028'0924—dc23
  [B]
                                      2013049983

W. W. Norton & Company, Inc.
500 Fifth Avenue, New York, N.Y. 10110
www.wwnorton.com

W. W. Norton & Company Ltd.
Castle House, 75/76 Wells Street, London W1T 3QT

1 2 3 4 5 6 7 8 9 0

To Peter and Laura,

For the gift of their childhood, mature wisdom,
and sustaining love,

To William E. Leuchtenburg,

For his friendship, scholarship, and inspiring example,

And to Joy,

For everything!

CONTENTS

THE
LITTLE GIRL
WHO FOUGHT
THE GREAT
DEPRESSION

Smiling through the Great Depression: Shirley Temple, 1935.
(Photofest/Twentieth Century–Fox)

INTRODUCTION

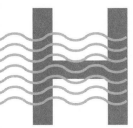er image appeared in periodicals and advertisements roughly twenty times daily, rivaling President Franklin Roosevelt and the United Kingdom's Edward VIII (formerly Prince of Wales and later Duke of Windsor) as the most photographed person in the world. Her portrait brightened a poor black laborer's cabin in lowland South Carolina, the mantel of the tumbledown house of a poor white childless couple in North Carolina, the living room mantel of preteen Andy Warhol's house in Pittsburgh, the recreation room of Federal Bureau of Investigation director J. Edgar Hoover's house in Washington, D.C., and the bureau of notorious numbers gangster Ellsworth "Bumpy" Johnson's Harlem apartment. A few years later her smile cheered the secret bedchamber of Anne Frank in Amsterdam as she hid with her family from the Nazis.[1]

Conventional histories of the 1930s draw their emblematic faces from the period's distinguished documentary photographers, such as Dorothea Lange's careworn woman known as "Migrant Mother." Yet the most popular and cherished images of the period were smiling ones, and the most popular and memorable of all were of the child actress Shirley Temple. At a time when movie attendance knit Americans into a truly national popular culture, they did not want a mirror of deep deprivation and despair held up to them but a ray of sunshine cast on their faces. In fact, such conspicuous demonstrations of confidence characterized the Great Depression, as President Roosevelt extended the politics of cheer deeply into the private lives of citizens and Shirley Temple did so into the private lives of even the youngest consumers. The complex and paradoxical effects of these efforts are with us still.

The emotional resiliency embodied in the smiles of Shirley Temple, Franklin Roosevelt, Bill "Bojangles" Robinson, and others in this decade has been largely taken for granted. Yet such smiling figures repay close investigation. They yield important insights into the character of American life during the greatest peacetime crisis in American history. They have broader implications for modern culture as well. "We can see emotional expressions as a medium of exchange," the sociologist Arlie Russell Hochschild has written. "Like paper money, many smiles and frowns are in circulation."[2]

The circulation of a new emotional currency during the Great Depression formed a little-understood but essential part of the nation's recovery, a sort of deficit spending with immense effects. In a time of great financial hardship, spending on amusements actually increased—eloquent testimony to its emotional necessity. Satisfying the craving of many deep in need of emotional loans and replenishments challenged political leaders and entertainers alike. The politician who succeeded most effectively was Franklin D. Roosevelt. The entertainer who did so most spectacularly was a little girl, Shirley Temple. Born in April 1928 in Santa Monica, California, to Gertrude and George Temple, Shirley began her film career at age three. Her performances attracted little notice until April 1934, the month she turned six. Then, with the release of Fox Film's *Stand Up and Cheer!*, she catapulted to stardom. But what distinguished her from every other Hollywood star of the period—and everyone since—was how brilliantly she shone. For the next six years, before she left Twentieth Century–Fox in 1940, she made twenty-two feature films. Through four of those years, from 1935 through 1938, she was the most popular star at the box office both within the United States and worldwide, a record never equaled. At the end of this energetic period of performances (which would continue at a lesser pace through the 1940s), she was still under the age of twelve.

In all of her major roles in the 1930s Shirley's central task was emo-

Shirley Temple holds an autographed portrait of FDR, November 14, 1935.
(© Bettmann/Corbis)

tional healing. She mended the rifts of estranged lovers, family members, old-fashioned and modern ways, warring peoples, and clashing cultures. She accomplished these feats not by ingenious stratagems but by trusting to her inexhaustible fund of optimism. No loss ever troubled her for long, even the death of a parent or reversal of fortunes. No scolding matron or miser could dampen her mood. Money could not buy happiness, she repeatedly reminded audiences, and, although she often wore exquisite clothes and bounced between cramped quarters and palatial settings, riches never turned her head. She treated the lowly with kindness and approached the mighty without intimidation. Characteristically lacking one or both parents, she relied not on institutional charity (frequently personified by desiccated killjoys) but on the doting protection that she magically released from hardened soldiers, harried executives, vaudeville veterans, impeccable butlers, imperious aunts, grumpy grandfathers, courting couples—almost anyone with a heart. A tireless worker when the situation demanded, she could spontaneously tap-dance with a partner such as Bill "Bojangles" Robinson and sing a cheerful ditty or a tender love song. While gracious and polite, she delighted in subverting stuffy decorum by sliding down a banister or popping a paper bag in a sepulchral men's club. She bubbled over with laughter, especially at herself. Amid gloom, she encouraged everyone to keep on the sunny side of life. Bromidic as philosophy, vacuous as social critique, her example was nonetheless immensely satisfying as entertainment. As such, it exerted a phenomenal appeal in an especially anxious decade, and it continues to remind us that Hollywood escapism in the Great Depression was never empty. Rather it brimmed with pleasures that both diverted and sustained moviegoers within the United States and through much of the rest of the world.

Like other movie actors of the period, Shirley Temple functioned as a persona effectively created, owned, and operated by the studio for which she worked, and most of her waking life was devoted to playing the part of a girl whom fans would find irresistible. Even as the Roosevelt administration sought to curtail exploitative child labor practices, it made a major exception for child acting, and both FDR and Eleanor Roosevelt heartily endorsed Shirley. Children still held an important place in the economy, but increasingly as consumers rather than producers, and particularly as beneficiaries of adult spending. As the most famous and commodified child in the world, Shirley Temple played a pivotal role in this revolution. She became a cultural fetish, whose likeness and outfits were endowed with magical properties, even as her role in producing that fetish was obscured.

Not only were Shirley and her parents transformed by Hollywood's star machinery, so too were her fans and their families. All came to view themselves and one another through the lens of celebrity. As a result, the rays of Shirley's star penetrated the deepest recesses of family life, recasting the terms by which parents valued their own daughters and those daughters imagined themselves. Within a year of Shirley's breakthrough in 1934, hers was the second most popular girl's name in the country. Twentieth Century–Fox staged promotional events, such as Shirley Temple look-alike contests and birthday parties, to solidify her bonds with individuals, families, and even entire communities, as when twelve thousand members of an Illinois town signed a congratulatory birthday telegram to Shirley. She quickly became the most adored and imitated child in the world. In Cuba contestants vied for the accolade of "la Shirley Temple Cubana." A Tokyo newspaper reported a young girl on the street discovered as "the Japanese Shirley Temple." Throughout the country and around the world, using every ploy that they could devise, movie theaters joined with merchandisers to promote Shirley Temple's latest film and licensed products. Her power and presence could be purchased in Shirley Temple dolls, dresses, underwear, coats, hats, shoes, soap, books, tableware, and similar items. Her face beamed from cereal boxes and cobalt blue plates and mugs. Ideal Novelty and Toy Company's Shirley Temple dolls accounted for almost a third of all dolls sold in the United States in 1935. Sheet music of her songs, such as "On the Good Ship Lollipop" and "Polly-Wolly-Doodle," led the sales charts. Newspapers around the globe bulged with Shirley Temple stories, as did movie magazines such as *Photoplay*, *Modern Screen*, and *Silver Screen*, each of which claimed a circulation of roughly half a million.[3]

Shirley's immense popularity reveals much about the ways in which Americans and many others around the world coped with the demands of this pivotal decade. The bright arc of her celebrity illuminates the dynamic relationship between the Hollywood film industry and movie fans, and between Shirley's performances and fans' dreams, as well as among those fans, the studio system, and the Temple family itself. Altogether, Shirley Temple allows us to explore the intricacies of Hollywood and consumer culture in the Great Depression more fully and freshly than any other figure of the decade. By placing Shirley Temple and her fans within the context of FDR and his constituents, we can see how popular entertainment as well as New Deal politics helped Americans to surmount the Great Depression. The forces set in motion by their smiling faces have shaped American life ever since.

CHAPTER 1
SMILE LIKE ROOSEVELT

In 1910 Gertrude Krieger and George Temple met at Henry K. Kramer's dancing cotillion for adults in Los Angeles. Actually, she was not yet an adult but a shy, willowy seventeen-year-old high school junior with jet-black hair. She loved to dance, and the large ballroom playing phonograph records gave her an irresistible outlet. Still, she nervously entered this public stage, and to steady her resolve, she came hand in hand with a female classmate.[1]

Soon a short, compactly built young man of twenty-two approached. Not her equal in height, he nonetheless had a muscular body, an easy smile, an affable manner, and a fondness for bad puns. A snappy dresser, belying his modest clerk's salary, he wore a three-piece suit and pearl-gray spats. He danced energetically if awkwardly, lead arm pumping up and down, no match for her in grace or practice. He immediately liked Gertrude and determined to make her like him. Gradually, she did.

Both had moved to Los Angeles in 1903 as children with their families, she from Chicago, he from Pennsylvania. Each had also lost a father and known financial uncertainty. By that fateful day in 1910 when George met Gertrude at the cotillion, he was still living with his mother and, along with his elder siblings, helping to support her. George and his sister, Grace, worked at the Southern California Edison Company, he as a clerk, she as a stenographer, while George's older brother, Herbert, clerked in a hardware store, and younger brother Francis soon took a job as a messenger. For her part, within a year of their first dance, Gertrude was helping to pay her family's bills as a stenographer.[2]

George and Gertrude married in 1913 and started their own household. Gertrude bore their first son, Jack (John), in 1915 and Sonny (George Francis Jr.) four years later. Yet family ties continued to bind. Gertrude's mother, Maude, chain-smoking, sharply opinionated, bossy, increasingly morose, would live with or near her daughter and son-in-law and be supported by them for the rest of her life. Both the Temple and Krieger families knew how parents and children often had to pull together to sustain one another.

Still, all about them they could witness the boom of Los Angeles's economy of oil, agriculture, maritime trade, banking, industrial manufacture, construction, moviemaking, and tourism. During the 1920s the city expanded by roughly eighty square miles through forty-five separate annexations. Newcomers poured into the county at the rate of 350 a day for ten years, and the city more than doubled its population from 577,000 to almost 1.24 million, making it the fifth largest in the country. Residents basked in what one journalist called "an easy optimism. . . . Anything seems possible; the future is yours, and the past?—there isn't any."[3]

George could confirm this optimism in the incremental improvements of his family's life. To aid his advancement, he supplemented his limited education with night-school and correspondence courses in typing, bookkeeping, and accounting. By 1920 he had inched his way up to chief clerk for Southern California Edison and lived with his wife and young sons at 419½ Ocean Front Avenue, along with other white transplants from the Midwest and East, in the suburban beach resort of Venice. A year later, the family moved a short way to what were probably larger quarters at 125 Breeze Avenue. And by 1927 they resided in a stucco bungalow with a radio in the living room and a car in the garage in the quieter town of Santa Monica. George now worked as assistant branch manager for California Bank, where the city and the country's speculative frenzy mounted almost day by day.

That year Gertrude Temple made a fateful resolution. In her mind it was not merely a hope but a determination: she and her husband would conceive a third child, that child would be a girl, ideally with naturally curly blond hair, and she would be named Shirley. The frustrated ballerina and movie-entranced mother launched her daughter's career in the womb by exposing her to classical music, uplifting literature, great works of art, scenes of natural beauty, and romantic films. Her resolution and faith in prenatal aesthetic influences tapped popular beliefs and placed her within a tradition of stage and screen mothers who claimed to have willed their children into existence.[4]

A dimpled, brown-eyed Shirley Temple was duly born on April 23, 1928. She immediately became her mother's pet project, displacing her older brothers as the center of Gertrude's life. George too delighted in indulging his little girl, and, at age forty, he could confidently anticipate his family and career humming smoothly onward. After all, the economy boomed as never before, and its future glowed brightly. A lifelong Republican, as was Gertrude, George could also feel the city, the state, and the country's government in the secure hands of the Grand Old Party. Indeed, the 1928 Republican presidential nominee, Herbert Hoover, himself a Californian and a self-made multimillionaire, epitomized sober, steady leadership.

Few national leaders in 1928 inspired confidence as did Herbert Hoover. For over a decade he had been one of the most respected figures in American government, and for almost two decades one especially praised for his ability to deal with calamities, whether of famine or flood. During the Great War, he spearheaded private food relief to German-occupied Belgium and coordinated American efforts to increase food supplies for U.S. troops and underfed allied nations, then organized food relief for millions starving in Central Europe at war's end and in famished Russia in 1921. When, in the greatest natural disaster in American history, the Mississippi River flood of 1927 created a vast inland brown sea a thousand miles long and fifty miles wide, Hoover again took center stage in directing public and private efforts to help victims and stamp out disease. As secretary of commerce in both the Harding and Coolidge administrations, he was perhaps the most dynamic of all cabinet officials. Had his public career ended then, he would have been celebrated in history as a brilliant administrator and one of the greatest humanitarians of his time.

In the context of the 1920s, Hoover's very colorlessness befitted his technocratic competence. The financial titan Bernard Baruch, who had served as head of the War Industries Board during the Great War, said admiringly, "To Hoover's brain facts are as water to a sponge. They are absorbed into every tiny interstice." A longtime friend and member of Hoover's cabinet, Ray Lyman Wilbur, likened Hoover's mind to a searchlight that he could turn full-blast onto any subject at will. "Sedate, laconic, undramatic, berating nobody, asserting nothing that his laboriously gathered facts and figures would not sustain," in the words of a Washington reporter, Hoover provided a figure of immense security amid the vicissitudes of the Jazz Age. In the public mind, he seemed to be a man who had "never known failure."[5]

The presidential election of 1928 was his first campaign for elective office, and Hoover's overriding theme was prosperity. In accepting the Republican nomination, he painted a vision of a nation steadily climbing on a broad, smooth highway through pastures of plenty. His honeyed words would quickly acquire a bitter aftertaste: "We in America today are nearer to the final triumph over poverty than ever before in the history of any land. The poorhouse is vanishing from among us. We have not yet reached the goal, but, given a chance to go forward with the policies of the last 8 years, we shall soon with the help of God be in sight of the day when poverty will be banished from this Nation."[6] Running against New York governor Alfred E. Smith,

Hoover achieved one of the most sweeping victories in modern American history. With 58 percent of the popular vote, he won forty states (including four in the hitherto solidly Democratic South) and 444 electoral votes to Smith's eight states and 87 electoral votes.

Less than eight months after Hoover's inauguration, beginning on October 23 and tracing a jagged but inexorable descent, the New York stock market crashed. By mid-November, the Dow Jones index of industrial stocks, which had climbed to a dizzying peak of 381.17 on September 3, plunged to 198.60 by the closing bell on November 13—a loss of 48 percent. By any measure, this was a panic.

Hoover, along with others in government, banking, and industry, tried to calm investors. Seeking to minimize the crash, he first termed it a recession, then, in preference to the term "panic," a depression. The country had seen depressions before, including the devastating Panic of 1893 and, most recently, the recessions of 1907 and 1920–22. Hoover thought the nation was in far better shape to deal with this one than it had been previously. In his annual message to Congress on December 3, 1929, he described the economy as fundamentally sound. The nation's woes, he made clear, were more psychological than structural. "The long upward trend of fundamental progress" had induced "over-optimism" and hence "a wave of uncontrolled speculation in securities, resulting in the diversion of capital from business to the stock market and the inevitable crash." Now giddy optimism had yielded to "unwarranted pessimism and fear." He reassured the nation that the Federal Reserve System, the strength of American banks, and the cooperative efforts of business institutions and state and local governments protected the economy from the depressions of earlier times. The panic was over. "We have reestablished confidence." Nonetheless, by the end of the month, industrial production had fallen 12 percent from its peak the previous June.[7]

As Hoover and others continued to beat the drum of confidence, the stock market revived and shuffled upward. By April 17, 1930, the

Dow Jones average had climbed nearly a hundred points (to 294.07), recovering almost 40 percent of its losses. Nonetheless, employment and national productivity had started to slide in the summer of 1929, months before the October stock market crash, and, together with credit and prices, they continued their slump. In early March Hoover predicted that "the worst effects of the crash upon unemployment will have been passed in the next sixty days." Again in May, as his sixty-day prediction came due, he declared the country had "passed the worst of the great economic storm."[8]

Hoover's calls for confidence in the fundamental soundness of the American economy and the character of the American people were accompanied by impatient dismissals of his critics. "Gentlemen, you have come sixty days too late," he snapped in June 1930 to one delegation of concerned citizens representing the National Catholic Welfare Conference. "The depression is over." In fact, the Depression was rapidly spreading across the globe, affecting virtually every important economy except the Soviet Union.[9]

By October 1930, Hoover's words changed somewhat, but his insistent tune and beat remained the same. Now, he acknowledged, "This depression is world-wide. Its causes and its effects lie only partly in the United States." Still, he emphasized the fundamental strength of American banking and business institutions to achieve new levels of prosperity for all. "I always have been, and I remain, an unquenchable believer in the resistless, dynamic power of American enterprise." At this time the humorist Will Rogers said, "There has been more 'optimism' talked and less practiced than at any time during our history."[10]

In fact, pessimism once again turned to panic. In November 1930 a rush of depositors overwhelmed Louisville's National Bank of Kentucky. The panic rapidly spread to affiliated banks in Indiana, Illinois, and Missouri, and then to Arkansas, Iowa, and North Carolina. By December the crisis of confidence forced New York City's Bank of United States to lock its doors in the largest commercial bank failure in American history up to that time. Although it was a private corporation, its name misled many to regard it as a national institution, further shaking confidence. The inability of the Federal Reserve System to mount a successful rescue deepened the dread. Still, the optimistic talk continued. Hoover and members of his cabinet, along with many leading industrialists and financial leaders, kept insisting that the worst of the Depression had passed and that recovery was imminent. Meanwhile, the gross national product declined from $181.8 billion in 1929 to 164.5 billion in 1930 and then to 153.0 in 1931. Jobs steadily disappeared. In 1929 only 3.2 percent of the labor force was totally unemployed. Their ranks swelled to 8.7 percent in 1930 and to 15.9 percent in 1931. The percentages of the partially employed grew even faster, as more and more industries cut production.[11]

Even Will Rogers's witticisms could not compete with some news stories. Toward the end of 1931 the journalist Edward Angly compiled a short book of roseate predictions by Republican officials and business leaders, interlarded with statistics of plunging markets and closing factories. It bore the mocking title *Oh Yeah?* and included the following entry attributed to Simeon D. Fess, chairman of the Republican National Committee:

> Persons high in Republican circles are beginning to believe that there is some concerted effort on foot to utilize the stock market as a method of discrediting the administration. Every time an Administration official gives out an optimistic statement about business conditions, the market immediately drops.[12]

In response, Hoover redoubled his cheerleading efforts. In March 1931 he appointed a new press secretary, Theodore Joslin, who tried to amplify the president's message. "Ninety per cent of our difficulty in depressions is caused by fear," Hoover insisted to Joslin. "What I want to do is to mitigate the effect of the recent crash and get back on to the road to recovery as quickly as possible. We must cushion this crash and we must restore confidence. And there should be confidence, for our country is fundamentally sound."[13]

For the last three years of his administration, Hoover, Vice President Charles Curtis, and cabinet secretaries maintained their chorus of confidence in the nation's economic health, even as the economy slumped and shrank. The mainspring of recovery, Hoover insisted, could not be the federal government. As he said in his December 1931 State of the Union Address, it lay with local governments (by now impossibly ill-equipped) and the isolated individual. In a radio speech four months later, New York governor Franklin Roosevelt directly challenged such a view when he called for governmental aid to "the forgotten man at the bottom of the economic pyramid."[14]

Meanwhile, in private, Hoover protested that he was unfairly blamed for the Depression when, as secretary of commerce and president, he believed he had done more than anyone else to avert the disaster. Profanely excoriating politicians of both parties and leaders of foreign governments, whom he regarded as the real culprits, he demanded, "Is it my fault that cheap politicians [and] selfish men over the whole world have refused to see the folly of their policies until it was too late?"[15]

No doubt in 1930, perhaps in 1931, possibly even into 1932, Hoover felt he had successfully dealt with far worse crises before in his career, restored hope, mobilized voluntary and governmental efforts, and, indeed, emerged a hero in the process. Yet as the economy's inexorable plunge continued, the limitations of Hoover's political vision and faith in voluntarism were severely exposed. By 1932 he grudgingly found himself forced to accede to innovations that he would earlier have regarded as dangerously radical, most notably the Reconstruction Finance Corporation, which provided aid to state and local governments and loans to banks, railroads, and other businesses. Although he had never been a strict exponent of laissez-faire capitalism, as he shifted his positions, he accompanied his moves with petulant stubbornness, exaggerating differences rather than aiming for common ground with others.

The deepening crisis starkly exposed the limitations of Hoover's personality. Born into a dour Quaker household in West Branch, Iowa, he lost his father, a tall, bearded, enterprising blacksmith who had risen to be a farm implements dealer, at the age of six. His mother lived for three more years, but from the time of his father's death through the rest of his childhood, he was shunted off to a series of uncles and other relatives, spending the last six working for his cold, calculating, and demanding uncle in Oregon. A profound sense of loneliness gripped him, and the chill of it lasted throughout his life.

As a mining engineer, manager, and financier, he quickly became a rich man, but success never thawed the laconic, brusque bearing of Hoover's youth or truly infused him with optimism. "If you want to get the gloomiest view of any subject on earth, ask Bert about it," his wife once said." The famous newspaper editor and Progressive Republican William Allen White described him as "constitutionally gloomy, a congenital pessimist who always saw the doleful side of any situation." Gutzon Borglum, the creator of Mount Rushmore, quipped, "If you put a rose in Hoover's hand it would wilt."[16]

From the beginning of his presidency, Hoover worked relentlessly, rising early in the morning and continuing to work into the night in bed, often waking up after two hours and working some more, sleeping only five or six hours. As the Depression engulfed him, he quickened his pace and slept as little as three hours a night. Members of his staff marveled at his stamina even as they feared he would collapse under the constant strain. The chief usher of the White House remembered, "He [Hoover] would go about, never speaking to any of the help. Never a good-morning or even a nod of the head. Never a Merry Christmas or a Happy New Year. All days were alike to him. Sunday was no exception, for he worked just as hard on that day if not harder than on any of the others. There was always a frown on his face and a look of worry."[17] In official meetings, said an associate, Hoover had a "persistent habit of not looking at one squarely when in conversation, and of doodling steadily the while. It gave one the impression that he was not much interested in what was being said and did not want anyone to know what he was thinking." As the economic crisis grew deeper, Hoover's mood also sank. After one particularly gloomy meeting, Secretary of State Henry L. Stimson confided to his diary, "The President was tired and . . . went through all the blackest surmises. . . . It was like sitting in a bath of ink to sit in his room."[18]

Hoover's doughy face was creased with a brow knitted in worry and a frown. He was distrustful and ill at ease with reporters, and the White House press corps fully reciprocated the feeling. As the Depression plunged further, his temper sometimes flared, so that one reporter dubbed him "our most peevish president." Hoover's press secretary, Theodore Joslin, wrote in his diary, "There is almost as much love lost between the president and the press as between God Almighty and the devil himself."[19]

Hoover disdained what he thought of as political theatrics, saying, "This is not a showman's job. I will not step out of character." True to his word, he was obstinately undramatic. In his speech accepting the Republican presidential nomination in August 1932, he all but extinguished applause, a British reporter noted, with his personality's "dispiriting influence . . . , his unprepossessing exterior, his sour, puckered face of a bilious baby, his dreary, nasal monotone reading interminably, and for the most part inaudibly, from a typescript without a single inflection of a voice or gesture to relieve the tedium."[20]

On the radio, he was even worse. "In his own mind, he had been elected to look after the nation's affairs, not to jabber into a microphone." His delivery made scant concession even to live audiences, and "the millions who listened over the radio were just eavesdroppers." Once, when asked by a woman if he did not get a thrill delivering an address over the radio, he replied, "The same thrill that I get when I rehearse an address to a door knob."[21]

The deepening economic crisis gradually transmogrified Hoover's reputation from expertise to ineptitude, from competence to incomprehension, from humanitarian savior to heartless bystander. For the rest of his long life Hoover protested that such characterizations were simplistic and unjust, but they stuck indelibly in public memory. His stiff bearing, immobile features, and shy, undemonstrative personality, refreshing in the context of 1920s ballyhoo and bluster, soon appeared to be a sign of cold indifference. A man of strong charitable impulses and personal tenderness, Hoover could not bear to look at the down-and-out people standing in breadlines or selling apples (including an estimated six thousand such vendors in New York City), let alone to greet and comfort them. Even in hindsight, he insistently regarded such desperate figures as emblems of opportunity. "Many persons left their jobs for the more profitable one of selling apples," he blandly wrote in his *Memoirs*.[22]

His appeals for good cheer came to seem feckless, even desperate, coming as they did from a man whose credibility was widely suspect and who was the embodiment of gloom. In February 1931 he told a reporter that "if the newspapers would quit talking about unemployment," the Depression would speedily lift. His remedy was simple: "What the country needs is a good, big laugh. . . . There seems to be a condition of hysteria. If some one could get off a good joke every ten days, I think our troubles would be over." He made similar appeals for a "resoundingly good new joke" to others, ranging from the old vaudevillians Joe Weber and Lew Fields to Will Rogers. He variously added that the country needed a "great poem" and a "good song."[23] To the rapidly swelling army of the unemployed, such prescriptions seemed as helpful as tossing a drowning man a whoopee cushion instead of a lifesaver.

For such feeble efforts, his own name became a sarcasm, mocking his 1928 campaign slogan "Vote for Prosperity" and his bromidic statements on the fundamental soundness of the American economy. Shantytowns were called Hoovervilles, freight cars providing shelter Hoover Pullmans, a newspaper warming the homeless a Hoover blanket, an out-turned trouser pocket a Hoover flag.

To many, the man who had brought food to millions of starving people earlier in his career now seemed deaf to the cries of want and misery throughout his own country. "No one is actually starving," he famously told a reporter in 1931, adding, "The hoboes, for example, are better fed than they have ever been. One hobo in New York got ten meals in one day." Rebuking such claims, the St. Louis blues musician Charley Jordan sang in his 1931 "Starvation Blues" of how he nearly had a square meal on a recent day—before a garbage worker came and hauled the trash can away.[24]

Around the country Americans were indeed dying from starvation and malnutrition, and, in contrast to Hoover's well-fed hobo, people ransacked garbage pails, fought over scraps in dumps, and begged on roads for food. Children frequently went hungry, at times eating only every other day, and they fell victim to deficiency diseases such as rickets and pellagra. In the Appalachian soft coal districts, miners and their families were often reduced to eating "bulldog gravy," a mixture of flour, water, and lard. In Philadelphia, during eleven days in April 1932, when no relief funds of any kind were available, one study documented how ninety-one families coped:

> One woman borrowed fifty cents, bought stale bread at three and one-half cents a loaf, and the family lived on it for eleven days. Another put the last food order into soup stock and vegetables and made a soup. When a member of the family was hungry, he ate as little as he could. Another picked up spoiled vegetables along the docks and except for three foodless days, the family ate them.

Another made a stew with her last food order, which she cooked over and over daily to keep it from spoiling. Another family lived on dandelions. Another on potatoes. Another had no food for two and one-half days. And one in ten of the women were pregnant and one in three of the children of nursing age.[25]

Because of his perceived insularity and aloofness, Hoover was ridiculed and despised as no other president had been since the days of the Civil War. Consumed by his responsibilities, he plunged into his reelection campaign only in October 1932, as he fought to preserve his policies from what he regarded as a woefully unprepared and ill-equipped opponent. Hoover privately thought Roosevelt was disqualified for the presidency on physical grounds alone, and the summer before the election his aides confidently predicted that the country would never elect a cripple. In the campaign, however, it was Roosevelt who seemed strong, vigorous, and magnetically confident, and Hoover who appeared weak, drained, even broken. As early as January 1932, when Hoover had been in office less than three years, *Time* magazine wrote that he had aged twenty: "His hair is greyer. His shoulders seem to droop in discouragement. The lines about his eyes have cut in deeper and those about his mouth have hardened."[26] In newsreels and newspaper photographs during the 1932 campaign, Hoover "invariably . . . appeared solemn and sad, an unhappy man, a man without hope. Instead of radiating confidence and good cheer in the presence of the economic crisis, his portraits made one want to sell short, get the money in gold, and bury it." As the campaign drew to a close, Hoover's deeply lidded red eyes and ashen expression gave him the appearance of a "walking corpse."[27]

By Election Day, the vaunted prosperity of 1929 seemed like another era. Real output had fallen close to 30 percent, and unemployment had reached at least 24 percent, or roughly one in four workers, not counting those working reduced hours. Despite this calamitous situation, Hoover professed hope: "The tide has turned and . . . the gigantic forces of depression are today in retreat." What the people should fear most, he emphasized, was a Roosevelt administration; in FDR's proposals for a New Deal he sniffed "the fumes of the witches' cauldron which boiled in Russia."[28]

Some crowds cheered, but many regarded Hoover sullenly or worse. On his final swing west in the closing weeks of the campaign, an angry mob menaced his train in Detroit, one of the cities hardest hit by the Depression, with an unemployment rate approaching 45 percent. Near Beloit, Wisconsin, his train ground to a standstill as a man was found pulling up spikes. At Elko, Nevada, the presidential railroad car was pelted with rotten eggs. Stink bombs greeted his entourage in San Francisco. As he prepared to cast his ballot near his home in Palo Alto, California, a telegram jeered, "Vote for Roosevelt and make it unanimous."[29]

The 1932 election turned Hoover's 1928 victory upside down. In 1928 Hoover had won the most colossal electoral majority in over a century. In 1932 his repudiation was devastating. In a Democratic landslide, Roosevelt carried all but six of the forty-eight states, for 472 electoral votes to Hoover's 59, and won 59 percent of the popular vote. In reporting the returns, *Time* magazine called Hoover "President Reject."[30]

The complex causes and cures of the Great Depression remain a vexed issue. The Depression was certainly not simply a crisis of confidence, as at times Hoover seemed to believe, but one of fundamental national policy and economic structures. Yet from the outset, numerous figures, including Republicans, Democrats, business leaders, and entertainers, agreed that the Depression was also an emotional crisis and that it needed to be addressed on emotional terms. Market economies are social institutions, after all, not simply constellations of natural forces. They depend on moral and social values, including confidence, trust, and expectations of stability.[31] All of these had taken a severe beating in the years since the stock market crash of October 1929. To reinvigorate these values was thus not a distraction or an escape. Because such values could be powerful forces in enlivening a paralyzed economy, to summon them forth was a potent political act.

For all the innovations of Franklin D. Roosevelt's extraordinary first hundred days in office, in which he sought to provide economic relief and recovery as quickly as possible, arguably the most immediate, essential, and enduring achievement was the fundamentally different emotional attitude he successfully projected: a contagious sense of optimism and purpose. As Frances Perkins, FDR's secretary of labor and longtime supporter, wrote in her memoirs, "When Franklin Roosevelt and his administration began their work in Washington in March 1933, the New Deal was not a plan with form and content. It was a happy phrase he had coined during the campaign, and its value was psychological. It made people feel better, and in that terrible period of depression they needed to feel better."[32]

Hoover and Roosevelt reflected not just two different understandings of the role of the federal government in the economy but also two fundamentally different conceptions of leadership, one bureaucratic, the other more charismatic. The contrast also revealed two markedly different appetites for aggressive innovation. It indicated two very different approaches to the popular media of the day. Hoover, in so many ways an embodiment of technocratic skills, approached the camera merely as a recording device and the radio as a transmitter. Roosevelt, cultivating his considerable charm and skills as an actor, brilliantly seized these same media and bent them to his own purposes. In so doing, Roosevelt helped to forge, as Hoover had devastatingly failed to do, a broad emotional alliance between the politics of the New Deal and broader national efforts, both populist and corporate, endeavoring to get people back on their feet, with renewed confidence, smiling once again, ready to work, to invest, and to spend.

Only a few weeks after Franklin Roosevelt's landslide victory, when the president-elect arrived at Warm Springs, Georgia, a reporter for the *Atlanta Constitution* observed, "After nearly a decade of grim visages and dour countenances the White House at Washington is about to adopt as its symbol a smile."[33] Indeed, Hoover's worried frown and Roosevelt's radiant smile epitomized their contrasting styles of presidential leadership. All that was warm, exuberant, ebullient, jaunty, optimistic, and hearty in FDR seemed cold, stiff, dour, pessimistic, and reserved in Hoover. Roosevelt's smile, and the voice, gestures, words, and spirit that accompanied it, were essential to his success, and a vital part of his political legacy. In fact, with Roosevelt the requisite emotional expression of American presidents permanently changed. Roosevelt grinned more effectively than any president before him, and he made a broad smile an essential element for every president since.

The basis of that smile was a natural gift, but its perfection was cultivated. Born in 1882 in Hyde Park, New York, to doting parents from families of immense wealth and privilege, Roosevelt enjoyed a childhood as different from Hoover's as imaginable. His father was a rich businessman with railroad and mining interests, who, in declining health, had abundant leisure to pursue his passion for horses and travel. His mother was not a dour Quaker minister but a patrician Delano Episcopalian. As an only child, he learned to charm adults and to hide or distract attention from physical and emotional discomfort. The villagers of Hyde Park, New York, treated Franklin and his family as local lords, doffing their caps when he and his father rode by, and addressing them as "Mister James" and "Master Franklin."[34]

Yet young Franklin was not a political natural. As a fledgling New York state senator, the man who became one of the greatest politicians in American history was notably lacking in charisma. Frances Perkins remembered "a vivid impression" of FDR when, as head of the New York Consumers League, she saw him in 1911 on the floor of the New York State Senate: "tall and slender, very active and alert, moving around the floor, going in and out of committee rooms, rarely talking with the members, who more or less avoided him, not particularly charming (that came later), artificially serious of face, rarely smiling, with an unfortunate habit—so natural that he was unaware of it—of throwing his head up. This, combined with his pince-nez and great height, gave him the appearance of looking down his nose at most people."[35]

Gradually, Roosevelt learned to shed his hauteur and to charm strangers and colleagues alike with a magnetic grin and ebullient personality. The transformation did not occur all at once. But by the time of the 1920 Democratic national convention in San Francisco, in which he received the nomination for vice president, he had learned, in Perkins's words, "how to feign the genial enthusiasm required to build the bridges he needed to advance his career."[36]

He envisioned that career with startling precision. In 1901, when Franklin was still a slender, narrow-shouldered, six-foot-one Harvard undergraduate, the elevation of his distant cousin (and future wife's uncle) Theodore to the presidency made him a role model, right down to his pince-nez spectacles. Franklin determined to follow TR's steps up the political ladder from the New York state legislature to assistant secretary of the navy to New York governor right on to the White House.[37] During the next two decades FDR steadily climbed the rungs according to plan, restively serving as assistant secretary of the navy in the Wilson administration, then in 1920 achieving national attention as the vice presidential candidate on the Democratic ticket (though suffering predictable defeat).

The sudden, apparently insuperable obstacle to achieving his goal, of course, was his contraction of poliomyelitis in August 1921. It was undoubtedly the great trial of his life, physically, emotionally, and professionally. While vacationing on Campobello Island, New Brunswick, with his family, he first experienced chills and fatigue, then weakness in one knee. Within two days he could no longer stand, and by the third, he was virtually paralyzed from the chest down, and the weakness extended to his shoulders, arms, and hands. His skin ached acutely. His vigorous body had suddenly become an inert throbbing mass. He lay in bed in excruciating torment, unable to sit up or turn himself from side to side, even to defecate or urinate without aid. His wife, Eleanor, who had not slept with him at least since her discovery in 1918 of his affair with her social secretary Lucy Mercer, now joined in an intense new intimacy. She shifted his body in bed, rubbed his back, buttocks, and useless legs, and inserted his enemas and catheter.[38]

For the next seven years, and, to a lesser degree, for the rest of his life, Roosevelt dedicated himself to his recovery. It was a long, arduous, painful effort. To keep his legs from bending grotesquely toward his hips as the paralyzed muscles tightened, attendants encased each leg in plaster and hammered wedges behind the knees in a torturous regimen lasting many days. Fitted with steel braces that weighed fourteen pounds and using crutches, he slowly mastered a rocking method of "walking," by which he swung one leg before him, regained a precarious balance, and then swung the other. He never complained. Indeed, he often exceeded his regimen and so did more harm than good. His greatest goal was to walk again unaided. It was a goal he never achieved but also one he never completely surrendered. Years later, Eleanor Roosevelt remarked, "You know that he has never said he could not walk."[39]

Recovery was a constant emotional and psychological struggle as well as a physical one. As Roosevelt toughened and thickened his upper body, acquiring the massive chest, back, arms, shoulders, and neck of a wrestler to assist in moving his heavy steel braces and shriveled, useless legs, so too did he develop new layers to his personality and manner. His reluctance to complain, easy smile, charm, talent for banter, and keen ambition—all were formidably brought to bear on his situation. He became supremely adroit at the social arts and psychological acts necessary to his recovery. These might be listed as a series of *d*'s: determination, discipline, denial, distraction, deception. Although he occasionally experienced waves of depression, he determinedly forced them down. In all of these, Roosevelt's smile was essential.

He used that smile from the outset. His doting mother, Sara, described in a letter her first meeting with her adored son after the illness:

> I got here yesterday at 1:30 and at once ... came up to a brave, smiling, and beautiful son, who said: 'Well, I'm glad you are back Mummy and I got up this party for you!' He had shaved himself and seems very bright and *keen*. Below his waist he cannot move at all. His legs (that I have always been proud of) have to be moved often as they ache when long in one position. He and Eleanor decided at once to be cheerful and the atmosphere of the house is all happiness, so I have fallen in and follow their glorious example. . . . They went into his room and I hear them all laughing, Eleanor in the lead.[40]

Similarly, his oldest son, James, then thirteen, later remembered how his father greeted his children from his sickbed, even as the paralysis still gripped his upper body: "He grinned at us, and he did his best to call out, or gasp out, some cheery response to our tremulous, just-this-side-of-tears greetings."[41]

In ensuing years, Roosevelt would perfect this hearty manner. Losing physical mobility and unable to command attention by his height as he once did, he learned to hold listeners by his powerful performance of geniality, confidence, and vitality. Waving his six-inch-long quill-stemmed cigarette holder to emphasize his points, pouring out stories, reminiscences, jokes, and gossip, he bathed listeners in a torrent of talk. Through his energetic voice, broad, expansive gestures, mobile face, ready laugh, and exuberant spirits, he gave an impression of great animation while sitting still. Keenly sensitive to potential embarrassment at his condition, he learned how to charm others and to sense their own foibles. Above all, he came to appreciate how powerful his example of triumph over adversity was, and, even to a degree among intimates, he learned to feign greater recovery than he had actually achieved.[42]

During his long convalescence Roosevelt continued to consolidate and extend his political power. When given the opportunity by the outgoing New York governor, Al Smith, to run for his post in 1928, after a brief hesitation, he seized it. As the Democratic presidential candidate that year, Smith was crushed in the Hoover landslide, but Roosevelt narrowly beat out his Republican opponent. FDR quickly put his own reform stamp on his administration and won easy reelection in 1930. Then, at the 1932 Democratic National Convention in Chicago, he deftly wrested the presidential nomination away from Smith and other rivals on the fourth ballot.

Also at the convention FDR's supporters snatched a theme song that was still warm from the grip of a Republican governor and proudly bestowed it on their candidate. "Happy Days Are Here Again" originated as the booming Technicolor finale number in MGM's largely black-and-white backstage musical *Chasing Rainbows* (1930), and it immediately became an anthem of cheer against the gloom of the Great Depression. Composed by Milton Ager in 4/4 time, the tune is eminently danceable as a two-step and even, in one 1930 rendition by Jack Hylton and His Orchestra, as a polka. Bidding farewell to gray skies and gloomy times, Jack Yellen's lyrics compel a smile as they greet the dawning of happy days.

California's Governor James "Sunny Jim" Rolph had made the piece his theme song, and the band played it in tribute to him at the 1932 Republican convention, in which he loyally supported Hoover. Nonetheless, after Roosevelt partisans triumphantly sang "Happy Days Are Here Again" as they clinched his nomination at the Democratic convention, the song became indelibly associated with FDR, and the phrase was a key one in Roosevelt's campaign. As much as his promise of a "new deal," it captured FDR's exuberant optimism.[43]

In the general campaign, barnstorming the country by train, speaking energetically and smiling broadly from the rear of his railroad car at each stop, Roosevelt attacked Hoover from every angle. "Roosevelt smiles and smiles and smiles and it doesn't get tiresome," wrote a reporter for the *Brooklyn Eagle*. "He can smile more than any man in American politics without being insipid." Yet not even all of FDR's admirers fully agreed with this assessment. In the words of two early analysts of the campaign, "Governor Roosevelt . . . almost overdid his charm; he smiled so broadly and he wagged his head so sincerely and spoke so appealingly and intimately that his more urbane admirers suffered acute distress. But the crowds liked him for all these posturings."[44]

By the time FDR took office on March 4, 1933, credit and credibility were at a low ebb. Industrial production as a whole had fallen by more than half since 1929, and in key industries such as steel and iron ore, the losses were far greater. Investment in new factories and machinery, $11 billion in 1929, was a meager $3 billion (in 1929 dollars) in 1933. Construction of new houses had fallen by more than 80 percent. Net income of farm production had declined by at least 70 percent. Total income of American workers in the form of wages and salaries was sliced by 42 percent from 1929 to 1933, and, of course, those cuts were quite unevenly shared, with millions losing everything. Overall income per capita had receded to where it had been three decades earlier, wiping out all of the gains since the 1890s. No one knows how many were out of work, but one in four, or fifteen million people, is a conservative estimate. Of these, millions were homeless, and many had turned migrants. The young suffered especially from unemployment, and the elderly also fared worse than the middle-aged. Those who suffered most of all in this respect were African Americans and

Hoover and Roosevelt en route to FDR's inauguration, March 4, 1933.
(Library of Congress)

other racial minorities, as prejudice, poverty, and political impotence ground them further down.[45]

The challenge for Roosevelt on Inauguration Day, then, was to embody a credible new spirit of optimism and to chart a new course in fighting the Depression, economically, politically, and emotionally. On their frosty drive together in an open car from the White House to the inaugural platform at the Capitol, Roosevelt attempted to make small talk, but Hoover wrapped himself in angry silence, his head down, his face grim, ignoring the cheering crowds lining Pennsylvania Avenue. "The two of us simply couldn't sit there on our hands, ignoring each other and everyone else," FDR later recalled. "So I began to wave my own response [to the crowd] with my top hat and I kept waving it until I got to the inauguration stand and was sworn in." The contrasting moods of the two men, if not Roosevelt's precise gestures, had been anticipated by the cartoonist Peter Arno in a drawing he prepared for *The New Yorker* several weeks earlier depicting Hoover's sour gloom and Roosevelt's gleaming grin. The drawing was scrapped by editors, however, after the February 15 attempt on Roosevelt's life in an open car, in which the gunman missed FDR but fatally wounded Mayor Anton Cermak of Chicago.[46]

Once at the Capitol, Roosevelt shed his overcoat, wishing to appear fit and energetic, and then "walked" to the rostrum, escorted by his son James. This apparently simple act of walking had been practiced for years as part of his performance of his own putative recovery, demonstrating his fitness for high office. Though his bout with polio was well known, the overwhelming public impression, carefully cultivated by Roosevelt, his family, and staff, was of a man who had achieved a triumphant victory over the disease. He remained paralyzed from the waist down, yet in the public mind he was merely lame. His very cane might seem a fashionable accessory, and his wheelchair was never mentioned. Photographers honored the injunction not to show the president being obviously assisted or carried, and Roosevelt himself went to great lengths to create a semblance of walking, one he could sustain only for a very short distance. He supported himself by his cane on his right side and tightly gripped the arm of a son or aide on his left, heaved one wasted leg forward in its heavy steel brace, resumed his balance, and then swung the other in a slow, toddling gait, head and torso rocking side to side. Always when performing this maneuver in public, he sweated profusely, no matter what the weather. He had his trousers cut long so their cuffs lapped the heels of his unworn shoes, covering the braces. So concealing his arduous effort, he made his way to the podium.[47]

Roosevelt's inaugural address is among the most famous in American history, and its most famous sentence spoke directly to the Depression as an emotional crisis: "The only thing we have to fear is fear itself—nameless, unreasoning, unjustified terror which paralyzes needed efforts to convert retreat into advance." The metaphor of paralysis could not have been a casual one for Roosevelt. Implicitly, he drew an analogy between his own determined recovery from polio, with all of its attendant fears, and the challenge of national recovery. After a broad survey of the devastated nation, he acknowledged, "Only a foolish optimist can deny the dark realities of the moment." He castigated the stubbornness and incompetence of leading financiers and mocked their tearful pleas for restored confidence. In rhetoric charged with biblical righteousness and militant patriotism, he pledged "action, and action now" in a bold, massive, and united attack on the obstacles to national recovery. If congressional measures were insufficient, he warned, he would then ask Congress for "broad Executive power to wage a war against the emergency, as great as the power that would be given to me if we were in fact invaded by a foreign foe." Of all the lines of his address, this one received the heartiest immediate approval.[48]

Roosevelt's great cymbal crash of a sentence facing down fear, his repeated drumbeats promising bold, decisive action, the strength and power of his address as a whole—these instantly brought the confidence that had eluded his predecessor. His voice, gestures, and bearing as well as his words instilled new hope. "Over the vast throngs there hung a cloud of worry, because of the economic and business outlook," the *New York Times* reported. "The new President's recurrent smile of confidence, his uplifted chin and the challenge of his voice did much to help the national sense of humor to assert itself." As the movie actress Lillian Gish said, the president seemed "to have been dipped in phosphorus."[49]

His confident spirit was contagious. Having languished under a sense of leaderless drift, politicians and much of the public were suddenly infused with vigor and purpose, akin to that of a nation at war. To address the financial crisis, FDR immediately declared a national bank "holiday" lasting a week and called Congress into special session, beginning Thursday, March 9.

So began the celebrated "Hundred Days," the most frenzied and productive in congressional history. The Hundred Days has sometimes been described as a one-man show, in which Roosevelt easily bent a pliant Congress to his will and vision. In fact, Roosevelt unleashed a pent-up demand for action from members of both parties, who reflected numerous interests and ideologies. As a whole, the break with the past was breathtaking. By the end of the session Roosevelt and Congress had decisively ended the banking panic, and they had created unprecedented institutions to manage vast sectors of the economy, including banking, agriculture, industrial production, and labor relations. With the Tennessee Valley Authority, they launched a massive government experiment in hydroelectric power, flood control, and regional development. They instituted the largest public-works program in American history and decisively committed the federal government to relief for the unemployed. They provided means to rescue homes and farms from foreclosure, insured small bank deposits, and established federal regulation of securities. Far from expressing a unitary political philosophy, Roosevelt pragmatically accommodated a host of contentious conceptions of the role of government, including fiscal conservatism and large-scale government spending, centralized government planning, public-private partnerships, localism, and states' rights.[50]

To be sure, many problems remained. Spending on public works and job creation, which in 1933 appeared startlingly bold, proved in retrospect to be insufficient. In fact, full recovery came only with the truly massive government spending required by the Second World War. Moreover, the deeply entrenched inequities based on racial discrimination went untouched. Only gradually and incompletely would African Americans' plight become a part of the New Deal. Yet in spring 1933, after many had despaired of the ability of the capitalist system and democracy itself to triumph over the economic catastrophe, Roosevelt had fulfilled his inaugural pledge. In the midst of the frenzied Hundred Days, California's Progressive Republican senator Hiram Johnson wrote, "We have exchanged for a frown in the White House a smile. Where there were hesitation and vacillation, weighing always the personal political consequences, feebleness, timidity, and duplicity, there are now courage and boldness and real action." Financial investors agreed. After trading resumed on the New York Curb Exchange on March 15, the stock ticker concluded the day with the joyful message "Goodnight . . . Happy days are here again."[51]

As Roosevelt won congressional support to launch his New Deal, he also made masterful use of the press and radio to appeal to the public at large. In previous press conferences, Hoover had insisted on written questions submitted in advance, as had Harding and Coolidge before him, and the antagonism between Hoover and the Washington press corps deteriorated to such an extent that he finally stopped giving press conferences altogether. Immediately upon taking office, a smiling and laughing Roosevelt invited accredited Washington correspondents (all of whom were white males) to the White House and announced a new policy of open press conferences twice a week in which all pertinent questions might be asked without advance notice. He poured on all of his considerable charm: shaking hands with each correspondent, calling them by their first names, holding his cigarette holder at a jaunty angle, smiling broadly, impressing them with his exact information and broad command of issues, lavishing confidences and "background information," delighting in the give-and-take of the exchange. The contrast with Hoover could not have been more complete. At the end of the session reporters broke out in spontaneous applause. "The press barely restrained its whoopees," one hard-bitten reporter wrote. "Here was news—action—drama! Here was a new attitude to the press! . . . The reportorial affection and admiration for the President is unprecedented." Although this euphoria inevitably cooled in time, Roosevelt made the White House, rather than Congress, the liveliest press beat in Washington. In the process he carried his message to a broad public and countered the stiff editorial resistance his programs faced from Republican newspaper publishers.[52]

Roosevelt's superb command of radio was still more novel. Radio had only recently become a truly mass medium, and ownership and use of radios continued to swell over the decade, much as television did in the 1950s.[53] As with television later, the very novelty of radio gave it special power. People listened with great attention and absorption, characteristically in groups with family or friends, and they responded actively, discussing the programs they heard and frequently writing letters to radio personalities, whether these were politicians, announcers, entertainers, or even fictional radio characters. Of all new forms of entertainment, radio most intimately brought people in their private settings into contact with public and commercial appeals. In the depths of the Depression, when the workings of the federal government seemed especially distant, impersonal, and opaque, radio provided an instrument to restore a sense of vital political community with millions of ordinary Americans.[54]

The transformative effect of radio began at the precise moment that Roosevelt became president. His was the first inauguration to be widely broadcast, and 450,000 letters and telegrams deluged the White House during his first week in office, compared with the average of 800 a day in the Hoover administration.[55] Some correspondents identified their professions: clergyman, attorney, businessman, banker, teacher, salesman, judge. Others placed themselves among the broad multitude of the American people, "undistinguished and unknown but a part of the vast herd known as The Majority," as one writer put it. They included people of all ages, all levels of education, and all areas of the country. These messages eloquently testified to the tumultuous response to Roosevelt's address from Democrats and Republicans alike. A man in Montgomery, Alabama, declared, "Your brilliant inaugural address, with the vigor and personality that radiated from it, has, in this part of the country, taken the people literally by storm. Everywhere there is a very definite and out-spoken feeling that at last, after wallowing in the trough without a rudder for four years, we have someone who is going to do things." A "small town one-vote Democrat" man from Clinton, Connecticut, wrote, "Thank God for this message of courage, confidence and decision; thank God . . . for the fresh hope you have inspired." He added, "The entire nation rejoices that the White House is again OUR White House, occupied by and presided over by friendly folks, who by their smiles, are encouraging all of us to smile again."[56]

Other writers echoed this stress on the contagious nature of FDR's smile and confidence. A Terre Haute, Indiana, man reported, "I feel certain that your inaugural address was happily received by eighty five per cent of our people. The thought of a 'new deal' has again renewed their hopes; the handshake, the smile and hospitality seems to radiate from most every one." A Cleveland man wrote, "To-day sitting among a gathering of the all but 'forgotten men' during your inaugural address, I seen those worried looks replaced by smiles and confidence, eyes fill up with tears of gratitude, shoulders lifted and chest out."[57]

As moist-eyed men smiled, some women openly confessed their joyous tears. A woman from Des Moines, Iowa, wrote, "As I listened to your acceptance speech today over the radio—I said to myself 'this is the very happiest day of my life' and I found tears on my face—tears of peaceful happiness despite the dreadful predicament the country is now in. Your words carried the honest, truthful conviction of your sincerity to my troubled, worried heart and comforted me." Writing in pencil on a small piece of paper, a self-described "Southern colored girl" working as a servant in New York City said that previously, "I never notice who or cared who was President," but that listening to Roosevelt's inaugural address on the radio, she was moved at first nearly to tears and then to cheerfulness. "Don't forget us colored people as you serve," she added.[58]

Responding to FDR's militant resolve to fight the Great Depression with all of the powers at his command, a number of correspondents compared Roosevelt to Lincoln. A man in Flushing, New York, who called himself one of the "common people," expressed confidence that "you will lead us all into a brighter day, and I hope be able to free the American people from slavery to that Master—Fear. A freedom far richer than Lincoln bestowed on the colored race." A woman in Dayton, Ohio, added, "I am still keyed up with emotion from hearing your voice over the radio at the inaugural. Thank heaven you gave us no pollyannaism. We have had enough of that. You talked as if the country were at war and it was the war spirit that answered you. It was as plain and appealing and exalted as Lincoln at Gettysburg. To my amazement several Republican friends have said the same thing. I did not vote for you but I believe in you heart and soul. That you know what you are talking about and will not lie to us."[59]

Again and again, listeners returned to the importance of Roosevelt's voice in instilling new hope. "*Your voice* and *your voice alone*, is the one force that will carry conviction, restore confidence and, I firmly believe, banish this all-pervading fear," a Rochester, New York, businessman wrote. An Arizona man expressed special appreciation for "these words spoken by you, with that clear and distinct voice, so clear so grand and with deep an[d] sincear [*sic*] meaning, to those millions of souls in our great country, who have lost all Faith Hope and Confidence in all former Leaders, and institutions of truth."[60]

Unlike Hoover, Roosevelt keenly appreciated the potential of radio to carry his voice and message directly into the homes of ordinary citizens and to enlist their support. He had used radio extensively as governor of New York, and over the course of his twelve years as president, he gave thirty-one radio "chats," as well as more formal addresses, as if "to a few people around his fireside." Such "fireside chats" may not strike modern ears as especially informal, but at the time they provided a sharp contrast with customary high-flown, extravagant political oratory.[61]

The first of these, and one of the most momentous, came eight days after his inauguration in the midst of the national banking crisis, shortly after the passage of the Emergency Banking Act, and on the eve of the first reopening of banks across the country. All of Roosevelt's efforts would be undone if panic broke out again and runs on the banks resumed. Repeatedly addressing his audience in his characteristic manner as "my friends" and using the most common words and idioms, he spoke slowly, simply, and directly.[62] "My friends," he began, " I want to talk for a few minutes with the people of the United States about banking. . . . I want to tell you what has been done in the last few days, and why it was done, and what the next steps are going to be." He proceeded to explain how banks depended on confidence and credit and how no bank, however sound, could withstand sudden, anxious demands for withdrawals by all depositors. He carefully described the reason for the bank "holiday," the reforms and restructuring that Congress had provided, and the stages by which banks would reopen. All the while, he spoke to his listeners as "you," not impersonally but intimately. Anticipating their questions and worries as if in conversation, he gave cogent answers in calm reassuring tones. He thanked them for their understanding, cooperation, and support. Concluding with a mild rhetorical flourish, he still maintained the tone and tenor of his message: "Confidence and courage are the essentials of success in carrying out our plan. . . . Let us unite in banishing fear."[63] The address lasted less than fourteen minutes.

Listeners' responses were immediate and overwhelming. To many, he seemed like a warm neighbor or relative, dropping into their homes to visit with them. A man from Iowa City, Iowa, wrote, "It was very cosy and friendly and cheery to have you with us last night. We invited some friends in 'to meet the President,' not forgetting to place an easy chair by the fireplace for the guest of honor, and when your voice came, so clear and vibrant and confident, we had but to close our eyes to see you sitting there with us, talking things over in friendly fashion." In a similar vein, a woman reported the remark of a young girl who had listened to Roosevelt's radio speech: "It seemed as if a Father were talking to me, and I felt like throwing my arms about his neck, he cheered me up so."[64]

From Chicago a man wrote to say, "You are bringing back Confidence and driving out the fear that has been gripping the people for the past three years." He related how he had lost his life savings in a bank failure and, married and past fifty years old, was now on sick leave with polio—a condition that he shared with the president. He concluded with a moving postscript: "Please pardon me for addressing you so familiar in some passages in this letter but your personality is such, and that kindly smiling face I see so much, on paper and that kindly voice I hear on the air, how can any human being keep from it. We all feel (us common people) that you are our friend, tho we may never meet face to face."[65]

Roosevelt's reassuring message dramatically quelled the banking panic. A judge from Syracuse, New York, listened to the chat with a group of Republican and Democratic friends: "When your radio talk began everyone seemed to become hypnotized, because there wasn't a word spoken by anyone until you had finished and as if one voice were speaking all spoke in unison 'We are saved.' The frantic individuals of a few moments before declared that they would leave their money in the banks and that they were not afraid of the future." Ruth Lieberman of Brooklyn listened to Roosevelt's chat with her parents: "My father, who is a determined pessimist, was airing his views on the banking situation. He was sure that the banks would never open— that he would never regain his savings. Then you spoke. For fifteen minutes Dad was silent, his brow wrinkled in thought. Then, when you had concluded your talk, he grinned sheepishly and said, 'Oh well, I wasn't really afraid of losing my money anyhow.'"[66]

FDRs "persuasive, almost melodic voice" was praised again and again. A reporter remarked in 1936 that it "contained an ineffable quality" which "makes it the most effective voice, the greatest radio voice, in America today. That quality is a timber, something soul-searching which reaches into you and plucks at you." "Like his picture," Professor Jane Zimmerman of Columbia University's Teachers College asserted, "his voice gives the impression of a genial smile."[67] A warm, relaxed tenor, the voice was lighter than the theatrical bass-baritones of many radio announcers. It was also one that he adapted to the new technology of the microphone, using it to develop a more intimate and informal style, analogous to the "crooning" of Bing Crosby, and a decisive break with earlier oratorical techniques, such as that of leather-lunged William Jennings Bryan, who prided himself on his ability to reach thirty thousand listeners in the open air without amplification.

Common listeners agreed. "Mr. President, you have an unusually fine radio voice," a Sierra Madre, California, woman declared. It "radiates so much *human sympathy* and *tenderness,* and Oh, how the public *does love that,* on the radio especially." From Milwaukee, Wisconsin, another woman wrote, "I am addressing you 'Dear Mr. Roosevelt' because you are so dear to the hearts of all of us, particularly to those who heard your address Sunday evening. There is that something in your voice conveying absolute sincerity and the positive assurance that we are to rise above all our difficulties in a very short time." A San Francisco woman added, "There is no radio announcer anywhere who has a better voice than you and I think it would be a great idea if you could and would give a short and brief talk on the current issue of the day over the radio whenever possible. It inspires courage and confidence to hear the truth 'straight from the shoulder.'"[68]

Nor did Roosevelt's patrician accent, with its inclination to drop *r*'s after vowels—so that he declared "we have nothing to *feah* but *feah* itself"—seem pretentious. At a time when many radio and film personalities spoke in a British-American manner, his accent carried authority but not affectation.

A large vocabulary intimidated listeners far more than did a voice marked by class and region, and FDR's clarity and simplicity won considerable praise. After the first fireside chat a man from Haskell, Oklahoma, wrote, "Although you have culture, aristocratic breeding and wealth you have one priceless gift, that of reaching out to the 'common people' with a deep sympathy and understanding, that goes into their hearts and you can talk their language and when you talked banking you talked banking so all could understand." An "old janitor" in Chicago remarked, "I know everything he talks about, even my boy could understand, no foolish words but *all good plain* talk, and our president is already helping the people." Will Rogers, himself a master of plain vernacular style, remarked approvingly, "He showed these radio announcers and our public speakers what to do with a vocabulary—leave it right in the dictionary where it belongs." Detailed analysis of Roosevelt's word choice shows he did just that: 70 percent of his words were among the five hundred most common in general reading material, and roughly 80 percent among the thousand most common.[69]

In these broadcasts, Roosevelt intentionally addressed each listener as "an intimate friend." Frances Perkins described how, as he spoke, "his head would nod and his hands would move in simple, natural, comfortable gestures. His face would smile and light up as though he were actually sitting on the front porch or in the parlor. . . . People felt this, and it bound them to him in affection."[70]

Such apparent simplicity took considerable effort. The fireside chats, Eleanor Roosevelt remembered, "entailed a great deal of work on Franklin's part. . . . I have known . . . Franklin to take a speech that had almost reached the final stages and tear it up and dictate it from the beginning, because he felt the others had not made it clear enough for the layman to understand. Franklin had a gift for simplification." Replying in 1942 to a letter asking him to give his radio chats more frequently, he wrote, "I suppose you know that every time I talk over the air it means four or five days of long, overtime work in the preparation of what I say."[71]

Roosevelt made equally skillful use of film newsreels. His was the first presidential inauguration to be carried as a sound newsreel, and he continued to appear in newsreels roughly twenty-six to thirty times a year through the 1930s, so that, as the actor Melvyn Douglas pointed out, "he was seen by more people in the movie houses than the two most popular Hollywood stars in any year."[72] Douglas, himself one of the most popular leading men in 1930s movies, paid tribute to FDR's great acting skill, as displayed in a 1936 newsreel in which Roosevelt greeted cheering throngs on a hot June day in Arkansas:

"He smiled his warm, inspirational smile. He was playing the role I think he liked best, leading man in a drama featuring People, Crowds, Speeches, and the Spirit of Pioneering. . . . FDR knew," Douglas added, "that millions of Americans would see the pictures and would feel happier if their President looked fit and healthy."[73] To that end, "he was the most cooperative presidential subject the newsreel cameramen had ever known."[74]

Journalists frequently compared FDR to leading actors. Marveling at his performance in the 1940 presidential campaign against Wendell Willkie, one reporter exclaimed, "He's all the Barrymores rolled in one." Veteran newspaperman William Allen White similarly told Roosevelt, "For box office attraction you leave Clark Gable gasping for breath."[75] These newsreels emphasized Roosevelt as a vigorous, dynamic personality rather than as a politician. An analysis of the *Universal News* during FDR's first two terms found him most frequently shown on trips (34 percent) or in nonpolitical ceremonies (30 percent). By contrast, his official speeches accounted for only 24 percent of his appearances. The newsreels also captured his mastery of humor—and his ability to reduce partisan attacks to absurdities. In 1938, receiving an honorary degree from the University of North Carolina in Chapel Hill, he confided, "You have heard for six years that I was about to plunge the Nation into war; . . . that I was driving the Nation into bankruptcy; and that I breakfasted every morning on a dish of grilled millionaire. (*Laughter*) Actually I am an exceedingly mild mannered person . . . a believer in the capitalistic system, and for my breakfast, a devotee of scrambled eggs. (*Laughter*)."[76]

Roosevelt relished this theatrical role. He once said to Orson Welles, "Orson, you and I are the two best actors in this country." On another occasion, when the sound squeaked in one of his newsreels, he quipped to Melvyn Douglas, who had costarred with Greta Garbo in three films, "That's the Garbo in me."[77]

To an extraordinary degree, in the early days of the New Deal it was Roosevelt's cheerful confidence, above all his smile, that people praised and emulated. "Smile like Roosevelt," a New York minister urged his flock: "The infectious smile of President Roosevelt should set the example for the entire people of the United States." Indeed, Roosevelt's smile became so fixed in the public mind in the early days of the New Deal that when in 1934 a painter bowed to the president's wish and removed a smile from his official portrait, the event made news. The artist, Ellen Emmet Rand, had "felt that the President did not look 'just right' without one." Pushing such a desire to the point of absurdity, in October 1933 the magazine *Vanity Fair* published a full-page photomontage of the grinning Roosevelt, so refracted as to assume a hallucinatory effect. Under the title "A Laughing Cavalier," the caption read, "For the first time in many years the Nation's Chief Executive is a man who understands the value of a grin."[78]

FDR's deep laugh also became celebrated. In contrast to Hoover, who never laughed aloud, Roosevelt easily burst into boisterous peals of mirth. "There never was another laugh like Franklin Roosevelt's," the writer Fulton Oursler remembered. "Over the chasm of the years I can hear it now clearly and distinctly—as joyous, hearty, rolling, thunderous laughter as ever was heard on this sorrowful globe." Such laughter, too, had its uses. His devoted secretary Marguerite "Missy" LeHand spoke of his infectious "political laugh," by which he could make everyone around him similarly erupt in mirth, even if the joke was a weak one.[79]

The leading Republican congressman Joseph W. Martin, a vigorous opponent of the New Deal, knew how beguiling FDR's smile could be and stood vigilant to revive fellow Republicans who fell under its spell. At one reception when Roosevelt turned on all of "his radiance," Martin recalled, "I could see the face of one of my men from Ohio lighting up like the moon. As quickly as I could manage I took him aside. 'Get rid of that moonglow,' I told him. 'Remember what we're up against in this fellow. Don't swallow all that hokum.'"[80]

In time some journalists voiced similar complaints. James L. Wright of the *Buffalo Evening News* grumbled, "Mr. Roosevelt is a man with the air of candor, but lacking in candor. He adroitly sidesteps and dodges. Unless one is hypnotized by being called by his first name, and will trade a presidential smile for a piece of news, he must admit that is so."[81]

For many of his opponents, indeed, Roosevelt's smile was especially galling, like that of a Cheshire Cat. The caustic critic H. L. Mencken referred to it as Roosevelt's "Christian Science smile," for him a damning epithet. Satirists quickly penned ditties such as "His Enigmatic Smile":

Twinkle, twinkle little Grin
Up above the world of din.
Never worried, so serene,
How I wonder what you mean.

In a similar vein, in 1935 the *Northwestern Miller* published:

I'm tired, oh, so tired, of the whole New Deal,
Of the juggler's smile and the barker's spiel,
Of the mushy speech and the loud bassoon,
And tiredest of all of all our leader's croon.[82]

Roosevelt, in turn, mocked his critics at a Gridiron Club dinner in December 1936, shortly after his overwhelming reelection, in which the Republican candidate, Alf Landon, carried only two states. Remarking on the newspaper caricatures of him, he said, "One morning, about the middle of October, I became curious about this man Roosevelt and I went to a beautiful, old mirror of the early Federal period and took a careful look at him in the glass. He smiled. I remembered that one of the most damning indictments that had been brought against him was that self-same smile. I smiled back. And after a careful examination I decided that all that this villain looked like to me was a man who wanted to be re-elected President of the United States."[83]

And where precisely were Roosevelt's smiles and friendly salutations leading? The adulation that showered Roosevelt, a response massively intensified by his masterful control of radio, alarmed opponents and concerned some observers, who saw in his emotional appeals the presence—or at least the potential—of a master manipulator bent on sinister, perhaps dictatorial ends. On the occasion of Roosevelt's second fireside chat in May 1933, the *New York Times* remarked appreciatively, "A wonderful new political instrument is placed in the hands of the President of the United States." Yet even while praising his use of radio to instruct and reassure the public, the writer observed, "He might use the radio to agitate or inflame. In the hands of an unscrupulous demagogue it might become a public danger." The ability to forge and shape public opinion, to invite a personal relationship with unseen listeners through impersonal means, the slippage between speaking *to* and speaking *for* the "people"— all carried disquieting implications at a time when the distinctly unsmiling Hitler had made radio a central instrument of Nazism. Roosevelt triumphantly claimed that through the bundles of mail he received daily, he was closer to public opinion than other politicians or reporters. ("Hoover got 400 letters a day," he said; "I get 4000.") Yet Father Charles Coughlin, the controversial and anti-Semitic "radio priest" who achieved significant political influence almost exclusively through his popular radio broadcasts in the early 1930s, made similar claims based on the letters he received. "I am not boasting when I say I know the pulse of the people." Similarly, Huey Long defended his autocratic control of Louisiana government, saying, "A man is not a dictator when he does the will of the people."[84]

The material and emotional needs of the Great Depression, together with the enhanced power of new media to reach a broad public, created new possibilities for charismatic leaders in the United

States and abroad. Even as it inspired millions, the very power of Roosevelt's warm voice and broad smile remained controversial. Under his administration the federal government, once a distant force for most American citizens except in time of war, massively extended its presence into their lives.

Yet while Hitler and Mussolini employed radio and other media to inflame, Roosevelt used them to inform. Mussolini's arrogant boast "The crowd does not have to know; it must believe" would have been regarded by FDR as the vilest sort of profanity. Hitler, Mussolini, and Stalin saw themselves as supreme embodiments of the popular will and taste.[85] Roosevelt never did. Instead of using the powers at his command to raise himself above his constituents or to stir their darker emotions, he embodied confidence in the ability of the democratic process to meet the greatest economic challenge the country had ever faced. To be sure, he could infuriate opponents with his mixture of cheer and calculation, patrician charm and democratic warmth, irrepressible optimism and immense emotional effort. But fundamentally, Roosevelt reasserted a broad emotional spirit that transcended partisan division. To return to Frances Perkins's phrase, he "made people feel better" when they greatly needed to do so. Hollywood provided considerable help in this effort, especially with its golden-haired discovery Shirley Temple.

CHAPTER 2
SUCH A HAPPY LITTLE FACE!

While banks failed and Hoover frowned, Gertrude Temple delighted in dressing and grooming her baby daughter. After Shirley lost her blond baby curls, her mother gave her weekly peroxide washes and set her hair in ringlets each night.[1] Then, when her daughter was barely three, Gertrude Temple enrolled her in Ethel Meglin's nearby dance studio, a magnet for mothers who were eager to launch their offspring into show business. Children at the studio automatically became "Meglin Kiddies," a talent pool that the former Ziegfeld Follies dancer exhibited in her annual Christmas revue and booked for stage and movie appearances. Three years earlier, Ethel Gumm had taken her three daughters to the studio, playing the piano to pay for lessons, and delighted in their movie debut the following year. The youngest of the sisters was the future Judy Garland.

Burning brightly as they did, the dreams of the vast majority of such mothers and their children faded and died, sometimes with agonizing slowness. The former child star "Baby Peggy" Montgomery, Diana Serra Cary, one of the most popular and lucrative child performers in 1920s silent movies, later observed that in the years when the child craze reached its height, approximately a hundred children and their families "poured into the Hollywood marketplace every fifteen minutes." Probably only one in fifteen thousand of these hopefuls earned as much as a single week's expenses in a year, she estimated. Roughly half packed their bags and went back home within a few months. A small fraction, "perhaps grubstaked by a husband's salary or a relative's nest egg . . . , might hold on for a year before giving up the fight. That left a small, fanatical corps of iron-willed survivors, women who preferred starvation and death to abandoning their dearly won positions before the very gates of fame."[2]

Shirley Temple's initial break was a small one. Shortly before Thanksgiving 1931, two men scouting for talent spotted Shirley at the dance studio. They were Jack Hays and Charles Lamont of Educational Films Corporation, one of the lesser movie studios collectively known

Gertrude and Shirley Temple. (Photofest/Fox)

as "Poverty Row" scattered along outer Santa Monica Boulevard west of Hollywood. After a screen test, Hays offered the Temple family a contract, under which little Shirley would make a series of one-reel comedy spoofs. She would be paid ten dollars a day, but only for the days of actual film shooting, two per short. Rehearsals were unpaid. Gertrude Temple would earn five dollars a week during filming for her services as Shirley's seamstress, hairdresser, and chauffeur. The contract bound Shirley to the studio for two years. If Educational Films lent her to other studios, the Temples would receive a percentage of her earnings. "Maybe by that time she will be worth a lot of money," Gertrude wrote her mother, Maude. "This all sounds like a fairy story."[3]

Little girls do not always fare well in fairy stories, however, and if the men at Educational Films were not wolves or ogres, neither were they fairy godmothers. Between December 1931 and early 1934 Shirley made eight one-reel movies (running ten to eleven minutes each) in the Baby Burlesks series and four in the two-reeler Frolics of Youth series. The casts consisted entirely of Meglin Kiddies, and the children were also obliged to pose for publicity photographs and advertisements. So Shirley Temple first smiled on the broad public anonymously from cornflakes boxes, candy-bar and chewing-gum wrappers, and cigar bands.[4] In addition, she acted in minor roles in several feature-length films, earning altogether only around a thousand dollars before her appearance in *Stand Up and Cheer!*[5]

The Baby Burlesks were aimed at adults rather than children, and Shirley's roles teetered on the cusp between innocence and flirtatiousness, characteristics that clung to her film persona. In the tradition of earlier children's impersonations of famous adult actors, such as those by "Baby Peggy" Montgomery in the early 1920s and by Jane Withers performing (beginning at age three) as "Dixie's Dainty Dewdrop" on Atlanta radio in the late 1920s and early 1930s, the shorts spoofed well-known feature-length movies, with young children caricaturing adult roles.[6] To heighten the absurdity of their mimicry, Jack Hays dressed the boys in huge diapers secured with giant safety pins.

The initial film of the series epitomized its brand of farce. *Runt Page* lampooned the tough-talking film comedy *The Front Page* (1931), which was based, in turn, on Ben Hecht and Charles MacArthur's play of 1928. The comic short begins with well-dressed adults drinking, talking, and laughing around a dining table as they appreciatively discuss *The Front Page*. Shirley Temple plays a little girl sitting in her high chair behind the table. As they talk, her head topples in sleep, and a compressed version of *The Front Page* unfolds in her dream. The scene is the press room of the county jail, where reporters play cards as they wait for a condemned man's execution, necessitated not so much by his guilt as by the rivalries of Chicago politicians. Little boys in diapers, collars, neckties, and hats stand in for adults who speak their lines in deep voices on the soundtrack, in many cases in thick ethnic accents. The effect is to provide viewers with absurd juxtapositions of image and sound: they see children and hear adults, so that the children seem like adult dwarfs and their doings provide ludicrous analogies to the tough-talking hard-boiled action. So when the character playing ace reporter Hildy Johnson (the name is burlesqued as Bilgy) speaks of taking a drink, the toddler playing his role takes a swig from a baby bottle. When the same character starts to leave the room with his suitcase and it falls open, baby clothes and paraphernalia spill out. Shirley appears relatively late in the action and has very few lines. The film purports to give viewers her dream, but it actually presents an adult fantasy about children who have nothing childlike about themselves except their bodies. The children literally go through the motions of adult characters without, presumably, comprehending anything about the drama they are enacting.

In other Baby Burlesks, the children speak their own lines, but the heavy-handed humor remains the same. A hip-bumping Shirley burlesqued actress Dolores del Rio's role as Charmaine de la Cognac in

Shirley as the vamp Polly in a production still for the Baby Burlesk
Polly Tix in Washington. *(Photofest/Educational Films)*

War Babies (a satire of *What Price Glory?*), Marlene Dietrich ("Morelegs Sweettrick") in *Kiddin' Hollywood*, Mae West in *Glad Rags to Riches* (in which she tap-danced and sang), and a strumpet bent on seducing a senator in *Polly Tix in Washington*. The child actors' broad gestures and mugging recall the silent-film era that had just ended.

However cartoonish these shorts were, making them was not child's play. Quite the contrary, they demanded strenuous effort from both mother and daughter. For her first film, *Runt Page*, finished in January 1932, three-and-a-half-year-old Shirley and Gertrude Temple shuttled back and forth from home to studio for weeks of unpaid rehearsals. Then, just as shooting began, Shirley's cold erupted in a painful ear infection. Gertrude rushed her to a hospital to have the eardrum lanced and stayed up with her all night. Gertrude begged producer Jack Hays for a rest, but he insisted that they be at the studio the following morning, or else Shirley would have to be replaced. If the film proved a success, he coaxed, then Shirley would star in the whole series. That day Shirley spent almost twelve hours in the studio. Recounting these events in a letter to her own mother, Gertrude concluded by confessing what she never revealed publicly: the link between her hopes for Shirley's film career and the family's financial worries. Immediately after saying how everyone anticipated that the movie would be a great success, she remarked on the empty shops and widespread unemployment in the Los Angeles area. Then she added, "George is also very worried, as our financial condition is pretty bad." Amid the wave of banking panics and depressed conditions, the abundant credit of the 1920s had slowed to a trickle. With her husband's position precarious, a lot of hopes rested on their daughter.[7]

Shirley might have just got her foot in the door of an outpost on Poverty Row, but Gertrude Temple imagined it as the first step on a stairway leading swiftly to the top. Anxious and excited, she seemed never to have doubted that the movies offered her daughter a golden opportunity. Hays had assured her that Shirley would have "a very good dramatic teacher," the use of a kitchenette, and a place to nap, so that her daily routine would proceed much as usual.[8]

These promises proved empty, however. Far from expert dramatic instruction, Jack Hays and Charles Lamont spoon-fed Shirley and the other child actors their lines one at a time and urged them to mug broadly. The children's job was not acting but mimicry, Shirley later observed. Gertrude coached her at home as best she could, urging her to "sparkle" and teaching her how to arch her eyebrows, round her mouth in surprise, thrust out her lower lip, and cock her head sideways with a knowing smile—gestures that would become characteristic in Shirley's later films.[9]

The set of the Baby Burlesks resembled a workhouse more than a day nursery. To threaten and punish uncooperative child actors, Lamont kept a soundproof black box, six feet on each side, containing a block of ice. An offending child was locked within this dark, cramped interior and either stood uncomfortably in the cold, humid air or had to sit on the ice. Those who told their parents about this torture were threatened with further punishment. When, nonetheless, Shirley confided to her mother, Gertrude Temple dismissed her report as a fanciful tale. A half century later, Shirley would still insist on its veracity, but it was not a story that Gertrude wished to hear. Lamont was equally ruthless behind the camera. In a *Tarzan* film spoof, *Kid in Africa*, for example, he concealed a tripwire to level the "savages" played by African American children. In filming *Polly Tix in Washington*, a terrified ostrich pulling Shirley and another child in a surrey careened wildly about the set before crashing into a wall. "This isn't playtime, kids," she remembered Lamont saying. "It's work."[10]

Looking back on her childhood from middle age, Shirley Temple Black agreed. Once she started in Baby Burlesks at age three, she observed, "[I] worked for the rest of my childhood." Though not solely the creature of the studio, "I went to work *every day*. . . . I thought every child worked, because I was born into it."[11]

Gertrude Temple, by contrast, insisted that her daughter's time at the studio was carefree recreation. "Motion-picture acting is simply part of her play life," she declared in 1935. "It is un-tinged with worry about tomorrow or fear of failure." Indeed, similar words were put in Shirley's mouth by a journalist the same year, when she supposedly told her "autobiography" as a seven-year-old: acting "is like playing a game of make-believe. That's the easiest game in the world to play. It is for me, anyway."[12]

This justification was a common, even threadbare, defense by parents and producers of child performers.[13] Such assurances constituted an implicit reply to an unnamable charge: that child acting, far from harmless play, in fact constituted a form of exploitative child labor. The defense of child acting as a legitimate activity, separate and distinct from oppressive child labor in textile mills, coal mines, glasshouses, tenements, street trades, and the like, had been fought by theatrical interests and the children's parents for over half a century. The position of the child actor was highly paradoxical, as one who fascinated audiences in the ability both to imitate adults and to portray the unique characteristics of childhood innocence. As the sociologist Viviana Zelizer has observed, such actors "were child laborers paid to represent the new, sentimentalized view of children."[14] Even very young children could score phenomenal triumphs in such roles, as they seemed not to work but to play—and earned far more for their families than most adults. One of the first American child stars, Cordelia Howard (1848–1941), appeared onstage at the age of four in *Oliver Twist* and soon afterward played Little Eva in *Uncle Tom's Cabin*, a part for which she became famous. Kate Bateman (1842–1917) began her acting career at age three in *Babes in the Woods*. A generation later, Elsie Leslie (1881–1960) launched her professional career as a four-year-old and achieved two of her greatest successes in dramatic versions of Frances Hodgson Burnett's *Little Lord Fauntleroy* in 1888 and Mark Twain's *The Prince and the Pauper* in 1890. In the first decade of the twentieth century, spectacular Broadway productions featuring children reached their height, led by *The Wizard of Oz*, *The Little Princess*, *The Blue Bird*, *Babes in Toyland*, and *Peter Pan*.[15] In the 1920s Hollywood brought forth Jackie Coogan, "Baby Peggy" Montgomery, and the popular Our Gang two-reelers, and legions followed in their footsteps. Film allowed child actors greater freedom of movement and intimacy of expression than did the stage. Moreover, the introduction of sound created new possibilities for giggling, sobbing, whining, shrieking, singing, and dancing.

Nonetheless, in the late nineteenth and early twentieth centuries, defenders of professional child actors frequently battled reformers who made little distinction between child performers on the legitimate stage and those performing in circuses or saloons.[16] Gradually abandoning arguments for the economically useful child, which had acquired a mercenary taint, such defenders claimed the higher ground of acting's educational benefits for children. They also extolled the realization of the playwright's artistic vision and the wholesome pleasures children's performances gave to the public. A pamphlet published in 1911 by the National Alliance for the Protection of Stage Children argued for uniform laws that would eliminate children's performances under hazardous, unhealthful, or indecent conditions while preserving their appearances on the legitimate stage. The authors sharply distinguished between "the few moments of mental effort of the stage child" and "the blind, constant and degrading toil of the little slave of the mill, whose drudgery dwarfs mind, body, and spirit." They spoke glowingly of "the emanation of the spirit of childhood; an emanation which only a little child can convincingly give forth." The pamphlet even leapt to the defense of stage mothers and fathers, often depicted as mercenary and demanding: "Parents of the child genius do not lose their parental solicitude by reason of their child's unusual talents." The wages that a child actor earned were entirely secondary, even though these children were "mostly little geniuses of the poor, or of those in moderate circumstances."[17]

Others objected, however, that the professionalization of child actors turned childhood itself into a commodity. "The idea of a professional child—a child in whose case simple childhood is the sole stock in trade," a writer protested, "is touched with sacrilege." Learning to perform childhood innocence, the child actor lost the unself-conscious spontaneity that was its essence: "One of the most inalienable and fatal attributes of the true show-child . . . [is that] it has learnt to watch itself, and will go so far as to make a study of its own emotions." Such critics nonetheless feared that the "capitalization of childhood's appeal" might be an irreversible trend.[18]

Shirley Temple's career proved to be a monumental step in precisely that direction, but it came within an inch of not happening at all. In September 1933 Shirley's modest prospects with Educational Films ended abruptly when Jack Hays filed for bankruptcy.[19] George Temple bought back the remainder of Shirley's contract, or so he thought, for a nominal sum. (After Shirley's success, Hays bedeviled him for years with legal suits.) Then, as Shirley and her mother viewed her last short for Educational Films in a Los Angeles movie theater around Thanksgiving, Shirley was spotted by or, more likely, thrust by her mother before the songwriter Jay Gorney, who was seeking a little girl to carry the song-and-dance number in Fox Film's *Stand Up and Cheer!*

Gorney was a composer with a political conscience and a talent for voicing the hardships and disillusionment of the decade. With lyricist E. Y. "Yip" Harburg, he had written the plaintive hit song of the Great Depression "Brother, Can You Spare a Dime?" (1932), based on a Yiddish lullaby he had known as a child.[20] In the voice of a "forgotten man" on a breadline, it traces the broken dreams, lost sense of fraternity, and withered pride of an American worker and veteran of the Great War, now friendless and spurned. Once he built railroads, towers, and dreams, the man remembers in a minor key. Then, brightening to a major key and a jauntier march rhythm, he recalls how, as a drummer boy, he trudged with other doughboys through the hell of the Great War. The song rises an octave to a loud, urgent C with its entreating, "Don't you remember? I'm your *pal!*" before its appeal collapses, no longer addressing the fraternal brother but the more impersonal "buddy," as he repeats the title plea, "Can you spare a dime?"[21] Introduced in early October 1932 in the Shubert brothers' *Americana* revue, the song also represented a moving rebuke to the violent dispersal three months earlier of the Bonus Army of World War veterans outside Washington, D.C. Indeed, the number served as an election-year riposte to Herbert Hoover, the figurative flip side of Roosevelt's "Happy Days Are Here Again." Bing Crosby's famous

James Dunn and Shirley in the "Baby Take a Bow"
number from Stand Up and Cheer! *(PhotoFest/Fox)*

rendition of the song was quickly issued by Brunswick Records, and by Election Day on November 8, less than five weeks after the song's Broadway debut, it was the most popular record in the country.[22]

Stand Up and Cheer! was already in production when Gertrude and Shirley Temple hurried to the Fox studio for a hastily arranged audition with Gorney and fellow songwriter Lew Brown. (The later report that she was among 250 children vying for the part was a publicity fabrication.) Shirley sang satisfactorily and then performed a dance routine that she had learned at Mrs. Meglin's. Suddenly she had a bit part, replacing a less winning little girl. Yet "Baby Take a Bow," the song-and-dance number by Gorney and Brown that Shirley performs in the film, was no paean to the forgotten man. On the contrary, all thoughts of the Depression are banished, and the carefree party of the 1920s remains in full swing. The number begins as a tribute by Jimmy Dugan, little Shirley's fictional father, in the persona of a boulevard-ier, to a supposed fiancée, "the future Mrs. Hemingway," who is the source of widespread attention. Wearing top hat and tails and carrying a walking stick, Jimmy sings the title lyric and dances with a single platinum blonde, then a cluster of scantily clad chorines. Recalling the much more elaborate dance sequences that Busby Berkeley made for Warner Bros., the camera moves to a series of close-ups on the chorines' faces and then, disorientingly, to doll-like figures in frilly dresses that turn out to be their knees and legs. Prepared for by this miniature scale, little Shirley, in a frilly, very short white organdy dress with red polka dots, emerges from her father's spread legs to become the new "baby" who is the source of everyone's tribute. With beaming smile, chest out, hands clenched, shoulders and arms moving to the rhythm, she returns the song's compliment, inviting her daddy to take a bow in turn. The two then perform the tap dance that Shirley brought from Mrs. Meglin's, and Jimmy scoops her up in his arms for a final embrace and kiss. In the course of the number, eroticism has been supplanted by cuteness, and the father-daughter bond is evidently sufficient protection from Shirley's flirtatiousness.

Shirley's place in the dance number is justified, as is the position of child actors generally, within the very storyline of *Stand Up and Cheer!* An important official must decide whether little Shirley Dugan's performance in her father's song-and-dance act should be exempt from a ban on child actors under the age of seven. "Shirley doesn't really work," protests her fictional father, played by James Dunn, an ex-vaudevillian himself. "She just sort of comes on at the finish, and she really loves it." Even here, however, his motives are decidedly mixed. He explains that his wife, who used to be in the act, has died, and little Shirley has taken her place. "Besides, I got to have her in the act with me," he insists. "She helps me over the rough spots. . . .

And look at her . . . she thrives on it." Winding up his appeal, he asks, "How's chances?" It was a catchphrase of the day, made all the more popular by Irving Berlin's song of the same title in the hit Broadway revue *As Thousands Cheer* (1933). Pressing her father's plea, Shirley fixes the official with luminous eyes and disarmingly lisps, "How's chances?" He can only scoop her up in his arms and reply, "I think chances are great." The conquest of an influential man's heart in this way would be a recurrent theme in Shirley Temple films.[23]

Arguments for the exceptional situation of child actors ultimately prevailed under the New Deal. The codes of the National Recovery Administration, one of the monuments of Roosevelt's Hundred Days,

"How's chances?" Shirley and Warner Baxter (with James Dunn in background) in Stand Up and Cheer! *(Photofest/Fox)*

which sought to place limits on child labor, made an exception for children in motion pictures, and, in any case, the Supreme Court struck down the codes as unconstitutional in 1935. The Fair Labor Standards Act of 1938 became the administration's most effective and enduring weapon against child labor, and it too made exceptions for children working for their parents outside of mining and manufacturing and for children less than fourteen years of age working in agriculture or newspaper distribution, or performing in motion pictures and the theater.

Anticipating Roosevelt's signature on this legislation, with its lustrous loophole for child actors, Twentieth Century–Fox arranged a brief meeting between Shirley Temple and President Roosevelt at the White House. He signed the bill the next day, June 25, 1938. Eleanor Roosevelt, the president's wife, had already met Shirley the previous spring in Hollywood and wrote in her syndicated column how impressed she was by Shirley's "natural simplicity and charm." "Why aren't you smiling?" FDR asked after Shirley was escorted into the Oval Office, trailing her tongue-tied Republican parents. "I thought you were famous for your smile." He spoke as one trouper to another. She was keeping her lips in place, she explained, because she had just lost a tooth.[24]

Not only did FDR and Shirley have the two most famous smiles in the country, but ever since the release of *Stand Up and Cheer!* hers had been associated with his confident leadership.[25] Together, they fought and licked the Great Depression. At least that was Hollywood's version of what happened. Fox released *Stand Up and Cheer!* in April 1934, just over a year after Roosevelt's inauguration, and it aimed to show how the entertainment industry was dispelling the gloom of the Depression right alongside the president. The face of the fictional president in the film is never shown, in compliance with White House policies protecting FDR's dignity. Nonetheless, speaking with unmistakably Rooseveltian inflection and cadences, and advancing Roo-

Shirley leaving the White House after her meeting with FDR,
June 24, 1938. Gertrude Temple and Shirley's bodyguard John Griffith
stand at left. (Harris & Ewing Collection, Library of Congress)

sevelt's most famous theme, he earnestly tells a theatrical producer named Lawrence Cromwell (played by Warner Baxter): "Our country is bravely passing through a serious crisis. Many of our people's affairs are in the red, and, figuratively, their nerves are in the red." As he endeavors "to pilot the ship past the most treacherous of all rocks, fear," the president intends "to dissolve that destructive rock in a gale of laughter." Accordingly, he appoints Cromwell to a new cabinet position, secretary of amusement, "whose duty it shall be to amuse and entertain the people—to make them forget their troubles."[26]

This premise, of course, was a transparent Hollywood self-justification. The fictional president regards commercial amusement not as frivolity in the face of the Great Depression but as a necessary and vital force in combating it. Hitching its wagon to Roosevelt's star, the film extolled innocent laughter as the best medicine for the economy, and healthful amusement as one of the highest forms of patriotism.

Opposition to the patriotic work of the new cabinet secretary in *Stand Up and Cheer!* comes from two quarters: conspiratorial businessmen reaping vast profits from the crisis, and stuffy senators placing their sense of dignity above the needs of the nation. Ultimately, the progressive forces of amusement triumph over the gloom and lift the country out of the Depression, emotionally and economically, but not without a struggle. Just when Secretary Cromwell's efforts appear defeated, the news comes, like a deus ex machina, that the Depression is over: "There is no unemployment! Fear has been banished! Confidence is reborn! Poverty has been wiped out! Laughter resounds throughout the nation! The people are happy again! We're out of the red!" Special credit for this sweeping victory goes to the Children's Division of the Department of Amusement. The smiling faces of Shirley Temple and other children have evidently done the trick.

Stand Up and Cheer! ends with vast parades through the streets of the nation—emulating the Roosevelt administration's determination to declare victory over the Great Depression. In summer and fall 1933,

Shirley celebrates "We're out of the red" in Stand Up and Cheer! *(Photofest/Fox)*

General Hugh Johnson, head of the National Recovery Administration, a major agency of the early New Deal, publicized reemployment efforts in various cities with spectacular parades of newly hired men and women, garbed in the attire of their trades. One such event in New York attracted nearly two million people. Using Fox's studio lot, *Stand Up and Cheer!* surpassed even Johnson's Blue Eagle ballyhoo as reemployed workers and civic and military organizations jubilantly celebrate national recovery. They include chorines, forest rangers, sailors, nurses, firemen, policemen, locomotive engineers, farmers, milkmen, housewives, office staff, miners, chefs, maids, schoolgirls, sanitation workers, postmen, men in kilts, soldiers, marines, railroad porters (led by Stepin Fetchit in top hat and tails), Boy Scouts,

Shirley in another view of the "We're out of the red" parade. (Photofest/Fox)

and others. Shirley Temple appears twice in close-up as she leads portions of the marching throng. What's good for the country, the film suggests, is good for Hollywood, and vice versa.[27]

Shirley's prominence in this triumphal march was prophetic. The hitherto obscure little girl, just six when the movie was released, had a relatively small part in the story and received only seventh billing. But she would play a major role in the history of Fox Film, Hollywood, the nation, and the moviegoing public in the years that followed. Her breakthrough came at a pivotal moment when movie audiences—and the film industry—needed her most. Although the movie as a whole, loosely structured and stuffed with vaudevillian gags, garnered mixed reviews, even jaded critics found Shirley irresistible: "Such a happy little face! With a dimple close to the laughing mouth. Such starry, friendly brown eyes!" a critic for the *Chicago Tribune* exclaimed. The *Boston Globe* agreed: "*She* has the most adorable smile and the most daintily poised charm of any little girl who has yet played in the talkies." The *Louisville Courier-Journal's* critic could hardly stay in his seat: "For once an infant prodigy appears upon the screen with such charm as to disarm any abhorrence of the usual nuisance. . . . Little Miss Temple is blonde, dimpled and all smiles but better than these attributes for picture taking she seems to know her power and it is very great right now. Not being overly tender about these matters I must confess nevertheless one wants to walk up to the screen and snatch her off it and hug her." Indeed, by one report, "a roomful of unsentimental Hollywood reporters (all male and all 'cold' to the usual run of precious child actors)" thought her performance especially impressive, and predictions arose that she would be one of the "big stars" to emerge that year.[28]

Film trade publication writers hugged her too. "The chief topic of conversation at home, at the office, at the club and wherever you go is Shirley Temple," the *Hollywood Reporter* exulted. And everyone rejoiced in her unaffected, natural manner. *Time* magazine emphasized how the "blonde and pretty" discovery had been chosen from two hundred child actors answering a general casting call. Yet she apparently had no previous training and had learned singing from imitating radio crooners and picked up most of her tap routine on the Fox lot. That she was supposedly only four and a half years old and the daughter of a Santa Monica assistant bank manager, not a theatrical family, enhanced her little-darling-next-door image.[29]

The 1934 breakthrough in *Stand Up and Cheer!* that ultimately led to Shirley's meeting with the real-life President Roosevelt came at a critical moment not only for the Temple family but also for Fox Film and the American film industry as a whole. That industry had enjoyed spectacular success in the two decades prior to 1933, but in the depths of the Great Depression it struggled to regain its footing. Prior to 1914 the majority of the world's films were made abroad. When the war disrupted European film production, American filmmakers leapfrogged ahead to capture the world market. Concentrating film production in the Los Angeles area, with its sunshine, temperate climate, and abundant land, and emphasizing maximum efficiency, American companies turned out films on a large scale much as Henry Ford made Tin Lizzies. By 1920 these companies produced 80 percent of the world's movies; by 1930, 90 percent.[30]

Dominating the industry were the "Big Five" motion picture conglomerates: Loew's, Inc., owner of the nation's largest theater circuit and the parent company of Metro-Goldwyn-Mayer; Paramount; Warner Bros.; Fox; and Radio-Keith-Orpheum (RKO). All of these integrated film production, distribution, and exhibition on a massive scale, nationally and internationally. Among the next rank of motion picture corporations, the "Little Three," Universal Pictures and Columbia Pictures were similarly organized, though with proportionally fewer theaters. The last of the Little Three, United Artists, functioned principally as a backer and distributor for independently produced films. Among the Big Five, most corporate capital was invested in movie theaters, not production, so that, as far as the film corporation presidents were concerned, studios made movies to accord with the needs of exhibitors, not the other way around. Together, these five corporations controlled most of the first-run movie theaters in the country, which screened new movies at least a month before lesser theaters, presented live stage shows and shorts as well as feature films, provided greater amenities, including air-conditioning, and charged premium prices. These advantages and their far greater seating capacity meant that the theaters controlled by the Big Five, although only 15 percent of all those in the country, garnered roughly 75 percent of all box-office receipts.[31]

Members of the Big Five developed regional concentrations and openly colluded with one another and the Little Three to their mutual advantage. They largely shut out independent products through block booking and blind bidding, whereby independent movie exhibitors were compelled to take a large, motley package of a company's movies sight unseen, including some as yet unmade, if they wanted to show the top films. Paramount controlled New England, the Upper Midwest, and the South; Warner Bros. presided over the Mid-Atlantic states; Loew's and RKO divided New York, New Jersey, and Ohio. Fox's greatest strength lay in the area west of Denver, but it included important holdings in Kansas, western Nebraska, Missouri, and Wisconsin, and presences in such cities as Philadelphia, Atlanta, and Detroit. Fox's flagship, the ornate Roxy Theatre, the "Cathedral of Motion Pictures," seated five thousand in its main auditorium in New York City's Times Square.[32]

Fox and other corporations established branch offices, agents, and control of theater chains around the world, making American films an overwhelming global presence and exponent of American values. Of these foreign markets, the largest lay in the United Kingdom, which had a robust movie attendance and a keen appetite for American offerings.[33] Despite pressure from various countries, most notably Nazi Germany, to restrict American film distribution and exhibition, by 1937 a reported 40 percent of the United States' major motion picture corporations' revenues came from abroad. Of these, Great Britain contributed 45 percent, the rest of Europe 25 percent, Australia and New Zealand a combined 12 percent, Latin America 11 percent, the Far East 5 percent, and all other markets 2 percent. In addition, Canada accounted for 5 percent of what was expansively considered the domestic market. The Motion Picture Producers and Distributors Association (MPPDA), the trade organization that sought to protect American interests, tried to anticipate material that would prove objectionable in foreign markets and served as the American film industry's representative with the U.S. Departments of State and

Commerce. Roughly half of this global market was English-speaking, and the rest viewed Hollywood films with subtitles, in dubbed versions, or, in smaller language markets, with printed summaries. By one 1938 estimate surveying movie theaters from more than eighty foreign countries, 70 percent of screen time was devoted to American films. In some countries the proportion reached as high as 95 percent.[34]

America's major film companies, riding the wave of sound that surged after the success of *The Jazz Singer* in 1927, initially gloated that they were "depression-proof." The industry did indeed remain profitable as late as 1931, but by 1933 nearly one-third of movie theaters in the country had closed their doors. Paramount had declared bankruptcy, and RKO and Universal had fallen into receivership. Fox Film was staggering badly. Within the past several years, the company had enjoyed a spectacular rise and suffered a crippling fall. By 1929 William Fox had built the enterprise from a chain of movie and vaudeville theaters to the largest motion picture production and distribution empire in the world. His aggressive expansion was heavily mortgaged, however, a gamble that he made confidently, betting on the appeal of innovative sound technology and extensive theater chains to attract new audiences. He lost the bet. An automobile accident in July 1929, the stock market crash that began in October, and an antitrust suit combined to topple him from his position as president and into bankruptcy. Without an experienced pilot, Fox Film Corporation foundered in debt until Sidney Kent took the helm in 1933 and steered it toward a 1935 merger with the brilliant Joseph Schenck's Twentieth Century Pictures.[35]

As the movie industry slumped, moreover, moral critics pummeled it from all sides. The very advent of talking pictures that garnered new profits also aroused a backlash against its perceived vulgarity, violence, and sexual impropriety—including titillating and coarse dialogue accentuated by sound. "Silent smut had been bad. Vocal smut cried to the censors for vengeance," the Jesuit priest Daniel A. Lord observed. "Sophisticated" fare that appealed to young adult urban movie patrons at the profitable first-run theaters shocked and angered parent-teacher associations, women's organizations, Protestant ministers, and other moral arbiters and pressure groups among the middle class, especially in small towns and rural areas. The famous Payne Fund studies bolstered these concerns. In a series of sociological investigations conducted between 1929 and 1933, they warned of the pervasive and troubling effects of movies on children and youth—ranging from loss of sleep to delinquency and crime. Joining the backlash against Hollywood's influence on the lives of children and their families, independent neighborhood exhibitors protested that they were forced by distribution contracts to book movies that their audiences found offensive. Various state and local censorship boards snipped objectionable scenes from Hollywood films, sometimes rendering them incomprehensible as a result, and calls mounted for censorship on a national level. Especially alarming to the major film companies, such federal oversight threatened to regulate their monopolistic business practices as well as their movies' content.[36]

Hollywood had endeavored to placate its critics and to attract investors with elaborate declarations of its own commitment to reform. To quell the rising moral panic, in March 1930 the Motion Picture Producers and Distributors Association announced a code of general moral principles and their applications for movie productions—much of it building on previous recommendations of major film executives. The code, drafted by Daniel Lord, emphasized conservative social, sexual, racial, and religious attitudes—above all, the rewards of virtue and punishment of vice. At the same time, it left open numerous possibilities for depictions of wayward figures, especially those struggling with sexual and criminal temptations before they either successfully resisted—or paid the awful price. Yet in the early 1930s many Hollywood films clearly lacked such a clear moral compass, and outcries persisted, until the MPPDA declared that, beginning on July 1, 1934, all of its members' films would require review and a seal of approval before being released. Appointing a prominent Catholic, Joseph Ignatius Breen, as head of this Production Code Administration (PCA), American movie titans successfully forestalled more draconian penalties.[37] That Shirley Temple's great breakthrough in *Stand Up and Cheer!* came only ten weeks before this demonstration of the film industry's moral rectitude was no accident. Like Breen's PCA, she represented an emblem of virtuous innocence for an industry scurrying for moral cover.

The film industry sought political cover as well. Just as *Stand Up and Cheer!* linked arms with FDR in celebrating national recovery, so did Hollywood promote a positive vision of American democratic life. This emphasis pervaded films of all sorts: gangster and detective thrillers, screwball comedies, melodramas, musicals, and westerns. Indeed, taken as a whole, 1930s Hollywood films stressed American rather than exotic locales, reaffirmed populist rather than elite values, and stressed the emotional virtues of resiliency, optimism, courage, and cheer. In such ways, Hollywood participated fully in the broad artistic and cultural enterprise of the decade, energetically encouraged by the New Deal and abundantly manifested in literature, art, music, drama, history, and other fields: the reaffirmation of vernacular forms, democratic values, and American traditions.

To be sure, a lighter tone and characteristic happy ending had long distinguished American cinema from its English and European counterparts. As early as 1909, the trade paper *Moving Picture World* advised exhibitors, "Give the public good cheer and watch the increased stream of dimes and nickels which will flow into your coffers." Explaining the dominance of Hollywood films in Great Britain in 1928, the future filmmaker John Grierson observed that American movies were optimistic and full of vitality, "bubbling vigor and . . . self-confidence," whereas their British competitors offered little encouragement or comfort to their audiences. He reported the tart observation of an American, "These English pictures don't make you feel any good."[38]

In the context of the Great Depression, to downplay dispiriting conditions became a conscious ideological choice. The Hollywood film industry treated political and industrial issues gingerly, aiming to affirm the essential rightness of American democracy and capitalism. The MPPDA considered these as much as they did personal morality. Even conventional melodrama had to be handled with care in the context of widespread poverty. Thus, in April 1932 Jason Joy, an administrator of the Motion Picture Production Code, wrote the MGM producer Irving Thalberg concerning *Faithless*, a movie about a rich socialite's loss of her fortune and descent into prostitution. The drama's moral issues, he believed, carried disturbing implications in the context of the Great Depression: "If it is to be suggested that the depression not only has stripped the nation of its wealth but has reduced its women to going on the streets as prostitutes to obtain the bare necessities of life, then our whole national life is depicted at a low point. There would be justifiable resentment of this insinuation, particularly in view of the rather heroic efforts being made by the relief organizations, individuals, and the government itself to take care of the needy."[39] In the released version of *Faithless*, a friendly policeman catches the heroine on the verge of her first pickup and sends her back to her husband and the path of virtue.

With the tightening of the Motion Picture Production Code in 1934 and also great pressure for political censorship from movie markets abroad, such restrictions increased. Martin J. Quigley, one of the Catholic architects of the code as well as a leading trade publisher, flatly asserted that movies with a political message "had nothing whatever to do with the amusement industry." Speaking to white southern theater owners in 1937, Quigley defended Hollywood's concentration on movies that fostered "contentment and happiness" as a bulwark against political radicalism. Communists and other radicals, he said, "want the film to be realistic—to deal with the facts of life in the raw. They are unhappy because the people are made happy in the theatres. They want the screen to shock and embitter patrons so that the ranks of the discontented will be enlarged, giving to them recruits in greater numbers to flock to their magical cures for what's wrong with the world."[40] Thus, Hollywood movies, in their very lack of sharp social critique, served a political purpose.

Ultimately, Hollywood not only succeeded in surmounting the immense financial, moral, and political challenges that arose in the early 1930s but went on to attain significant growth, nationally and internationally. This achievement held immense cultural significance. During the Great Depression, the greatest worldwide economic crisis in history, movie attendance rose. In a time of scarcity, spending flowed far beyond dire necessities, pouring into sites of drama, abundance, vitality, and emotional relief. Hollywood's stupendous supply of entertainment met avid and widespread demand.

Yet accurately estimating that attendance, even within the United States, remains difficult. A 1936 survey asked adults how often they went to the movies, and, if they were parents, how often their children attended. Among respondents, 13 percent said they attended movies more than once a week, 24.9 percent attended once a week, 12.1 percent went more than once a month, 13.2 percent went once a month, 21.1 percent attended less than once a month, and 15.7 percent never went.[41] A 1937 survey indicated that 50 percent of Americans regularly attended the movies. (By contrast, only 7 percent of French citizens did.)[42] Another study, published in 1939, gave a more conservative estimate of the American moviegoing population. Noting that weekly movie ticket sales amounted to 85 million in a nation of 130 million, the author judged that many of these sales represented repeat visitors, so that perhaps only 40 million truly had a movie habit.[43] More recently, the film historian Lary May has carefully examined inflated industry figures and concluded that in 1929, weekly movie attendance was 37.6 million. In 1931, by cutting ticket prices, exhibitors pushed ticket sales to 45.1 million a week. Box offices languished in 1932 and early 1933, the nadir of the Depression, but the weekly average of patrons increased to 54.6 million by 1941 and over 70 million by 1945.[44]

Beginning in 1933, exhibitors erected smaller, more economical movie houses across the country at the rate of a thousand a year. They expanded beyond their base in urban middle-class areas to cultivate less-developed markets, including urban working-class neighborhoods and cities and towns in underserved regions, such as the South, the Northwest, and the hinterlands in general. Previously, many small towns lacked proper movie houses at all and relied on shops and other facilities to screen films on Friday and Saturday nights. The construction of new theaters, together with the lifting of Sunday closing laws in many areas, allowed movie theaters to serve as important social centers and sites of civic renewal, open six or seven days a week. They sponsored numerous popular gatherings, from bank nights and amateur hours to high school graduations, charity drives, and club events. Although viewers did not shed their distinctive class, racial, and ethnic consciousness in the theaters, they had a sense of participation in a broadly shared social activity, national mass culture, and imaginative life. Yet these theaters were not equally accessible to everyone. Even though movie attendance increased among young adults from Southern and Eastern European backgrounds, racial segregation remained widespread. Nonetheless, eight hundred new theaters catering to African Americans opened in the 1930s, as did more theaters welcoming Mexican Americans.[45]

To an extraordinary degree, those with any money to spare in the Great Depression spent it at the movies. During the golden age of Hollywood, between 1930 and 1945, the movie industry received eighty-three cents out of every dollar spent on entertainment. Furthermore, precisely because moviegoing was such a popular activity, those who could not afford a ticket often found themselves socially isolated. "Two people can't be friends when one is working and making money and the other is unemployed," said one man in 1935 who had long been out of work. "It just don't work out. The people who have the money don't want to stay at home and do nothing all the time. They want to go to a movie or take a ride, and they can't be expected to treat the other couple." A similar "shadow of humiliation" fell on the children of the unemployed. For instance, rather than confess to his movie-going friends that his mother did not have a cent to give him, a boy of eight said, "Mother doesn't want me to go to movies, but she gave me some money for candy instead."[46]

Movie theater design itself shifted in the direction of egalitarian-ism. The ornate motion picture palaces of the 1920s, built in styles evoking aristocratic and oriental fantasies, with exotic trappings, boxes, balconies, loges, and differential ticket prices, now acquired the taint of the profligate capitalist order that had led to economic collapse. Theater designers in the Depression favored smaller, sleeker, self-consciously "modern" structures, in which, literally and figura-tively, everyone sat on the same level. Movie theater names changed too, expressing the new democratic and nationalistic ethos. Popular 1920s names, such as Alhambra, Granada, Tivoli, and Rialto, gave way to Roosevelt, Washington, Lincoln, and Liberty.[47]

Shirley Temple exerted a special appeal on this expanding movie market in small towns and rural areas as well as big cities. Yet even after she won the part in *Stand Up and Cheer!*, Fox Film was not quite sure what to do with her. Right after filming the "Baby Take a Bow" number, the rotund head of Fox studios, Winfield Sheehan, pressed a minimum contract onto George and Gertrude Temple for Shirley. They happily signed, with Shirley earnestly printing her own name, four days before Christmas 1933. Shirley would now receive $150 a week, plus an additional $25 a week for her mother's assistance, with

Gertrude, Shirley, and George Temple beam over a lucrative new contract with Fox, July 1934. (© Bettmann/Corbis)

an option to renew the arrangement for seven years. Soon thereafter, Sheehan had Shirley's birth certificate altered, subtracting a year from her age, a common practice with child performers, so that she would seem still younger and more prodigiously talented. This deception fooled not only the public but Shirley herself, who discovered her true age from her mother only in 1941, when she turned thirteen.[48]

The contract itself lasted only half a year. Almost immediately after the release of *Stand Up and Cheer!*, various figures from Educational Films and elsewhere laid claim to Shirley's earnings. With the help of a lawyer, Loyd Wright, and after a good deal of public bluffing, the Temples negotiated a new seven-year contract with Fox in July 1934. Under its provisions, Shirley would receive $1,000 a week, and Gertrude Temple $250 a week for her services as hairdresser. In addition, bonuses for each completed picture beginning at $15,000 and rising to $35,000 would accrue in trust accounts on Shirley's behalf. Perhaps to make this agreement attractively tangible to a six-year-old girl, Fox also provided her a scooter, a doll carriage, a skipping rope, picture books, blocks, and a game of jacks.[49]

Preserving the image of little Shirley as mistress of her own destiny, a *Newsweek* article showed her signing the contract and beaming at the camera as her parents smiled approvingly. In a drawing for *Vanity Fair* the caricaturist Miguel Covarrubias imagined still more smiles, as a confident Shirley signs the contract with a large *X*, thus exaggerating her childishness, to the rapacious delight of toothy film moguls. The golden-haired girl with precisely fifty-six curls appeared to have the Midas touch.[50]

Fox Film executives were eager to secure an exciting new child actress, even if she proved to be only a shooting star. Under pressure from their chief creditor, the Chase National Bank, they needed to make appealing movies under tight budgets. And so Winfield Sheehan, eager to exploit his new gold mine before it petered out, placed Shirley Temple in as many feature films as he could. After *Stand Up and Cheer!*, he quickly lent her to Paramount for major roles in *Little Miss Marker* and *Now and Forever*, in addition to assigning her brief appearances in other Fox films. The hectic pace continued with two more starring roles in Fox productions, all released before Christmas 1934.

Stand Up and Cheer! gave Shirley Temple the break her mother had dreamed of, but the movie that established her as a star was the first of her two Paramount pictures, *Little Miss Marker*. Based on a Damon Runyon short story, it revolves around the question, what is a little girl really worth? Once again, Shirley plays a motherless little girl, but this time she almost immediately loses her father too. A well-spoken man, now destitute and desperate, he pleads with an off-track bookmaker to take his little daughter as security for a twenty-dollar bet.[51] In the argot of bettors, she is his "marker," his IOU. The bookmaker

Adolphe Menjou as Sorrowful Jones appraises Shirley
as Marthy in Little Miss Marker. *(Photofest/Paramount)*

Sorrowful Jones (played by Adolphe Menjou) at first turns him down flat. But Shirley's Marthy instantly pierces through his callous facade to see into his emotional depths. Looking intently at him, she says, "You're afraid of my daddy. Or you're afraid of me. You're afraid of something." She has identified fear as the chief obstacle to a healthy sentimental economy as Roosevelt did for the financial one. Sorrowful lifts her up and returns her searching gaze. "Take his marker," he tells his astonished assistant. "A little doll like that is worth twenty bucks, any way you look at it." The clerk, nicknamed Regret, replies sardonically, "She ought to melt down for that much."

When her father loses his wager, instead of reclaiming his daughter, he turns on the gas in his room and kills himself. Little Marthy, an unredeemed IOU, becomes Little Marky, punning on the word "marker." A sweet little girl left to the custody of hardened men is a situation rich in comic possibilities. Sorrowful quickly wins his money back by joining a betting pool in which each of his cronies guesses Little Marky's weight. As the men pass her around and heft her, the explicit comparison is with picking up and fondling a voluptuous woman. The "little doll" is thus also a marker for a grown-up one. But one might see this as an attempt to place Marky on the scales by which these men customarily determine value—in terms of money and, at times, sex, but not sentiment. Sorrowful wins the bet when, on her own initiative, Marky conceals a large saltshaker in order to confirm his estimate of her weight. Then, reluctantly contemplating turning over Marky to the police, Sorrowful sees a way to get still more money from the girl: he makes her titular owner of a racehorse, the true owner, Big Steve, having been temporarily suspended from racing because of infractions.

Sorrowful might be said to be not just a bookie but a comic version of the disillusioned, untrusting economic man of the Depression, with a single worn suit, no family, and no woman on whom to lavish gifts or affection. The film has already suggested that his stinginess sank his romance with the beautiful nightclub singer Bangles Carson (played by Dorothy Dell). Emotionally as well as financially, he is a tightwad.

As Little Marky, Shirley melts his frozen feelings and also loosens his purse strings. When Bangles orders new clothes for her, Sorrowful pays for them without complaint. Soon he moves out of his spare apartment (a "fleabag" in Runyon's story) to a spacious new one with a modern kitchen, a large living room, and at least two bedrooms. Still later, he buys a new suit (Menjou himself had the reputation of being the best-dressed man in Hollywood) and makes a resplendent appearance. The economics of consumer spending and sentiment turn together.

In *Runt Page* and, to a large extent, in the "Baby Take a Bow" number in *Stand Up and Cheer!*, the "make-believe" of Shirley Temple's characters had been in the service of adults. But in *Little Miss Marker* her capacity for make-believe is part of her distinguishing childish innocence. Orphaned by her father's suicide, she is sustained by a book of Arthurian legends. She projects their titles and attributes onto the raffish characters about her, with unintentional mock-heroic effect. The gamblers pin their hopes on Dream Prince and similar horses, or, like Sorrowful, Regret, and Bangles, they no longer truly dream of anything. When Marky starts to adopt their tough talk and to give up on her fairy tales, they avidly seek to restore her faith and sense of wondrous innocence by arranging an elaborate Arthurian ball. These doubly depressed adults need the emotional qualities of childhood, including the ability to play and pretend, every bit as much as children do. In staging a costume ball for Marky, they ironically pay tribute to her priceless innocence as many American parents did with their own children—by lavishing her with treats in order to relish her response.[52] The plot contains still more twists and turns, but ultimately Marky repairs the broken relationship between Sorrowful and Bangles—and even turns the gangster Big Steve from a heel into a hero.

The work of emotional repair of adults' relationships, and especially the repair of the sentimental economy of men, became a strong and abiding theme in Shirley Temple's films. In the midst of the Depression a consecrated sense of childhood as a refuge from the anxieties of adulthood held immense comfort. The image of an adorable girl helped adult men and women to recall nostalgically their own childhoods and savor a vision of domestic bliss. In Shirley Temple's feature films in 1934, including *Little Miss Marker, Now and Forever, Baby*

Take a Bow, and *Bright Eyes*, caring, often emotionally wounded men receive a second chance to resume upright lives and to gain the love and admiration of a child—and the love and admiration of a woman as well.

Contributing to Shirley Temple's popularity in the Great Depression was the widespread sense of shame and humiliation that her movies addressed. Vivid instances of this shame, especially as it related to the loss of male authority, emerged in one study of the effects of unemployment on fifty-nine white Protestant families in a metropolitan area near New York City in the winter of 1935–36. All the men had been out of work since 1931. "The hardest thing about unemployment," one man said, "is the humiliation within the family." He felt "very useless to have his wife and daughter bring in money to the family while he does not contribute a nickel. . . . He feels that there is nothing to wake up for in the morning and nothing to live for. He often wonders what would happen if he put himself out of the picture. . . . Perhaps she and the girl would get along better without him." The same man "intimates that they have fewer sex relations—'It's nothing that I do or don't do—no change in me—but when I tell her that I want more love, she just gets mad.'"[53]

Another out-of-work man in the same study said, "Before the depression, I wore the pants in this family, and rightly so. During the depression I lost something. Maybe you call it self-respect, but in losing it I also lost the respect of my children, and I am afraid I am losing my wife." "There certainly was a change in our family," a third unemployed man confided, "and I can define it in just one word. I relinquished power in the family. Now I don't even try to be boss. She controls all the money, and I never have a penny in my pocket but that I have to ask her for it."[54]

Pride thus became an overarching issue in the face of economic hardship. Surveying the plight of the poor around the country for the Federal Emergency Relief Administration, a key New Deal agency, the former journalist (and confidante of Eleanor Roosevelt) Lorena Hickok repeatedly encountered the reluctance and often refusal of people to register for the relief they so desperately needed. "God, how they hate it," she wrote of unemployed white-collar workers applying for relief in Birmingham, Alabama, in 1934. An engineer confided, "I simply had to murder my pride." An insurance man added, "We'd lived on bread and water three weeks before I could make myself do it." "It took me a month" to apply for relief, a lumberman told her. "I used to go down there every day or so and walk past the place again and again. I just couldn't make myself go in."[55] Although these people and their families may not have seen Shirley Temple's movies, they nevertheless expressed feelings that were pervasive in this decade and that accentuated the sense of vulnerability of all but the most financially and emotionally secure.

Thus, viewers of even a slight Shirley Temple movie, *Baby Take a Bow*, might find in it aspects of their own defeats and dreams. Eager to reunite Shirley Temple and James Dunn after their success in *Stand Up and Cheer!*, Fox's Sheehan cast them in a remake of the studio's 1928 silent comedy-mystery *Square Crooks*. Two ex-convicts, Eddie and his friend Larry, are determined to go straight, work hard, and attain their visions of domestic happiness, which for Eddie and his wife, Kay, means a dream house in Yonkers and a child in the nursery. Yet their shameful past dogs the two men. They are hounded by a suspicious detective, who gets them fired from their jobs, and tainted by the unwelcome return of a ruthless criminal with the ominous name of Trigger Stone. The emotional anchor and radiant source of unconditional love in the movie is Eddie's daughter, Shirley. Affectionate and trusting, she effortlessly penetrates her parents' emotional evasions. She can tell when her mother is worried, she confides, because then "you look sick, and, when you look that way, it makes me want to cry." In the sort of emotional grooming that characterizes so many of her films, Shirley coaxes a smile from her mother, confident that happy feelings will quickly follow. It is a lesson that Kay applies in the very next scene with Eddie, chasing away her own tears with a smile as he says approvingly, "Now it ain't gonna rain no more."

With her father, Shirley is a fount of affection and an eager playmate. At her birthday party, they perform a song and dance, "On Account'a I Love You," in which they celebrate the foods and pleasures they enjoy together. In the number Shirley is always the center of the camera's attention, and her father's upper body is at times cropped from the picture frame. Wearing a very short, frilly dress and with her chubby legs and full cheeks, she seems scarcely more than a toddler, making her dancing ability seem almost preternatural. As Eddie, James Dunn heightens this doll-like quality, lifting her effortlessly and, at one point, pretending that she is his ventriloquist's dummy. Even so, he in no way upstages her, as he performs elementary steps, falls over, and closes their song flagrantly off-key. As she sings, Shirley kisses and hugs him repeatedly, and the number ends in a further shower of smooches. *Baby Take a Bow*, like *Little Miss Marker*, proved to be among the most popular movies of the year.[56]

It is a striking measure of shifts in cultural attitudes that such flamboyant cuddling between Shirley and the fathers and father-figures in her films, deeply suggestive of pedophilia and incest to many critics today, clearly delighted Depression audiences. Even though Shirley's first film shorts, the Baby Burlesks, outrageously played on her infant coquetry, the English novelist Graham Greene was unique among 1930s critics of her feature films in pointing to their scarcely sublimated erotic appeal to middle-aged men. "Watch the way she measures a man with agile studio eyes, with dimpled depravity," Greene wrote in 1937. "Adult emotions of love and grief glissade across the mask of childhood, a childhood skin deep. . . . Her admirers, middle-aged men and clergy-men, respond to her dubious coquetry, to the sight of her well-shaped and desirable little body, packed with enormous vitality, only because the safety curtain of story and dialogue drops between their intelligence and their desire." Determined to silence such scandalous sneers, Twentieth Century–Fox officials sued Greene, contending that he libeled the child and accused them of procuring Shirley for immoral purposes. The company knew that if Shirley's flirtatiousness lost its veil of innocence, her career would be ruined. Their highly paid counsel Sir Patrick Hastings refused even to read the "beastly publication" in court, remarking that it was "one of the most horrible libels one can imagine about a child 9 years of age." Lord Chief Justice Gordon Hewart agreed, calling Green's article a "gross outrage." Not only did he require the weekly *Night and Day* that published the offensive piece to pay £3,000 in damages, he also ordered Greene personally to pay an additional £500, as well as threatening him with criminal prosecution.[57]

A fan letter from a self-described "two-time loser" just out of the penitentiary when he saw *Baby Take a Bow* testified to a much more protective fatherly response. "I knew it was hokum all the time I was looking at it, but Kid, you got to me," he wrote. "This can't be such a tough world as long as there is people like you in it." Shirley gave him an emotional and moral center, he said: "I just wanted to tell you you taught me a guy can go straight if he has got a reason for it, and you are going to be my reason from now on. I am going to see every one of your pictures just like you were my little girl."[58]

The tumultuous year of 1934 concluded with the release of *Bright Eyes* just before Christmas. The story was especially written for Shirley, unmistakable tribute to her star status. So too were the simultaneous introductions of various products licensed in her name, including the first Shirley Temple dolls by Ideal Novelty and Toy Company. For movie exhibitors and merchandisers alike, the Christmas season represented their best hope of the year to get truly out of the red, and Shirley could help them do so.

As in *Stand Up and Cheer!*, *Little Miss Marker*, and *Now and Forever*, Shirley is already half-orphaned at the beginning of the movie, and in time she loses her mother as well. The questions propelling the story are, where will she live and who will care for her? Such a plot had a long history in sentimental melodrama but an especially sharp pang in the Great Depression. After the death of Shirley's acclaimed aviator father in a plane crash, his fellow pilot and best friend, and Shirley's godfather, Loop Merritt (played, in his third pairing of the year with Shirley, by James Dunn), strives to take her father's place as the little girl's protector and pal. A bachelor, he was once jilted by the socialite Adele Martin, and the wound has never healed. In order to provide a home for her little girl, Shirley's self-sacrificing mother, Mary, has taken a job as a live-in maid with a loveless, snobbish, mercenary family, J. Wellington and Anita Smythe, their insufferably bratty daughter, and Mr. Smythe's rich, irascible Uncle Ned.

As Christmas approaches, Mary and the other household servants contrive to make it a special celebration for Shirley, as do Loop and a band of irrepressibly jovial young aviators at the airport barracks, who dote on the little girl. Thus, in what was still the depths of the Depression, Christmas becomes another occasion of consumerist delight, like the fancy-dress Arthurian ball in *Little Miss Marker* and Shirley's birthday party in *Baby Take a Bow*. Money alone may not be able to buy happiness, but materials lovingly bought and arranged— an elaborate birthday cake from a bakery, a beautiful doll and carriage, a lavishly decorated Christmas tree—trigger the wondrous surprise and gratitude of a sweet little girl and vicariously thrill her adult benefactors. Presumably, taking a child to this very movie, which opened in first-run theaters just before Christmas, gave similar pleasure to millions of viewers. As a model child, Shirley was also an exemplary consumer, and the movie provided ample opportunities for merchandising tie-ins. As the trade paper *Motion Picture News* noted appreciatively, "This sure-fire box-office attraction will draw in any locale and affords timely exploitation possibilities surrounding Shirley's Christmas party sequence."[59]

Shirley thaws flinty Uncle Ned (Charles Sellon) in a production still for Bright Eyes.
(Photofest/Fox)

The great foil to Shirley's wondrous innocence, sweetness, and love in the movie is the Smythes' daughter, ironically named Joy and memorably played by eight-year-old Jane Withers, who became a child star in her own right in Fox's B movies.[60] Pampered and spoiled, she is mean, loud, and destructive. Rather than cherishing dolls, she "kills" one and proposes to "operate" on Shirley's with a knife. When Shirley speaks trustingly of what Santa Claus might bring her for Christmas, Joy interrupts, "There ain't any Santa Claus. . . . My psychoanalyst told me."

On Christmas Day, as Shirley's mother rushes toward a trolley to take her daughter a special cake, she is struck and killed by a passing motorist. There ensues a melodrama of contending custodians for Shirley. Mr. and Mrs. Smythe, contemptuous of this servant's daughter, would cheerfully pack her off to an orphanage. Yet Shirley has penetrated the flinty exterior of Uncle Ned to his soft heart (as well as the tender heart of his niece Adele, Loop's erstwhile fiancée), and he is determined to adopt her. To remain in his good graces and his will, the Smythes agree to lodge Shirley in their home—but only temporarily, they tell each other. Opposing both the obnoxious Smythes and imperious tactics of Uncle Ned is Loop. He willingly risks his life in a perilous flight to earn the money to give Shirley a home with him. At the conclusion of a custody hearing, a grandfatherly judge takes Shirley on his lap and, guided by her desires, constitutes a new family comprising those who love her most: Loop; his repentant fiancée, Adele; and regenerate Uncle Ned. Spurned and furious, Mrs. Smythe gives her daughter a slap in the final scene, to the delight of critics, exhibitors, and, quite probably, many viewers.[61]

In the course of the story Shirley is lifted or caressed by at least fifteen men, each of whom is utterly smitten by her infectious mixture of jollity, candor, and affection. The most famous scene is that in which Shirley performs the song "On the Good Ship Lollipop." It is part of the Christmas party that Loop elaborately stages for her, including taxiing around the airport on the newly introduced fourteen-passenger, twin-propeller Douglas DC-2. The number is in many respects a distillation of the vicarious pleasure taken by adult men—and, presumably, the moviegoing public—in the performance of childhood innocence, whimsy, and delight. Although the song is ostensibly from the perspective of a child, like Shirley Temple's movies as a whole, it is in fact a vision of childhood innocence carefully constructed by adults. To the accompaniment of composer Richard A. Whiting's skipping rhythm and hopping ornaments, the lyricist Sidney Clare traces a magical flight to a land of sweets before landing in dreamland. (Sheet music of the song quickly sold over 400,000 copies, and it reached the position of number three on the charts in February 1935.)[62] Supposedly to a recording over the airplane radio, Shirley performs the song with practiced assurance and broad pantomimic gestures. The dozen aviators (played by members of the University of Southern California football team) become a male chorus, singing an accompaniment as they present her with huge lollipops and boxes of candy. At one point they lift her and pass her gently down the aisle. The scene is a celebration of childhood innocence, but, as in Shirley's previous films, that innocence contains an implicit contrast with a romantic adult alternative.

The popularity of the movie, the paternal affection it aroused, and its possible erotic subtexts were all suggested in a letter to the weekly trade paper *Motion Picture Herald*. In the section "What the Picture Did for Me," in which small-town independent movie theater exhibitors reported on their successes and frustrations, Herman J. Brown, manager of the Majestic and Adelaide theaters in Nampa, Idaho, gushed, "I am infatuated with this little elf. This picture left me helpless in a new kind of love. I am wild to be my best girl's father. Something James Barrie [author of *Peter Pan*] perhaps can understand but a terrible amour for an old gent like me. I should pay to run these Temple pictures but instead this one paid me like anything. Let us all join Fox in thanking Heaven for Shirley."[63]

Still another letter to the "What the Picture Did for Me" section testified to the equally enthusiastic but far less ambiguous response of a special audience of adult men, the inmates of the New Jersey state penitentiary in Trenton. The prison's recreational director described how the movie "went over 100 per cent. I saw plenty of tears mingled in between the numerous laughs. The men got a great kick out of the antics of the spoiled rich kid, a part which Jane Withers played to perfection, but their hearts were delivered on a silver platter to Miss Temple!" In the next few years the director reported similarly enthusiastic receptions by the inmates to other Shirley Temple movies, including *Captain January*, *Stowaway*, *Heidi*, and *The Little Princess*.[64]

In 1941, six years after these prisoners laughed and wept watching Shirley Temple in *Bright Eyes*, the writer-director Preston Sturges made his brilliant film *Sullivan's Travels*. It is a picaresque tale of a fictitious Hollywood director, John Sullivan, who, dissatisfied with his ephemeral though lucrative comedies, travels incognito in search of material to portray the authentic experience of the downtrodden and destitute. Though initially frustrated in his efforts, Sullivan ultimately succeeds all too well: he is convicted of assault and sentenced to six years on a southern chain gang. One evening he and the other prisoners attend a movie at a small African American church. As they shuffle to the pews, the black preacher and congregation conclude singing "Go Down, Moses." Watching a Mickey Mouse cartoon, the entire audience—congregants and convicts, blacks and whites—is united in uncontrollable laughter, and Sullivan has a secular revelation. Comedy is not trivial but humanly necessary, and movies that lift the spirits of the depressed may provide a balm as sustaining as a hymn. The immediate point for Preston Sturges's character—and for the real-life prisoners who laughed and wept at *Bright Eyes*, as well as countless other viewers in the Great Depression—was not to change the world but to summon the emotional resources simply to persevere in it. In all her 1930s movies beginning with *Stand Up and Cheer!*, Shirley Temple helped them to do so.[65]

CHAPTER 3
DANCING ALONG
THE COLOR LINE

By Christmas 1934 Shirley and her proud parents could look back on the most astonishing year of their lives. Their talented daughter had vaulted from obscurity to worldwide fame. George and Gertrude Temple, so recently worried about making ends meet, along with countless others, giddily reeled in their new riches. Shirley had chased the gloom from their lives and, momentarily at least, lifted the spirits of untold millions. Two months later at the annual banquet of the Academy of Motion Picture Arts and Sciences, toastmaster Irwin S. Cobb was still in a Christmas mood as he bestowed a special miniature statuette on Shirley in tribute to her box-office power. "When Santa Claus did you up in a package and dropped you down Creation's chimney," the triple-chinned humorist said as he presented her diminutive Oscar, "he brought the loveliest Christmas present that I can think of in all the world."[1] Yet already this golden child was hard at work in another astonishing year of film fame, one in which she had an extraordinary new dance partner, Bill "Bojangles" Robinson.

From the moment of her breakthrough in 1934, Shirley Temple's smiling charm was set against the smiles of emotional deference and buffoonery of African American adults. In *Stand Up and Cheer!* Stepin Fetchit (the stage name of Lincoln Perry) performed his signature role of a lethargic, mumbling fool, and Tess Gardella appeared as her blackface character Aunt Jemima. In *Little Miss Marker* Willie Best played the janitor Dizzy Memphis, a slow-witted character similar to Fetchit's, and Mildred Gover served as Sarah, Bangles Carson's deferential maid. Fetchit and Best continued to appear in Shirley Temple films and to serve as fools and foils to her poise, intelligence, and courage. Other comforting mammy figures came forth, including the irrepressible Hattie McDaniel in *The Little Colonel*.

Yet the African American actor who most memorably contributed his emotional warmth to her movies was the great tap dancer Bill "Bojangles" Robinson. Beginning with the release of *The Little Colonel* in late February 1935 and *The Littlest Rebel* nine months later, they were paired in four films, and the combination of their radiant smiles and infectious cheer delighted moviegoers, white and black.[2] It also gave special prominence to what had hitherto been a minor aspect of Shirley Temple's movies: the emotional work of African Americans in lifting white spirits in the Great Depression.

For when a smiling Bill Robinson entered Shirley Temple's movies, it was to enact the racial politics of the mythic plantation South. An essential aspect of that performance, dating back to antebellum blackface minstrelsy, was a broad smile. That smile complemented FDR's grin of confident command and Shirley Temple's smile of innocent trust. It signaled contentment, servility, and simplicity, from a race white viewers believed to be without ambition or high intellect. Such performances assumed new prominence in the early twentieth century, appearing everywhere from souvenir photographs to Hollywood films to national advertising campaigns in which a beaming Aunt Jemima sold pancake mix and a grinning Rastus cooked Cream of Wheat. Amid the uncertainties of the Great Depression, such performances of sunny servility still held enormous appeal for whites both as testimonies to continued racial deference and as examples of spiritual fortitude. As the novelist Ralph Ellison later observed, "If blacks could laugh (even if only laughing to keep from crying), who could dare to frown?"[3]

In fact, of all racial and ethnic groups, African Americans were the most devastated by the Great Depression. They were the most vulnerable economically—working principally as sharecroppers and tenant farmers or as unskilled or semiskilled workers and domestics—and also the least powerful politically. In the early 1930s more than half lived in the rural South, where collapsing crop prices forced many to hunting, scavenging, or begging in order to survive. In southern cities African Americans suffered too, victims of the contracting economy and racist demands that scarce jobs be reserved for whites. By 1932 more than half were out of work, and further racist discrimination in the administration of relief pushed some close to starvation. In northern cities African Americans fared only slightly better. Though they suffered less overt discrimination in receiving relief, like their southern counterparts, they were the last to be hired and the first to be fired. In the early New Deal, FDR's administration substantially kept African Americans out of the game, as it was far more eager to appease powerful white southern politicians. Yet in 1935, the New Deal began to address the plight of African Americans in substantive and symbolic ways.[4]

Northern African American voters responded decisively to the modest gains they achieved under the New Deal. In the 1932 election they had maintained their historic support for Republicans by a two-to-one ratio. In the 1936 election, by contrast, in what became a permanent shift, three-fourths of the northern African American vote went to FDR.[5] Bill Robinson anticipated this historic change. He supported Roosevelt at least as early as 1930, when he performed at a benefit for FDR's gubernatorial reelection campaign. An autographed photograph of the president hung prominently in Robinson's Harlem apartment, and it was quite likely one sent to him by FDR through their mutual friend Shirley Temple.[6]

Fifty years older than Shirley (and ten years older than her father, George), Robinson had perfected his virtuosic performances over a long career as an entertainer. During the Great Depression he reached his peak of popularity. Yet in a society still saturated with racial prejudice, Robinson inevitably found himself dancing along a color line as dangerous as any high wire. In appearing on stage and screen before overwhelmingly white audiences, he knew he was performing not simply songs and dances but his race as well. His jokes onstage acknowledged that fact. He frequently quipped that he was "having the best time I've had since I was colored," and his anecdotes often involved blackface minstrel humor.[7]

Like Shirley Temple, Robinson began as a child performer—but under quite different circumstances. An orphan on the streets of post-Reconstruction Richmond, Virginia, he learned how to smile, dance, and charm white patrons as a bootblack in order to survive. He and his brother lived with their grandmother, a former slave and a strict Baptist, who disapproved of dancing. At the first opportunity he ran away to Washington, D.C., and moved from street performer, dancing for pennies, to pickaninny roles in minstrel-inflected touring shows such as *The South before the War* and *In Old Kentucky*.[8]

The story of Robinson's theatrical discovery carefully appealed to comic racial stereotypes. Supposedly, in 1903 he was an aspiring dancer waiting tables at the Jefferson Hotel in Richmond. With his mind more on an impending amateur night performance than the task at hand, he spilled a dish of soup over a diner's jacket. Profusely apologizing, Robinson reportedly wailed, "Gee, boss! I'm goin' to quit dis here waiterin' an stick to dancin'. I'se a tap dancer, I ain't no waiter." The soaked guest turned out to be the rising vaudeville manager Marty Forkins. On the lookout for new talent, Forkins went with Rob-

Bill "Bojangles" Robinson. (© Bettmann/Corbis)

inson to an amateur night performance, was impressed by this "colored boy"—and managed him ever after. In fact, Forkins only became his manager after Robinson had already performed jokes and skits for a dozen years with George Cooper as one of the very few African American acts on the Keith and Orpheum circuits. The story, couched in stereotypical dialect that stressed Robinson's comic ineptitude and racial deference, helped smooth Robinson's transition under Forkins to becoming the first African American solo performer in major vaudeville houses.[9] Billed as the "Dark Cloud of Joy," he continued his ascent, becoming with the revue *Blackbirds of 1928*, a consistent Broadway headliner.

A headliner, but still one dancing along the color line. For one vaudeville tour, Forkins's office suggested this publicity ploy: "THE MECHANICAL DANCING SAMBO is still a standard mechanical toy. You know the colored fellow who steps when he is wound up. Get one of your stores to make a window display of these mechanical toys with a sign in the window reading in effect 'THESE FELLOWS CAN DANCE, BUT YOU OUGHT TO SEE BILL ROBINSON AT THE RKO THEATRE.'"[10]

Just as Robinson was reaching the peak of his stage career, the advent of sound created vast new possibilities for Hollywood films, including a new medium for tap-dancing. Quickly thereafter, the stock market crash and the Great Depression whetted appetites for cheering, stylish performances that tap dancers' infectious rhythms, percussive variations, fast, intricate footwork, delicate balance, and exuberant energy satisfied in abundance. Emerging variously out of the blackface minstrel tradition, vaudeville, nightclubs, and Broadway revues, tap-dancing became the rage in the 1930s. Ethel Meglin's dance studio, where Shirley Temple and Judy Garland took lessons, was one of hundreds of such schools where white children learned to tap. Still, no one did it better than Bill Robinson, and the "Dark Cloud of Joy" was soon appearing in Hollywood films.[11] In the single year of 1935, when he teamed up with Shirley Temple, he danced in five.

The differences among these roles expose the workings of the color line in Hollywood. In African American specialty numbers, carefully embedded in movies with otherwise entirely white actors, Robinson strides and dances through black Harlem, elegantly dressed and self-assured.[12] He smiles radiantly, twirls a walking stick, and carries himself with magnetic confidence. Because such possibilities were so rare in Hollywood films, African American moviegoers savored them. At a theater catering to black audiences in Kansas City, Missouri, on a hot August day in 1935, a "restless audience sat through the news-reels, the shorts," and the bulk of RKO's musical revue *Hooray for Love* awaiting the precious eight and a half minutes of Robinson's performance in a Harlem sequence, "Living in a Great Big Way." The specialty number treats a common plight of the Great Depression, a tenant's eviction. As a jazzy orchestral introduction evokes a Harlem street scene, a beautiful, young light-skinned African American woman (played by nineteen-year-old Jeni Le Gon) follows her furniture down the steps of her former apartment and sits on the sidewalk. Her blues last but a moment, however, as the mayor of Harlem (Bill Robinson's honorary title) strides resplendently from his office, beaming like the morning sun.[13] Urging her to count her blessings, he coaxes a smile that makes her "the richest gal in Harlem." Then, to the snappy number "Living in a Great Big Way" by Jimmy McHugh and Dorothy Fields, they join in a vivacious song and dance, claiming the beaming smile and prestige of the president ("I'm a Franklin D. Roosevelt"). Now feeling like a million dollars, she somehow persuades the landlord to relent. Meanwhile, Robinson continues the song's gently swinging beat in a scat number with Fats Waller (in his first film role), then does an exuberant and increasingly virtuosic solo to the admiration of swaying black onlookers—and a white policeman directly behind him. "When Bill's Harlem scene flashed, the applause was deafening," wrote a correspondent for the African American *Chicago Defender* newspaper. "It was as if Bill was on the stage in person, smiling in response to the welcome, as if he knew and understood that he was the asset necessary to the happiness of the audience. . . . Many sat through the picture twice and many grumbled because there wasn't more to see," the reporter noted, "but the manager smiled in understanding."[14]

Bill Robinson's specialty number in Paramount's *The Big Broadcast of 1936* is, if anything, still more exuberant than "Living in a Great Big Way." As a stylish patron in a barbershop brought to his feet by the infectious taps of the Nicholas Brothers and a swinging band version of the Ralph Rainger and Richard A. Whiting tune "Miss Brown to You," he becomes the Pied Piper of Harlem, leading everyone into the street in joyous dance. Here his authority comes not specifically from his office, as in "Living in a Great Big Way," but from the entirety of his dress, demeanor, and expansive emotions and gestures, and he has an unmistakable masculine allure. Although such scenes are carefully circumscribed within their films and undoubtedly contain stereotypical elements, they nonetheless suggest what the emotional possibilities of full citizenship in America might be.

Robinson had brought tap-dancing up on its toes, making the older flat-footed buck-and-wing style seem leaden. Holding himself upright and making little use of his hands and arms, he danced principally from the waist down but with a clarity, precision, and intricacy to his steps that defied imitation. Though he occasionally leapt upward, he was not acrobatic. Instead, he often concentrated on close rhythms in which his feet came only an inch above the floor. Although he devised no new steps, he arranged them superbly. The jazz historians Marshall and Jean Stearns have described his footwork in his stage shows:

Sandwiched between a Buck or Time Step, Robinson might use a little skating step to stop-time; or a Scoot step, a cross-over tap, which looked like a jig: hands on hips, tapping as he went, while one foot kicked up and over the other; or a double tap, one hand on hip, one arm extended, with eyes blinking, head shaking, and derby cocked; or a tap to the melody of a tune such as "Parade of the Wooden Soldiers"; or a broken-legged or old man's dance, one leg short and wobbling with the beat; or an exit step, tapping with a Chaplinesque waddle.

Instead of metal taps, he danced in split clog shoes, which had raised wooden heels and wooden half-soles, loosely affixed for greater flexibility and tonality.[15]

Adding to the virtuosity of his feet, Robinson projected a radiant, joyful personality, especially with his eyes and smile. About five feet seven inches tall, he retained a well-proportioned figure throughout his life, despite his daily regimen of quarts of ice cream. He also dressed sumptuously. In his stage appearances, he favored top hat and tails. His personal wardrobe would have furnished a small haberdashery. In 1936 it reportedly included "forty or fifty suits, numerous shirts made to order . . . thirty pairs of shoes . . . six overcoats . . . dozens of hats," and "dozens of walking canes that are gifts from all over the world." He wore a ten-carat diamond ring and affixed his tie with a six-carat marquise diamond. "There's no use in going through life as if you were in a funeral procession," he told a *New York Times* reporter. "After all, there's a lot of fun in it, so why grump and grouse? Why not dance through life?"[16]

Robinson's success led to more integral roles in three Twentieth Century–Fox films of 1935, but bigger roles meant placement in scenes dominated by whites. He is stripped of his power, prestige, virility, and belonging. He can still sustain a smile and embroider the most mundane domestic task with elegant and exuberant virtuosity, but a sense of white supervision is never absent. The genealogies of these performances are as palpable as if the ancestors' portraits hung on the walls. His impeccable dress is now the uniform of his office as butler and a tribute to the wealth of his white employer, harkening back to

Bill Robinson leads the dancing throng in the "Miss Brown to You"
number from The Big Broadcast of 1936. (Photofest/Paramount)

the Uncle Tom of the Tom shows, in which the radical message of Harriet Beecher Stowe's novel was quashed. And when white onlookers cluster around Robinson's dances, regarding him as an exotic figure, there emerge the ghosts of a hundred blackface minstrel performers going back a century to Thomas D. Rice.

Producers for In Old Kentucky with Will Rogers and revivals of The Little Colonel and The Littlest Rebel with Shirley Temple cast Robinson not in a black metropolitan present but in a mythic white southern rural past, in which all African Americans are servants and either formally or practically enslaved. These films' music emphasizes not uptown swing and sophistication but down-home folk tunes—at least as mainstream whites understood them, for in fact they leaned heavily on blackface minstrel material. Indeed, both *In Old Kentucky* and *The Littlest Rebel* include scenes of racial masquerade, in which Will Rogers's and Shirley Temple's characters black up. The scent of magnolia blossoms contains the sting of burnt cork.[17]

As a house servant in the film *In Old Kentucky*, Bill Robinson lifts the simplest of tasks in kitchen and dining room to an elegant performance, the sort to which Charlie Chaplin might have aspired if he could tap. Yet, instead of Chaplin's dreamy lyricism, Robinson suggests a man for whom dance is as natural as breathing and rhythm as basic as a pulse. There is no ignoring the fact that he restrains the expansive mood and movements of his Harlem dances. He may caper, but he does not swagger. Unselfconscious and unobserved, except by the camera, he nonetheless retains the demeanor of a servant in a white man's home. When his employer, a horse trainer named Steve Tapley, played by Will Rogers, walks into the kitchen at the end of the scene, Robinson's bubble is instantly popped.

Later in the film, when Robinson's character is brought from the kitchen to perform before white ball guests, he is introduced as the "boy" of "Mr. Tapley's." The smile he affixes and holds throughout his dance has a labored, almost ghastly quality, unlike his smiles in "Living in a Great Big Way" or "Miss Brown to You." The ballroom remains the property of the formally dressed white men and women who stiffly watch his performance, and, under the circumstances, his effort to please and placate them becomes an eloquent measure of the continuous emotional deference demanded in the Jim Crow South— and interracial scenes in Hollywood. How much more circumscribed, then, should we expect the performances to be when Robinson dances with Shirley Temple in *The Little Colonel* and *The Littlest Rebel*?

In these two costume melodramas Robinson aided Shirley as she mended not only individual hearts but implicitly the heart of the nation. Ostensibly concerned with cleavages between North and South during and after the United States' greatest calamity, the Civil War, the films provided both refuge and resilience for those experiencing the national ordeal of the Great Depression.

Although the war is over in *The Little Colonel*, it remains an emotional wound in need of healing. Based on the 1895 story by Annie Fellows Johnston and set in postbellum Kentucky, the film is, in the words of one critic of the day, "all adrip with magnolia whimsy and vast, unashamed portions of synthetic Dixie atmosphere.[18] The stony heart that Shirley's character must soften in this melodrama is that of cantankerous ex-Confederate Colonel Lloyd, who clings to the planter vision of the Old South and vows "confusion to all her enemies." Such enemies include his daughter's fiancé, who is doubly damned in the old colonel's eyes as not only a Yankee but a former Union soldier— and one bearing the name of Sherman at that. When she defies her father's command and leaves with her lover, Colonel Lloyd melodramatically declares his door forever barred to her. Played by Lionel Barrymore, the colonel embodies all of the stereotypes of the Kentucky gentleman, including white suit, walking stick, and luxuriant white locks, eyebrows, mustache, and goatee, as well as a violent temper, brutal racism, and the status to indulge both freely.

Six years later, as Sherman pursues investments in the West, Colonel Lloyd's daughter returns to a cottage near her father's house, now with her own young daughter, Lloyd Sherman, the "little colonel," played by Shirley Temple. The child's honorary rank has been bestowed by a western general in recognition of her conquest, "completely unarmed, except for . . . [her] golden curls, brown eyes, and dimples," of the hearts of an army regiment. Back in Kentucky, the little girl, proud of her honorary title, swaggers around the plantation. It is amply staffed with an array of African American servants, for whom life seems unchanged since slavery. She orders the young black children about in her games. Stereotypical pickaninnies, they

Shirley blacks up to hide from a Union soldier in The Littlest Rebel.
(Photofest/Twentieth Century–Fox)

serve as foils to her imperious defiance of old Colonel Lloyd and innocent targets of his wrath. The girl's mammy, played by Hattie McDaniel, generously dispenses cookies, folk wisdom, spirituals, and simple
piety. Yet she remains a lovable inferior, comic in her illiteracy and
great girth.

As Colonel Lloyd's butler, Walker, Robinson preserves much of the
tradition of blackface minstrelsy in which he had served his theatrical
apprenticeship. Still, he remains more the author of humor than the
object of it. Certainly he had little opportunity for self-assertion in his
lines, but he expressed himself eloquently with his feet. Indeed, when

he dances, his authority, artistry, and wit are supreme. In the most memorable scene in the film, the justly celebrated staircase dance in which Walker aims to coax the colonel's granddaughter up to bed, Robinson adapted his signature stage routine from a collapsible set of stairs with five steps on each side to a flight of fifteen steps up to a landing and then ten more to the top. He gave each step a different pitch, so that the stairway became, in effect, a drum set on which he could create elaborate rhythms and patterns. Robinson gave various accounts of his inspiration for his stage version. At times he said it originated when, as a boy, he danced up the wide steps of a Richmond house in which his mother worked. At others he said the idea came in a dream, when the king of England was awaiting him at the top of a flight of stairs, and he danced up them to receive a crown. Robinson undoubtedly told these stories to bolster his claim to have originated a dance that, in fact, long antedated him, and that King Rastus Brown claimed he stole, though Robinson gave it his inimitable stamp. But such stories also point to the way in which the dance could be at once the exuberant delight of a maid's son and an assertion of nobility.[19]

Stock minstrel materials pervade the sequence, from the anthology of tunes Robinson hums as he dances (including "Old Kentucky Home," "Carry Me Back to Old Virginny," "Old Black Joe," and "Year of Jubilo") to the dancing couple's abrupt retreat when Colonel Lloyd appears. Yet Robinson's virtuosic dance on the master's flight of stairs is also an improvisational flight of freedom.[20] In his ability to endow a simple nursery rhyme and hackneyed minstrel tunes with dazzling artistry and vitality, he shows his refusal to be defined as simply a servant. Indeed, he suggests an alternative to Colonel Lloyd's authority, one based on the power to delight rather than denounce. Instead of commanding, he charms. Instead of stamping his foot in exasperation (a gesture shared by Colonel Lloyd and his granddaughter), Robinson's Walker teaches her how to tap it. "I want to do that too," the

Bill Robinson and Shirley join hands in a production still
for the staircase dance from The Little Colonel. *(Photofest/Fox)*

little girl says after Robinson's solo dance. He takes her hand with courtly grace and leads her in a stair dance exquisitely attuned to her talent.

By every indication, Bill Robinson and Shirley Temple had great respect and affection for one another. She cherished his warmth and talent, and he never lost a chance to praise her. Photographs of her took pride of place in his dressing room and in his apartment. Nonetheless, as the African American jazz pianist Hazel Scott later recalled, "He had no illusions about a Black man's privileges. He knew that *only* as her butler, her trusted servant, could he take the hand of the little golden haired child and teach her to dance."[21]

In teaching Shirley the dance, Robinson pared it down and showed her how to keep her steps close and precise. To gain an extra tap or step, he had her kick the stair riser with her toe. As an adult, she remembered, "Every one of my taps had to ring crisp and clear in the best cadence," and she repeated her routine until she got each tap just right. Yet this was the opposite of drudgery. "The smile on my face was not acting; I was ecstatic."[22] Robinson's recording of the pair's taps for the soundtrack perfected the performance, here as elsewhere giving her steps a precision that they lacked.

Ultimately, the little girl proves to be fully her grandfather's equal in courage and his instructor in forgiveness. Together, they foil dastardly swindlers, bent on extorting the deed to her father's valuable land, and Colonel Lloyd, softened by his granddaughter's blend of honey and vinegar, is reconciled with his daughter and son-in-law. In the closing scene, as the black-and-white film bursts into pastels and the soundtrack plays "Dixie," the family is joyfully reunited in a Technicolor embrace.[23]

The *New York Times*'s Andre Sennwald, while chiding Fox's "ruthless . . . exploitation of Miss Temple's great talent for infant charm," still noted that the Radio City Music Hall audience "applauded 'The Little Colonel' for eleven seconds after Miss Temple faded out in Mr. Barrymore's arms." Small-town audiences were equally enthusiastic, as exhibitors reported in the "What the Picture Did for Me" section of *Motion Picture Herald*. "The color sequence left the audience gasping it was so beautiful," J. R. Patterson of the Majestic Theatre in Fort Mill, South Carolina, wrote, and exhibitors from Oscoda, Michigan, Montpelier, Idaho, Tilbury, Ontario, and Lebanon, Kansas, all agreed.[24]

In setting and theme, *The Little Colonel* was a prelude to Shirley Temple's last film of 1935, *The Littlest Rebel*. Having reunited her unreconstructed grandfather and his Union veteran son-in-law in the earlier film, she was ready to patch up the ultimate American family quarrel, the Civil War. As a theatrical property, *The Littlest Rebel* was already old-fashioned in 1911 when Edward Peple created it as a four-act melodrama, starring the child actress Juliet Shelby (later known as Mary Miles Minter). By November 1935, when Twentieth Century–Fox released its film version, it had become "a claptrap skeleton," calculated to serve as a sequel to *The Little Colonel* by reuniting Shirley Temple and Bill Robinson in another moonlight-and-magnolias story of sectional cleavages set in the South.[25]

Edward Peple's version of *The Littlest Rebel* is another reminder of how the road to reunion between North and South was paved on the backs of African Americans. As Peple wrote in the foreword to the novelized version, "This story deals, not with the right or wrong of a lost confederacy, but with the mercy and generosity, the chivalry and humanity which lived in the hearts of the Blue and Gray, a noble contrast to the grim brutality of war." As for the enslaved portion of humanity whose condition lay at the heart of the conflict, Peple appeared to think freedom was a great mistake. As another of her slaves prepares to run away to the Union army, the noble plantation mistress tells her faithful but feckless house slave, Uncle Billy, that her chief concern is for their welfare: "It makes me sad to see them leaving one by one. They are such children, Uncle Billy; and so helpless without a master hand."[26]

Following Peple's play, a generation of silent films, including D. W. Griffith's *The Birth of a Nation* and a version of *The Littlest Rebel*, plowed this fertile ground of racism, well fertilized with the manure of nostalgia. The coming of sound amplified the message with unconvincing southern drawls, blackface dialect, and minstrel music. King Vidor's *So Red the Rose*, based on Stark Young's novel and released less than a month before the Fox production of *The Littlest Rebel*, included slaves enthusiastically cheering their master as he leaves to fight the infernal Yankees.[27] The climactic and most lucrative production of the decade was David Selznick's version of Margaret Mitchell's *Gone with the Wind*, released in December 1939. More than these films, *The*

Littlest Rebel was calculated to please northern and southern whites alike, while offering the barest crumbs of consolation to African Americans. As the trade paper *Variety* observed, "All bitterness and cruelty has been rigorously cut out and the Civil War emerges as a misunderstanding among kindly gentlemen with eminently happy slaves and a cute little girl who sings and dances through the story."[28]

The Littlest Rebel was a romance on several levels, and the terms of these romances reveal much about the emotional needs of the film market in the midst of the Great Depression. As the country faced widespread unemployment, want, and uncertainty, the film reminded moviegoers how Americans had endured far worse in the Civil War and recovered. Shirley plays the part of Virginia, the devoted daughter of invincibly honorable Confederate Captain Herbert Cary, and Bill Robinson serves as their steadfast enslaved house servant Uncle Billy.

In the waning months of the Civil War the Confederate cause is all but lost, but, as little Virgie, Shirley wins the heart of every good man she meets. Apart from her doting father, her first great conquest is the Union commanding officer, Colonel Morrison, who captures her father, despite her best efforts to conceal him. Even so, he is deeply touched by news that her father only returned to attend Mrs. Cary in her final illness. Morrison has, he reveals, his own little girl much like Virgie, and the father-daughter bond is stronger than sectional division or the dictates of war. Instead of taking Virgie's father prisoner, Morrison tells his foe how he might find a spare Union officer's uniform and transport his daughter safely to Richmond, pledging him only not to spy on Union operations in the process.

The innocent conspiracy is quickly foiled, however, and Cary is arrested as a spy, and Morrison as a traitor. Awaiting execution in adjoining cells, they bond in a show of cheerfulness with Virgie during her daily visits. To Uncle Billy's banjo accompaniment, she sings the minstrel staple "Polly-Wolly-Doodle," giving the chorus a special twist for Depression audiences as she banishes "Mr. Gloom."

By this time, Virgie regards Colonel Morrison as a "second daddy" and lovingly kisses him near the mouth, just as she does her father.

The other romance in *The Littlest Rebel* is between little Virgie and Uncle Billy. Yet here the roles of little mistress and servant are kept firmly in place. He can teach her dances and act as her guide, but their affection is determinedly kept within the boundaries of innocent playmates—at least as that bond was represented in the mainstream white press. Nonetheless, one African American movie theater glee-fully promoted Bill Robinson and Shirley Temple as an interracial cou-ple: "SHOT AND SHELL COULDN'T PART THESE SWEETHEARTS!" Among the African American patrons in Oakland, California, watch-ing the couple was a ten-year-old boy, the future artist Robert Cole-scott. "What if America's sweetheart had been a black girl?" he later wondered. "What would it mean to a white man to see himself as a Bill Robinson, caught in that image and playing second fiddle to a black girl?" The impish painting that sprang from these subversive ques-tions was *Shirley Temple Black and Bill Robinson White* (1980), the title gleefully punning on Shirley Temple's married name.[29]

Although Uncle Billy was a thoroughly contented and credulous slave in the original play, his character acquired more dignity in the film version, while still staying within the stereotype of a courteous and steadfast Uncle Tom. To take but one instance, early in the film, Uncle Billy, explaining the Civil War to little Virgie, reports that he heard a white gentleman say, "There's a man up North who wants to free the slaves." When she asks what that means, he replies, "I don't know what it means myself." As *Variety*'s reviewer observed, the line "is spotted and delivered by Bill Robinson in such a way as to possibly cause northern eyebrows to tilt. Just a slight tilt."[30]

As a foil, Willie Best played the "coon" part of James Henry, a ludi-crously simple-minded, lazy, and easily frightened young slave.[31] Rounding out the slave population on the plantation are the patient, loving Mammy (Bessie Lyle) and a group of children, who are tongue-tied in little Virgie's presence. Their bashful ignorance and Virgie's noblesse oblige fully accredit the plantation myth of the Old South.

Still, just as in *The Little Colonel*, Robinson's character is most able to proclaim his authority and dignity through his virtuosic dancing. When Uncle Billy and Little Virgie turn buskers to raise their train fare to Washington in an effort to free her father, they perform a dance shuffle on the plank sidewalk. Robinson initiates skipping crossovers, back flaps, and other steps, tunes, hums, and interjections, and Shirley imitates him. White onlookers quickly cluster around the odd couple, and once again, as in the ballroom performance in *In Old Kentucky*, Robinson is not simply a dancer but a racial exhibit. The racial imitation and masquerade at the heart of blackface minstrelsy are epitomized in this duet, which culminates in another staircase dance.[32]

Robinson's status as dance instructor to little Virgie in this scene amused rather than threatened white viewers. A critic in the *Atlanta Constitution* wrote, "To see Shirley imitating Bill Robinson, not only in tap steps but in gestures and cast of countenance, is to see one of the most laughable sights on the screen." The African American *Chicago Defender*, by contrast, was delighted to see Shirley Temple "truckin' on down" with Bill Robinson as if fresh from a Cotton Club revue.[33]

In the original play of *The Littlest Rebel* a ragged and emaciated Virgie finally appeals to General Grant to pardon her father and Colonel Morrison. In the film version a notably plump, well-dressed Virgie and Uncle Billy take the matter directly to the White House. Soon they are ushered into Lincoln's presence. The president, played by Frank McGlynn Sr., who made a career of Lincoln roles, rises from his desk, shakes Virgie's hand, and then extends his hand to Uncle Billy. It is the film's one explicit if fleeting suggestion of the dignity and freedom owed to African Americans, and it was intended to emphasize Lincoln's magnanimity rather than Uncle Billy's equality. At first Billy fails to grasp the president's hand, because, presumably, a white man has never extended his hand to him before. (In a line later cut from

Shirley and Bill Robinson truckin' on down in The Littlest Rebel
(Photofest/Twentieth Century–Fox).

the script—could it have been at the request of Bill Robinson?—he
says incredulously, "I'se a slave.")[34] Then he shakes it.

Lincoln takes Virgie over to his desk and gently extracts the facts
of the case from her. When she describes how her mother "went away,"
Virgie breaks into sobs, and Lincoln sympathetically lifts her onto his
lap. Ultimately, the president dispatches an order to General Grant,
freeing her father and Colonel Morrison. Virgie has won the greatest heart of all. An early draft of the script had Lincoln writing his
Gettysburg Address while still under her spell, but the veteran script

doctor Raymond Griffith protested that viewers' credulity would snap. "If you ever even suggest that Shirley Temple was the inspiration for the Gettysburg Address," he warned, "they'll throw rocks at us."[35]

In the film's concluding scene, we see Virgie and the bars of the jail behind her. Then the camera pulls back to reveal a long table, covered with a cloth and the remnants of a banquet celebrating the officers' pardons. She is singing "Polly-Wolly-Doodle," with the men joining in. Cary and Morrison rise on each side of her in the final chorus and simultaneously plant kisses on her cheeks.

Like Shirley Temple's smile and sunny disposition, Robinson's virtuosity was repeatedly portrayed as a natural gift rather than a product of work and craft. Robinson himself shrewdly played the part of the naive artist for white journalists. "I don't know how I do it," he told the New York Times's S. J. Woolf. "I just dance. I hear the music and something comes into my head which I just send down to my feet. And that's all there is to it." Woolf observed, "He brings up pictures of those happy-go-lucky darkies who lolled about columned plantation homes—who danced because they had no cares and who sang because they couldn't help it." Another white interviewer noted approvingly, "His southern upbringing and innate modesty makes [sic] Bill tactful about observing Jim Crow laws, written and unwritten."[36]

Racist constraints on Robinson deeply offended African Americans who admired his artistry. The avid proponent of the Harlem Renaissance Alain Locke declared in The Negro and His Music that "for two generations the American Negro dancer has been in vaudeville chains. His accomplishments within such a narrow compass of routine foot work and acrobatic eccentricity have only been possible through sheer genius; but what . . . [a host of dancers, including] Bill ("Bojangles") Robinson could have done in a freer medium with more artistic background can only be imagined." Locke continued, "A Bojangles performance is excellent vaudeville, but listen with closed eyes, and it becomes an almost symphonic composition of sounds. What the eye sees is the tawdry American convention; what the ear hears is the priceless African heritage."[37]

Whites and blacks joined in celebrating not only Robinson's artistry but also his tireless philanthropy. He performed at numerous charitable and police benefits and gave generously to the poor and needy, to African American hospitals and orphanages, and to civic efforts on behalf of playgrounds in Harlem and a traffic light at a dangerous intersection in his hometown of Richmond, Virginia. To African Americans, however, Robinson was not merely a specialty act and a comfortingly sunny personality but one of the greatest stars of stage and screen, as well as a spectacular rags-to-riches story, a stature that earned him both adulation and scrutiny. For black newspapers and many of their readers, his presence in a movie was reason enough to attend, and they regarded him as fully the costar of Shirley Temple, not merely a supporting player.

Nonetheless, a subject of heated, if largely subterranean, debate among African Americans was whether his role as a model Negro (from the white point of view) was compatible with being a "race man." Attending a stage revue in which Robinson told the racial jokes that had long been a staple of his act, a black youth heckled, "We don't want to hear that old 'Uncle Tom' stuff. . . . We came here to see you dance."[38]

The journalist and critic Ralph Matthews fumed, "The big names among Negro performers are only those who have appealed to the whimsicalities of the white race and conformed to their idea of what a Negro should be." Robinson, he said, was "always presented as an old Uncle Tom" in his films with Shirley Temple. Yet, while castigating Hollywood's timorous deference to southern white racial prejudice, Matthews did not blame Robinson himself. Renzi B. Lemus, the venerable head of the Brotherhood of Dining Car Cooks and Waiters, saw the issue in terms of protecting African American jobs. Accordingly, he rushed to the defense of Robinson and similar actors. "Why not leave Bill Robinson alone?" Lemus asked, arguing that black actors working in Hollywood were far preferable to grease-painted imitations. The latter had often claimed major African American roles as late as the mid-1920s.[39] Thus, African American pride and frustration with Robinson inevitably reflected the larger problem of claiming respect, wealth, opportunity, and a measure of happiness in 1930s America.

Robinson rarely answered his critics directly. Still, in an interview with a black journalist, he declared, "There are so many who innocently feel that I haven't my race at heart. This is not true. I am a race man! And I do all in my power to aid my race. I strive upon every turn to tear down any barriers that have existed between our two races and to establish harmonious relationship for all."[40]

Nonetheless, Robinson knew the truth of Paul Laurence Dunbar's poem "We Wear the Mask." His grin hid at least as much as it revealed, including the dedicated practice and discipline by which he achieved his virtuosity and also a hot temper dating back to his childhood. His given name was Luther, but he appropriated his brother Bill's name instead in a boyhood fight and went by it for the rest of his life. His very nickname, Bojangles, pointed to that temper, deriving from "jangler," meaning a quarreler or squabbler, though this meaning too was masked in reports to the white press.[41] His temper only occasionally flared onstage in response to hecklers, but offstage it was much more in evidence. The "Dark Cloud of Joy" could turn stormy in his encounters with Hollywood directors and producers.[42] More generally, his quarrelsome nature, his gambling habits, and the racial tensions of American life all led to scrapes with blacks and whites alike. His body bore scars from razor and knife slashes, and a bullet fired in 1898 remained lodged in his knee. By the time of his success with Shirley Temple, he habitually carried a gold-inlaid, pearl-handled .32 caliber revolver, a pistol permit, and affidavits from numerous police chiefs and eminent officials as a kind of passport through white America. Robinson managed to keep most of his fans, the white ones especially, from seeing all of these dimensions. Again and again, white critics lauded this irrepressibly jolly man who was part of "a naturally jovial race."[43]

No doubt they would have been surprised to hear Robinson's outburst at a New York Yankees baseball game when he was in his mid-sixties. As his third wife, Elaine, recalled, "Bill was betting some man a hundred dollars that someone would hit a home run. This big [white] man in the back yelled, 'Oh, sit down. We don't want to touch your dirty money.' And Bill couldn't believe that the man had said that. He yelled back, 'Dirty money? Yeah, pretty, white Shirley Temple money. That's where I got it. Teachin' white Shirley. It's filthy, dirty money!'"[44]

At last, a golden opportunity to press for African American rights did emerge when Robinson met President Franklin Roosevelt. Not allowed to plead for his people to President Lincoln as Uncle Billy in *The Littlest Rebel*, when Robinson stood face-to-face with Roosevelt, he seized the moment. "By the way, Mr. President, I see you got some kind of New Deal going," he said, undoubtedly smiling all the while. "Just remember, Mr. President, when you shuffle those cards, just don't overlook those spades."[45]

When in 1949 Robinson died at the age of seventy-one, he received one of the largest funerals in the history of New York City. An estimated half-million mourners lined city streets for eight miles as his flag-draped hearse slowly rolled from Harlem's Abyssinian Baptist Church through Times Square to the Evergreens Cemetery in Brooklyn. At the funeral, Adam Clayton Powell Jr., the church's pastor and first African American congressman from New York, eulogized Robinson. "Bill was a credit not just to the Negro race but to the human race," the civil rights leader said. "He was Mister Show Business. He was Broadway. And who is to say that making people happy isn't the finest thing in the world?"[46] The question was rhetorical, of course, but it pointed to Robinson's effort and achievement, even as it aimed to forestall black criticism.

Criticism came quickly, nonetheless. Five days after Robinson's funeral, a letter to the editor of the *New York Amsterdam News* declared, "Although it is unfortunate that Bill Robinson died, the type of entertainer who died with him is well gone. Recognizing that Bill began his career many years ago in an altogether different age, it is understandable that he would have played the 'Uncle Tom' role to gain fame and fortune. But in the opinion of many he portrayed that role when it was wholly unnecessary." Writing in the *Chicago Defender* in 1953, four years after Robinson's death, Langston Hughes more eloquently expressed the same impatience: "Uncle Tom did not really die. He simply went to Hollywood. . . . Long ago in America," he continued, "the stereotype of the Negro as a humorous clown was born. That shadow of the South is still over the Negro in professional entertainment. A superb dancer like the late Bill Robinson told jokes shaming his people because he danced in that shadow."[47]

The difficulty of assessing Robinson's example remained, and central to that difficulty was the nature of his smile. Was it a sign of his emotional strength or weakness? Was his ability to sustain it as he danced along the color line with Shirley Temple a triumph or a surrender? African Americans debated such questions during Robinson's lifetime and still more so after his death. Whatever their individual answers, his smile was emblematic of the emotional work that African Americans had been expected to perform through the Great Depression and of their growing refusal to do so. That smile compressed volumes of African American history and resilience, artistry and accommodation, pride and pain. It was a history that the young Shirley Temple could scarcely imagine.

CHAPTER 4
THE MOST ADORED
CHILD IN THE WORLD

"I used to sleep with a clothespin on my nose, and two cotton balls," Oprah Winfrey once recalled. "And I couldn't breathe and all I would do is wake up with two clothespin prints on the side of my nose, trying to get it to turn up. I wanted Shirley Temple curls; that's what I prayed for all the time." The paradoxes of modern celebrity are many. That Oprah Winfrey, born in rural Mississippi in 1954 and rising out of a broken family, poverty, racism, and sexual assault to become the most admired and richest African American woman of her generation, ached as a little girl to look like Shirley Temple is by no means the strangest.[1]

Crucial to Shirley Temple's amazing fame in the Great Depression—and its endurance for generations—were the strong bonds forged between vast, diverse publics and the adored curly-haired child. Celebrity and fans became inextricably linked in the chains of the Hollywood empire. Although such fans have frequently been portrayed as passive, they participated actively and creatively. Yet the choices presented to them were distinctly limited, just as were those of the Temple family in working within the studio system. All were captivated by processes larger than themselves. For the star system served as a key agent in a larger consumer system, and Hollywood's golden age must be understood as an integral part of the development of a modern consumer culture. That culture especially transformed the United

States, penetrating deep into the lives of children as well as adults, and it was rapidly changing the lives of families around the globe.

Even today, the breadth and depth of Shirley Temple's fame in the Great Depression remain astounding. The top box-office star in the world for four consecutive years, from 1935 through 1938, she exerted a personal appeal for many moviegoers that no adult could match. Stimulated at every opportunity by Fox Film and later Twentieth Century–Fox representatives and their allies among film distributors, exhibitors, the press, magazines, merchandisers, and advertisers, her worldwide fame rivaled any celebrity's of the time. In the mid-1930s her fan clubs comprised 384 branches with a total of 3,800,000 members. Had they been a city unto themselves, it would have been larger than any in America other than New York. On the occasion of her seventh birthday, twenty thousand admirers in Bali gathered to pray for her good health. A Japanese movie magazine filled two issues solely with photographs of Shirley and sold a million copies. Remarking how deeply American movie culture had penetrated the interior cities of China, the writer Lin Yutang observed: "A street peddler with Shirley Temple postcards always does a roaring business before schools and at luncheon hours." Even in 1940 with war raging in Europe, the German satirical magazine *Simplicissimus* gently spoofed Shirley Temple's fame, depicting the child star in the front row of a schoolroom as she responds to the teacher's instructions to the class to write their names, "No, ma'am, I'm not giving any more autographs!" With only modest exaggeration, a 1939 Hollywood trade paper marveled, "There is no country in the world, both civilized and uncivilized[,] where at some time or another her pictures have not been shown. In the Orient she is called 'Scharey,' in Central Europe it is 'Schirley,' but throughout the English speaking world 'Shirley Temple' stands as a universal symbol of childhood. No child in history has been so well known or universally beloved."[2]

This status of universally beloved child was one that the studio and its representatives assiduously cultivated. Almost from the moment of her 1934 breakthrough, Shirley served as a goodwill ambassador for Twentieth Century–Fox and the Hollywood film industry in general. In this capacity, she met President Roosevelt and Eleanor Roosevelt (the latter twice), the Australian prime minister, the daughter of a Japanese ambassador, the son of Benito Mussolini, the Chilean navy's chief of staff, who named her an official mascot, three Russian polar flyers, and Prince Purachatra Jayakara of Siam, among many others. She greeted the most celebrated thinker of the century, Albert Einstein, a Jew who fled his native Germany in 1933, the year that Adolf Hitler came to power. When she met the distinguished conductor Leopold Stokowski, he held her face in his hands and pronounced her "a divine instrument." After meeting her, the British novelist and historian H. G. Wells declared, "She totally disarms you—she lifts you off your feet." To visit her was to commune with the radiantly cheerful embodiment of American girlhood, and many made the pilgrimage.[3]

The ultimate honor that the studio could bestow was to have Shirley sit on the lap of visiting dignitaries. Shirley sat on hundreds and became a connoisseur. California governor Frank Merriam's lap was "surprisingly bony," the powerful financier and future New York governor and United States vice president Nelson Rockefeller's not the most comfortable, but Federal Bureau of Investigation director J. Edgar Hoover's "outstanding as laps go. Thighs just fleshy enough, knees held calmly together, and no bouncing or wiggling." The two formed an unlikely friendship that lasted for decades.[4]

Just as celebrities in many fields basked in the glow of Shirley Temple's attention, others shivered in her shadow. The great composer Arnold Schoenberg, another Jewish émigré from Nazi Europe, was incensed that the neighboring Temple family house was a featured attraction on a tour of Beverly Hills homes, but not his own. In modern celebrity culture, a diminutive child star easily dwarfed even a giant of modern art music.[5]

Beyond such celebrities, and far more important to Shirley Temple and Hollywood, lay the vast moviegoing public. She was a consistent favorite among children. Indeed, one reporter noted that "Shirley Temple would play to more persons if children would leave the theater after seeing one show. They stay all afternoon, while hundreds stand in line outside."[6]

Yet she was also a favorite among American adults. A 1937 poll published in *Fortune* magazine provides the best snapshot, however blurred, of the character and extent of this audience. Respondents to an opinion poll placed her overall as the second-most-popular movie star, a hair's breadth behind Clark Gable. Women as a whole declared her their absolute favorite, and among men she ranked second, right behind Clark Gable and ahead of William Powell. Among moviegoers between the ages of twenty and forty, her ranking slipped to fourth (still placing her first among actresses and ahead of Norma Shearer and Myrna Loy), but among those over forty, she soared to number one. Further sifting the poll data, *Fortune* concluded, "Shirley Temple is the darling of the Middle West, Northwest Plains, Southeast and Southwest, also of rural districts and cities of 2,500 to 25,000. Housekeepers (of course), proprietors, farm labor, and retired gentlemen like her best of all. Her strength is appearance and personality."[7] Not surprisingly, she exerted her greatest attraction not on younger adults living in cities but among those living in the small towns and rural areas of the American heartland. These were the "unsophisticated" audiences to which independent movie exhibitors catered, the sort who celebrated their successes and lamented their disappointments in *Motion Picture Herald*'s "What the Picture Did for Me."

Although half of all Americans in the mid-1930s attended the movies on a regular basis, the poorest Americans were unlikely to see Shirley Temple movies. Yet it is a testimony to her cultural centrality that even they, black and white alike, might admire, even cherish, her image. An interviewer for the New Deal's Federal Writers' Project visited Gabriel Meyers, a black laborer and grandfather of twelve, in his unfinished four-room cabin, built of rough lumber, near McClellanville in the South Carolina lowlands. Holding pride of place in the modest but neat home where he lived with his wife and one grown daughter were two photographs, one of Gabriel, the other of Shirley Temple. Another such interviewer saw a picture of Shirley Temple on the mantle of the tumbledown house of a fifty-five-year-old white textile mill worker and his wife, John and Lizzie Pierce, in Wake Forest, North Carolina. Asked if she liked to see the child actress's movies, the woman replied, "Hon, I've never saw her. . . . I never did take up no time with picture shows and amusemints of that kind." The couple was childless, and the husband confided, "When I see the fine young girls of today I wisht I had a daughter of my own."[8]

The wish to have a daughter like Shirley Temple swept American families in the 1930s, and many expressed those wishes in naming their newborns. When Gertrude Temple chose the name of Shirley for the daughter that she hoped would be a star, that name ranked as the tenth most popular for girls in the United States. This ranking changed little until 1934, the year of Shirley Temple's sudden popularity, beginning in late April with the release of *Stand Up and Cheer!* Then the name rose to number four. In 1935 and 1936 it was the second-most-popular girl's name in the country, and it remained in the top five through 1939. Its popularity strikingly accorded with Shirley Temple's reign as box-office champion.[9]

The desire for a personal link with a figure of radiant confidence and cheer also drew countless parents and children, as well as those wishing for a child, to Shirley Temple movies. Since the establishment of Hollywood as a movie capital in the second decade of the twentieth century, women in particular had formed the backbone of movie culture, and they represented the heart of Hollywood's fans. By the beginning of the 1920s, Hollywood stars were far more than merely

actors: they were models of modern selfhood, transcendent personalities to be admired and emulated. Although the Great Depression
dimmed many women's (and men's) own dreams, they stubbornly
retained those on behalf of their daughters. A little girl with a big
personality could win their hearts and shape their ambitions. Beginning in 1934 and throughout the 1930s, Shirley Temple glowed as the
supreme model of American girlhood, whose personality and appearance entranced those mothers and daughters as did no other figure in
the twentieth century.[10]

Hollywood and the numerous media and industries that depended
on it had learned how to stoke the dreams of women, men, and children in the 1920s, and they redoubled their efforts in the Great Depression. Just as there was a Shirley Temple formula to her films, so there
were formulas governing publicity, all of them based on her adorable
appearance and personality. Publicity campaigns operated simultaneously at multiple levels—from the intensely local to the global—to
make Shirley's presence ubiquitous and her spell unshakable.

The press played an indispensable role. Hollywood and surrounding Los Angeles was the third largest news source in the country, with
more than 350 newspaper and magazine correspondents, including
one from the Vatican.[11] For Shirley, her popularity meant that everything that she did was news: catching a cold, losing a tooth, changing
her hairstyle, traveling to Hawaii or across the country, appearing
at a theater. Studio press releases papered the world, so that readers
would see similar accounts and photos of the beaming star whether
they lived in Hoboken or Havana, São Paulo or Singapore, Ottawa
or Osaka.

Shirley Temple's birthday on April 23—her age consistently reduced
a year—provided one such occasion. The first party, held in April
1934, less than three weeks after the release of *Stand Up and Cheer!*,
was a modest affair by later standards, but the guests invited to the

Fox studio restaurant were carefully selected to ensure the greatest publicity. All were the children of newspaper reporters, and the event was chronicled even in Japan.[12]

After Shirley's rapid ascent, scarcely a newspaper reader, movie-goer, or shopper could fail to miss the occasion. Indeed, all were invited to participate. In April 1936, coinciding with the release of *Captain January*, Twentieth Century–Fox orchestrated a series of events at movie theaters, department stores, and organizations around the country and abroad, more than nine hundred parties in all. "Shirley says, 'Everybody come to my birthday party!'" ran a typical newspaper advertisement. Ideal Novelty and Toy Company, maker of the authorized Shirley Temple doll, proclaimed this the "biggest non-Christmas toy event in history." In addition to dolls and dresses, merchants displayed a host of less expensive Shirley Temple items: songbooks, paper dolls, coloring books, sewing cards, soap, and other novelties. Twentieth Century–Fox publicists arranged for a torrent of congratulatory telegrams from fans to flood the Temple home in Santa Monica. Many came from entire communities: a wire from one Illinois town bore twelve thousand signatures, another ten thousand. Some fans sent presents, dolls especially, so that Shirley Temple acquired an extensive collection despite herself. Altogether, she received 135,000 greetings and gifts.[13]

On the big day Shirley got several cakes: one from her New York fans, a second, in the shape of the Tennessee State Capitol, from that state's governor, and a third from the Hotel Biltmore in Los Angeles. The colossal scale of greetings, gifts, cakes, and parties blurred the border between the cute and the grotesque. To preserve a semblance of normality, publicists emphasized that the cake that Shirley actually cut at her birthday party was a homemade one and the gifts that she prized most—a pony, a bicycle, and a turquoise ring—came from her family. The Temples also announced that almost all of the gifts that their daughter received were donated to charity.[14]

Shirley in her new hairstyle celebrates her "ninth" birthday, 1938.
(© Bettmann/Corbis)

Always welcome copy for newspapers, Shirley was the special darling of movie fan magazines, which numbered more than a dozen in the United States by 1934, the largest achieving circulation of roughly half a million each, in addition to dozens more abroad. In 1935, her first year as an established star, she garnered the most coverage in feature stories, interviews, and photographs in the top eleven fan magazines. She also appeared on nine of these magazines' covers, surpassing all competitors except for Claudette Colbert, with ten. Like the movie industry as a whole, such magazines saw declining sales in the early 1930s, and almost all of these publications cut their price to ten cents. Also, like the Hollywood studios, they faced growing moral outcry against false and salacious stories, such as gossip about the marriages and divorces of Jean Harlow, as well as photographs of scantily clad actresses. To quell such critics, Will Hays's Motion Picture Producers and Distributors Association imposed restrictions on fan magazines similar to those of the code governing the film industry. Henceforth Hollywood studios and magazines worked hand-in-glove to preserve a star's carefully constructed image. Studio publicists regularly supervised interviews and approved stories, and many magazine writers also served as studio publicists themselves. Magazine publishers and studio executives were keenly aware that the film and fan industries could flourish if united—and likely fail separately. Fan magazines thus embraced Shirley Temple with much the same calculation as did Hollywood producers. Her cheerful innocence gave them a welcome attraction who appealed to the widest variety of readers without a whiff of indecency.[15]

Indeed, so sure were they of Shirley's impeccable purity that studio publicists and journalists often wrote with tongue in cheek as if she were a femme fatale. In this spirit, immediately after Shirley's breakthrough in 1934, Fox launched a series of full-length ads in trade newspapers, spoofing Hollywood gossip stories. One breathlessly declared, as if probing the marriage prospects of a high-society celebrity, "Cornered by reporters here today, Shirley Temple broke the silence which she has maintained about her future plans. 'I am going to appear next,' she said, 'in the Fox picture Baby Take a Bow with Jimmy Dunn and Claire Trevor.' Declining to discuss rumors of her engagement to the Prince of Wales, La Temple rushed to the studio restaurant for an ice cream cone." In a similar vein, an article in Modern Screen began, "Shirley Temple is due to wreck more American homes than the combined devastation of the depression and the torrid electrons of every siren on the screen today." The threat, it emerged only several paragraphs later, was that mothers around the corner, reading about the munificent contract that the Temple family had signed on behalf of their delightful daughter, would grab their own cherished child and, abandoning home and husband, head directly to Hollywood.[16]

In cities and small towns, in the United States, Canada, and much of the rest of the world, Fox Film and later Twentieth Century–Fox representatives united with distributors, exhibitors, merchants, manufacturers, community organizations, and schools, seeking at every possible opportunity to create tie-ins ("tie-ups" in the phrase of the day) between Shirley and her fans. Exhibitors energetically used every bit of ballyhoo that they could imagine to draw people to the movie house. Frank H. Ricketson Jr., president of Fox-Intermountain Theaters in Denver and a veteran of Howard Hughes's movie theater chain, filled a book with extensive advice to theater managers on how to drum up movie attendance. A manager, Ricketson insisted, must be a "showman," one who knows how to book an attractive bill and to stimulate public desire, "to make the public believe that it is necessary to happiness." Such demand could be achieved only by concerted appeals, including newspaper articles and advertisements, radio spots, billboards, film trailers, and the like. Managers also staged a variety of "giveaways": premiums, contests, drawings, and similar stunts, often in tandem with local merchants and organizations.[17]

One of the most popular of such stunts was the Shirley Temple look-alike contest. From 1934 through the rest of the decade, Fox and later Twentieth Century–Fox publicists promoted such contests extensively, enlisting the efforts of local movie exhibitors, newspapers, department stores, and other retailers in the process. Shortly after Shirley's breakthrough in 1934, a manager of a movie theater in Des Moines, Iowa, teamed up with a photo studio specializing in children's portraits. Girls who sat for the photographer could have their likenesses displayed in the lobby of the theater as it ran Shirley's latest movie, *Baby Take a Bow*, and moviegoers voted for the one who most resembled Shirley. At the same time, a Brooklyn manager joined with the newspaper *New York American* to host a Shirley Temple look-

Nine contestants in a Shirley Temple look-alike contest, sponsored by
Fox Film and the Daily Telegraph, *Sydney, Australia, October 2, 1934.*
(Photograph by Sam Hood, Dixson Galleries, State Library of New South Wales—
DG ON4/814 s, reproduced by permission)

alike contest with Pekinese puppies as prizes. Other look-alike contests awarded top contestants a pass to Shirley's latest movie and an
autographed photo of the star. That fall in Sydney, Australia, Fox Film
and the *Daily Telegraph* newspaper raised the stakes, offering contestants a first prize of a hundred pounds. Similar contests were held in
other cities of the British Empire, including Bombay, India.[18]

Nor were such contests confined to English-speaking countries. In
April 1935, still less than a year after Shirley's breakthrough, a journalist in Havana interviewed three young Cuban veterans of Shirley Temple look-alike contests. The first of these, a five-year-old girl
named Myrna with golden curls and brown eyes, had already won first

prize in several competitions in which she not only had to look like Shirley but also had to demonstrate her "command of the enchanting arts" practiced by "Hollywood's kid." A second, only four years old, could re-create Shirley Temple's gestures exactly. The third, despite her golden hair and an enchanting smile, possessed more of Shirley's temperament than appearance and had a string of second-place awards in Shirley Temple contests, rather than the coveted first prize. The influence of Shirley Temple, the Cuban journalist favorably noted would serve to "de-countrify" Cuban children.[19]

The search for the "Cuban Shirley Temple" was reiterated in other countries around the world. In May 1936 the "French Shirley Temple," winner of a contest sponsored by the Paris film weekly *Pour Vous* that attracted three thousand look-alikes, journeyed with her mother to Hollywood as the guest of Twentieth Century–Fox to receive Shirley's personal congratulations. Although not yet six years old, the curly-blond Parisienne and her mother confessed that they were contemplating her own film career.[20]

As far away as Japan, newspapers repeatedly reported on Shirley Temple look-alikes. "I'm Shirley Temple," declared one seven-year-old actress, half Japanese and half Russian. Two other Japanese articles warned of a scam in which a man tricked several families out of their money by telling parents that their child could become a child actor more popular than Shirley Temple.[21]

Thus, in a great whirling circle, spun by publicists, journalists, eager parents, and their daughters, Shirley Temple became a global standard of what a little girl should be. A chart, carried by newspapers and purportedly devised in consultation with leading California educators, invited readers to "Test Your Own Child" in the ability to live up to Shirley's sterling example. Among ten questions, it asked: "Does your child receive praise without being spoiled? seem at ease in the presence of strangers? admit errors without trying to blame others? lead in group activities? make friends quickly?" In a decade in which "personality development" became the prime concern of child-rearing advice, not only Shirley's appearance but her personality demanded imitation. In a similar spirit the movie fan magazine *Silver Screen* reported that many readers had found that they could "only make their daughters willingly eat their spinach, or drink their milk, because Shirley Temple does so." Older sisters taught younger ones "good manners and neatness . . . by setting Shirley up as an example." Teachers instructed pupils in obedience by the same tactics. Accordingly, the magazine invited readers to "write a letter telling us how Shirley Temple's influence has helped in the up-bringing of some little girl you know." First prize was a Shirley Temple doll, with a carriage and accessories. As a final thought, the magazine added, "Neatness will be considered."[22]

All of these Shirley Temple contests—and the broader desire to imitate Shirley Temple—linked girls and their families throughout the world with Hollywood and the consumer industries surrounding it. Such imitations vividly demonstrate the active engagement of moviegoers with their favorite actors. They also indicate the emotional needs that viewers brought to the theater and the stories that sustained them.

In actively encouraging imitation of Shirley Temple, promoters exploited a fundamental appeal of movies for children. Even before the onset of the Great Depression, the desire of children and adolescents to imitate, consciously and unconsciously, the characters, plots, and gestures of the movies had attracted notice—and considerable concern from moral guardians. The most extensive investigation of the impact of movies on youth, the famous Payne Fund studies, stressed how powerfully the influence of film permeated the imagination and everyday play of children. Although the studies were flawed in many respects, their fundamental finding that movies deeply enthralled the young has never been seriously questioned. In one of these studies, *Our Movie Made Children* (1933), Henry Forman wrote,

"The mirror held up by the movies is gazed into by myriads of adolescents and even young children in their secret thoughts, in their broodings, their daydreaming and fantasies—they want to be like the people in the movies." Drawing on the studies' extensive interviews and questionnaires describing how children imitated the movies in their play, from cowboys-and-Indians games to Rudolph Valentino's torrid seductions, Herbert Blumer observed, "For the time being the child assumes a new role. All phases of his make-up thoughts, intentions, interests, vocalizations and gestures reflect the role which he is acting." Thus, if we consider play as a kind of acting, movies made performers out of most children. From this perspective, we may see Shirley Temple as leading a vast throng of child actors, imitating the little girl who began her own career parodying adults in Baby Burlesks.[23]

Imitation took many forms. Tap-dance schools in the 1930s bulged with would-be Shirley Temples. Fred Kelly, a brother of the great dancer Gene Kelly, recalled the legions of such girls in the family's dance studios in Pittsburgh and Johnstown, Pennsylvania: "Every time Shirley Temple made a movie, our studio enrollment doubled." Soon "we had one hundred girls in our studio who all looked exactly like Shirley Temple! . . . In one of our shows we did a big 'Shirley Temple' finale number. Mother went down to the local department store in Johnstown and talked to the owner of the store. She bought a gross of dresses, different colors. When the finale of the show happened, every girl came out in a dress that had a big bow on the back, all with their hair in bouncing curls, and they all looked just like Shirley Temple!"[24]

The journalist and essayist A. J. Liebling satirically imagined the grim traffic of little Shirley Temple look-alikes and their belligerent mothers to the offices of voice, dancing, and theatrical instructors: "Often several of the Shirleys and their mothers find themselves in a[n elevator] car together. The mother's upper lips curl as they survey the other mothers' patently moronic young. The Shirleys gaze at each other with vacuous hostility and wonder whether their mothers will slap them if they ask to go to the bathroom again. All the Shirleys have bony little knees and bitter mouths and . . . will undoubtedly grow up to be ax murderesses."[25]

Such caricature aside, emulation of Shirley Temple sprang from many needs. Shirley's charm, courage, cheer, and charisma delighted countless children and their families, and by imitating her they could momentarily bathe in the glamour of Hollywood, however remote their homes. In her sunny reminiscence "Carefree," Eileen Bennetto recounts how, growing up in a small country town in northeast Victoria, Australia, she eagerly anticipated movie matinees on Saturday: "It was our own special world, the theatre filled with screaming, whistling kids, and not an adult in sight, except occasionally the manager who came down to threaten us." Of all the actors, "Shirley was our undoubted favourite, and the streets were filled with Shirley Temple look-alikes, with sausage curls, short frocks with puffed sleeves, and patent-leather shoes with taps on them."[26] Here imitating Shirley Temple appears to be as joyous a pleasure as watching her onscreen, and one spontaneously enacted by children without mediating adults. Under Shirley's spell, everyday sidewalks could become Hollywood sets.

Yet "carefree" is not the word that characterized most people's lives during the Great Depression. The economic crisis, as we have seen, carried massive emotional ramifications, and among the children drawn to Shirley Temple in the 1930s were those who most craved a portion of her indomitable spirit. Shirley's repeated triumphs of healing, of building new families out of once broken hearts, spoke to audiences everywhere. Her feats carried special power for those yearning for deliverance from their families' miseries: poverty, prejudice, divorce, abandonment, alcoholism, derangement, sexual abuse—all of the woes of childhood. The darkest of these troubles, of course, never appeared in Shirley's films, but viewers in need could easily adapt her plots to fit their individual circumstances.

Reminiscences prepared decades later reveal precisely how individual girls invested Shirley Temple with their own deep longings, often in collaboration with their mothers. Such accounts, of course, are interpretations as much as recollections, but common patterns clearly emerge across region, nation, religion, ethnicity, class, and individual circumstances.

The painter Ruth Kligman, who first became famous as the muse and mistress of the action painter Jackson Pollock, gave special prominence in her 1974 memoir to her experience in a Shirley Temple look-alike contest. One of twin sisters, Ruth was born in Newark, New Jersey, in 1930, to a mother still in her teens. Her father, a local con man, never lived with the family, and her mother's Russian Jewish parents spurned them. She remembered a childhood racked with sadness and paranoia: "My mother was always crying, always unhappy about facing the outside world . . . wanting to be something else. She cried, I cried, and my twin sister cried, we all cried in a kind of horrible unison. I never knew what was wrong. But the outside world represented terror."[27]

From such misery the local movie house provided a rare haven of happiness, and Ruth, who later acquired the dark beauty of a Hollywood star, attended avidly. Once her mother learned of a statewide Shirley Temple look-alike contest, sponsored by the *Newark News*. To enter, aspirants needed to provide a photograph, and, it went without saying, it had to include some semblance of Shirley's famous curls. So Ruth's mother laboriously curled her dark-eyed twin daughters' dark-brown hair, garbed them in Shirley Temple dresses, and had them photographed at Bamberger's massive Newark department store, "our big faces smiling and our bodies back to back in the pose making us look like Siamese twins." The next week Mrs. Kligman proudly escorted her curly-coiffed daughters to a large hall for the preliminary judging. Four decades later, Ruth Kligman still ached from the episode: "I think it was the biggest room and the largest assortment of people together I had ever seen. . . . Every little blonde girl in the state of New Jersey was there that day, from all the hundreds of suburbs, all those sweet-looking little girls with curls and thin bodies and gold lockets around their necks, and the mothers looked so good, so wealthy and well dressed."[28]

Ruth's mother pushed her twin dark-eyed brunettes forward, certain that they would win, only to be blocked by an official who refused even to let them enter. "But my daughters are beautiful, and twins," she protested. "Come on now, you're not being fair." "Now, lady, be reasonable," he replied firmly. "They're not the type." Across an immense chasm, Ruth longingly viewed those contestants who were the type: "Girls who had fathers that loved them and mothers who didn't work. They lived in homes and had back yards and roller-skated and had brothers. We were foreign. Our grandmother couldn't read or write and spoke with a heavy accent. . . . And the screaming at my grandmother's home every day; these people talked sweetly to each other, they didn't scream and hit and cry." Furious, Ruth's mother left the hall with her rejected daughters. She cursed "the goddamn bastards, and we didn't feel anything except utter sadness and confusion and somehow ashamed, ashamed of being Jewish and dark and chubby and different. It was somehow clear: the world was for them, not for us."[29]

At roughly the same time, halfway across the continent in Omaha, Nebraska, Dorothy Coomer (later Dorothy Weil) similarly longed for the happiness that Shirley Temple embodied. A year and a half younger than Shirley, Dorothy was the daughter of a dreamy, at times depressed middle-class mother who, in her family's eyes, had married beneath her, and a tough, distant father with a body scarred from fights. He had worked on the river boats, sold patent medicine, and in the Great Depression often fruitlessly searched for a job. Dorothy's mother had flirted with suicide, and their marriage had fallen apart. Living with her two children in an Omaha hotel, she turned to the

Muse Theater across the street to sustain her spirits. Both Dorothy and her mother succumbed to Shirley Temple's spell. "I saw every Shirley Temple movie that came to the Muse," Dorothy Weil wrote. "Shirley was so adorable, the ideal every little girl compared herself to." Dorothy cherished her modest collection of Shirley Temple products like icons: "I had Shirley Temple paper dolls with ermine coats and muffs and ruffled skirts. I had a Shirley Temple mug: blue glass with Shirley's image in white." Blind to the gulf between her daughter's appearance and Shirley's, "in a totally misguided moment," Dorothy's mother "curled my lank locks and entered me in a Shirley Temple look-alike contest, in which I received the twenty-fifth and last prize." Her mother also insistently displayed Dorothy to her friends, dressed in a full-skirted taffeta frock. Yet "the clothes were not what I envied about Shirley Temple." Rather, "it was the way that, in story after story, through the sheer power of her personality, she brought her parents together and mollified crusty grandfathers who had cut their daughters off for marrying the wrong man."[30] Viewing Shirley's films through the lens of her own desires, Dorothy saw her own story and the promise of deliverance.

Meanwhile, in North Dakota, Kathy Plotkin stood uncomfortably before a gas stove as her mother styled her hair into Shirley Temple curls using a marcel iron. The device "was held over a gas flame until hot enough to curl hair—and sometimes burned it, causing an aroma not unlike scorched chicken feathers." Kathy fared better in her Shirley Temple look-alike contest than Ruth Kligman or Dorothy Weil did in theirs, winning an honorable mention and her picture in the fan magazine *Photoplay*.[31]

Shirley Temple's pin curls created an international fad, and at times it marked a cultural divide between the power of Hollywood and moral authorities. When she was a Catholic schoolgirl in Dublin, Ireland, Ita Bridget Bolger remembered, "there was one great hairstyle . . . the imitation of Shirley Temple, a mass of little ringlets all over the head."

As in many other cities, the local newspaper, the *Evening Herald*, held a Shirley Temple look-alike contest: "There were rows of photographs of girls every night—they all had the hair in curls but very few of them looked like Shirley Temple." One of Ita's friends made the mistake of carrying her imitation to school. She arrived one morning with her normally straight hair in a Shirley Temple permanent. "Oh, consternation," Ita remembered, "the nuns didn't like it one bit. Terrible show of pride; so the mother was sent for, and she arrived in the next day with the hair all frizzy, because it had been permed, but no longer quite like Shirley Temple's."[32]

Yet the great majority of retrospective accounts testified to the myriad ways in which imitating Shirley Temple provided relief from hardship. One of the most striking comes from Beatrice Muchman, who fled from Berlin to Brussels with her Jewish family, the Westheimers, to escape Nazi persecution. In 1939 her parents were living in cramped quarters, working illegally, and arguing frequently as they desperately tried to find a way to the United States. In Berlin Beatrice's mother had been a fashion designer and, perhaps expressing her own thwarted ambitions, dreamed that her daughter would become a movie star. She made beautiful clothes "seemingly from nothing" for six-year old Beatrice and "would wrap my hair around thick wooden rollers to give me curls in the style of Shirley Temple." For Beatrice, as for millions of other girls, "Shirley Temple was the person I most wanted to be." Her example stimulated Beatrice's own play-acting. "During those tension-filled times, my world of make-believe was a warm refuge that my mother encouraged." All too soon Beatrice had to put such acting to use, as she became one of the "hidden children," Jews passing as gentiles, in order to escape the Holocaust, in which her parents died. Masquerading as the niece of a Catholic woman in a Belgian town, she assumed a new name and a Catholic identity. "Although having to change identities was a bit confusing," she wrote, "I enjoyed the idea of playing a real game of pretend." At age nine she took her first Catholic communion. She basked in the attention and the pleasure of a special dress, veil, and patent leather shoes. "I felt like a little movie star," she wrote.[33]

Another star-struck Jewish girl who cherished Shirley Temple's smiling example as she hid from the Nazis was Anne Frank. Her family had fled Frankfurt, Germany, in 1933 and established a new life in Amsterdam. Then in 1940 the Nazis occupied the Netherlands and initiated increasingly repressive policies targeting Jews. These included, beginning in January 1941, a prohibition against their attendance in movie theaters. Anne had avidly gone to the movies, including Shirley Temple and Deanna Durbin films, and she dreamed of becoming an actress. No longer able to see films directly, she devoured each week's issue of *Cinema and Theater* magazine that her family's confidant Victor Kugler bought for her. In July 1942 the Frank family went into hiding in a secret annex of an office building, where they remained for more than two years, until they were betrayed and shipped to concentration camps. "Our little room looked very bare at first with nothing on the walls," Anne wrote in her diary, "but thanks to Daddy who had brought my film-star collection on beforehand, and with the aid of a paste pot and brush, I have transformed the walls into one gigantic picture. This makes it look much more cheerful." Prominent among these pictures was the beaming smile of Shirley Temple.[34] Anne Frank died in the Bergen-Belsen concentration camp in March 1945, only weeks before the British liberation.

Imitating Shirley Temple as a film personality frequently involved imitating her as a consumer. Hollywood had long served as the handmaiden of modern advertising and of consumer culture more generally. From the dawn of the star system in the second decade of the twentieth century, the film capital became the center of new fashions and a new ethic of self-expression. Actors capitalized on this prestige by endorsing products, thus conferring the luster of their personalities. Beginning in 1916, Mary Pickford, the star with the most famous

Winsome Jackie Coogan, among the most highly merchandized
movie stars of the 1920s. (© Bettmann/Corbis)

curls prior to Shirley Temple, appeared in a series of advertisements for Pompeian skin cream, chocolates, and cigarettes. By the 1920s Hollywood stars, fashions, and decor exercised a considerable influence on American buying habits.[35]

Child stars, as well as adults, cast a spell that captivated consumers. Jackie Coogan, the most popular child actor of the 1920s after his success in Charlie Chaplin's *The Kid* (1921), leased his name and image to a host of products, including dolls, lunch boxes, peanut butter, pencil sets, an Erector set, records, stilts, and a line of clothing. Woolworth's dime stores hawked piano sheet music with theme songs from his silent movies, his winsome face on the cover, in one instance beseeching, "Buy me and take me home. I'll be a good little boy," above his signature. Anticipating the Shirley Temple craze of the 1930s, Jackie Coogan look-alike contests became a staple of Saturday movie matinees—with first prize often a Coogan product.[36]

The onset of the Great Depression did not stifle such efforts. On the contrary, advertisers and merchandisers tightened their alliances with Hollywood, determined to get consumers spending once again. Marketers hungrily eyed the juvenile market as a vast frontier, hitherto hazily mapped and fitfully explored. By some estimates children under the age of eighteen affected a third of all merchandise sold in the country. During the 1920s advertisers and merchandisers increasingly realized that children held both the keys to the juvenile market and a hand on the door to purchases by their families. If children could be coaxed to open these doors, vast fortunes lay ahead. Yet prior to the 1930s merchandisers conceived of the child as a smaller and less independent customer, not as a unique type of consumer whose perspective needed to be carefully cultivated. They noted children's delight in premiums and clubs but did not concentrate on the psychology of children as they did on mothers. In the 1930s this situation changed dramatically, so much so that one historian has declared this a turning point in the history of childhood. Manufacturers, merchants, advertisers, and others, including many in the movie industry, sought to make the perspective of the child a vital element in consumer markets. Mothers and other adults were not ignored in this effort, but no longer would the child consumer be addressed principally through them. Rather, at every turn, marketers celebrated the "natural" and "healthy" desires of the autonomous child—and used these qualities as the basis for a new commodification of childhood.[37]

A key text in this effort was E. Evalyn Grumbine's *Reaching Juvenile Markets: How to Advertise, Sell, and Merchandise through Boys and Girls* (1938). As assistant publisher and advertising director of *Child Life* magazine, a twenty-five-cent monthly with a circulation of more than

150,000 that addressed a "quality market" of children up to age thir-teen, Grumbine could speak authoritatively on the subject. By selling to and through children, she emphasized, advertisers and merchants could vastly expand their sales and raise a new generation of con-sumers. Grumbine built on Alfred Adler's theories of child person-ality development as well as Progressive notions of active learning, stemming from the work of John Dewey, and adapted them for mar-keting purposes. Whereas Adler and Dewey sought the realization of the child's full potential and growth into a democratic society, guided by wise parents and teachers, Grumbine concentrated on the child's sales potential and development into a consumer economy, guided by helpful marketers. Building on the work of child psychologists, she minutely divided the child market into age groups (infancy to three, four through six, seven through nine, and so on) and, beginning at age ten, by gender as well. From age three onward, she contended, each group had characteristic psychologies that marketers could use to their advantage, especially if they addressed children directly. Grumbine justified such appeals not as crass exploitation but rather as nurturing children's growing sense of independence. Encouraging their desires for heroes of their own age, and satisfying their instinct for collecting, for membership in clubs of their own, for the lure of a reward, for choosing their own clothes and the like—all might be seen as progressive activities. She took for granted that the consumer economy would be integral to their health and happiness.[38]

Capturing the independent child's interest meant harnessing that child's insistence. "The particular toy or game or doll that a child wants he will eventually get," Grumbine observed approvingly, "for if he makes up his mind to have a certain thing, ninety-nine times out of a hundred mother or father will buy it if it is at all possible." The parent would do so not with gritted teeth but with a gladsome smile, Grumbine added, savoring the satisfaction that "by grant-ing these requests he is contributing to the happiness of the child."

Reversing earlier conceptions of the children's market, she portrayed the child as the active agent in determining a purchase and the adult as the passive consenter.[39]

Thus, juvenile market promoters believed, a "new type of child" had emerged by the mid-1930s, more self-reliant and observant than in the previous generation. These qualities had been cultivated not only by new modes of education but also by the increased presence in children's lives of radio, comic-strip, and movie personalities, especially child stars such as Shirley Temple.[40] "Every hamlet in the country has its movie theater," Grumbine wrote, "and the children, even those who must sit on mother's lap to see, know Shirley Temple, Deanna Durbin, Jane Withers, and the other heroines of the screen as intimately as the small playmate next door. In their fertile young imaginations they, too, are stars and would shine as lustrously in their own circles. Hence the appeal of the merchandise bearing the names of their 'fashion mentors'—an appeal of which the manufacturers have taken full advantage with profit to themselves and the stores."[41] The most adored child in the world, Shirley was also the model child consumer.

She was ideally cast for the part. Self-reliant, enthusiastic, and adorable, she exemplified the child whom no adult with a heart could refuse. She aroused the passionate imitation of girls from toddlers to early adolescents around the world, the admiration of many boys, and the affection of mothers and fathers alike. Little wonder, then, that she figured conspicuously among Grumbine's examples of effective advertising and merchandising. Not only did Grumbine note the success of department stores in encouraging girls and their mothers to participate in Shirley Temple events, such as birthday celebrations and Christmas greetings, she also investigated the specific ways in which objects associated with Shirley changed family's buying habits. Interviewing children about their response to premium offers, she spoke with an eight-year-old girl named Carol. "I got a Shirley Temple drinking cup with Bisquick," Carol reported. "Mother got the

Bisquick because I wanted the drinking cup." Carol said that her family used Bisquick "all the time now" and that her mother continued to buy it even when no premium was involved. Similarly, as Grumbine reported, Quaker Oats used Shirley Temple extensively in its 1937 advertising campaign on behalf of Puffed Wheat and Puffed Rice cereals. In a two-pronged assault on children and their mothers, Shirley's image appeared in ads in juvenile and mass-circulation magazines as well as on advertising cards on buses, subways, and trolleys.[42]

Even advertisements aimed squarely at mothers, such as one in the April 1937 issue of *Ladies' Home Journal*, often emphasized the point of view of the child. "This is *my* cereal!" a beaming Shirley Temple proclaims, as she munches dry Quaker Puffed Wheat right from the box. Quaker Oats encouraged other children to be equally assertive, while reassuring mothers of the cereal's nutritional benefits.[43]

Other promotional schemes lauded by Grumbine turned children from consumers to sales representatives in their own right. One of the largest magazine publishers in the country, Curtis Publishing, appealed to girls' desire for belonging by establishing a Junior Girls' Club. By selling subscriptions to *Saturday Evening Post*, *Ladies' Home Journal*, *Jack and Jill*, and other Curtis magazines, they could earn cash or prizes, such as a Shirley Temple doll. Other magazines and newspapers, including *Parents Magazine*, made similar offers, potentially linking mothers and daughters as a sales team.[44]

No sentimentalist, Grumbine thought of Shirley Temple's popularity as a fad that would inevitably run its course. Child consumers might be independent, but they were also fickle. So she advised manufactures to exploit fads quickly, before they peaked. Selling through Shirley Temple was a race against time.[45] Yet Shirley's power on behalf of advertisers, merchandisers, and manufacturers directly corresponded to her power as a box-office star, and while it lasted it was immense, transforming the juvenile market as thoroughly as she did the movie industry.

A major element of this transformation occurred in children's fashions. Shirley modeled stylish children's outfits in virtually all of her movies, even those in which her protectors' circumstances were supposedly modest. No less a figure than Twentieth Century–Fox's vice president in charge of production, Darryl Zanuck, observed that her fans wished to see her well dressed. In a script conference for *Little Miss Broadway* he noted, "We should give her as many changes of costume as we possibly can, and all her dresses should be very smart and pretty. We should have the feeling that Pop and Barbara would keep the child well dressed, even if they had to sacrifice on other things."[46]

Through her movie wardrobes Shirley helped dress designers mark a sharp divide between the juvenile and adolescent markets. Although she was beyond the toddler stage even in her early Baby Burlesk film shorts, she perpetuated a toddler look through the 1930s and popularized it for the children's fashion industry, including Big Sister versions for girls up to age twelve. Such dresses had the additional virtue of being easy to manufacture. A fashion industry reporter noted enthusiastically, "They follow one pattern almost invariably: a skirt (about the size of a postage stamp) that falls in soft pleats from a round collar of a contrasting material or appliqué; no belt— Shirley wisely favors the pinafore fashion which shows off a small round tummy to best advantage; and, for trimming, a bow of baby ribbon or an appliquéd nursery figure. Even her party frocks use no trimming except touches of hand embroidery and edgings of narrow lace."[47] In addition to emphasizing the lack of a waistline, her dresses were exceedingly short. Even when she was standing, they scarcely extended beyond her panties.

Shirley Temple dresses dominated the girls' fashion industry in the mid-1930s. In addition to the popularity of those clothes and accessories authorized to bear the Shirley Temple name, countless other lookalike versions proliferated, illustrated in advertisements and catalogs by girls with hair and features closely resembling the child star's and

Shirley models an accordion-pleated dress. (Photofest/Twentieth Century–Fox)

often striking one of her characteristic poses. Such was the case with the largest department and mail-order concern in the country, Sears, Roebuck. A pioneer in mail-order sales to rural Americans since the 1890s, the company aggressively expanded into urban retail outlets beginning in 1925 and continued to do so through the 1930s. By the end of the decade, it accounted for 1.5 percent of total retail sales in the United States. Following Shirley's phenomenal ascent in 1934, she played a starring role in Sears catalogs. In a page devoted entirely to Shirley Temple fashions, the fall 1935 issue breathlessly declared, "In big city stores they're going like wildfire! Shirley and her cute clothes have stolen everyone's heart; no wonder every little girl wants to wear the same styles!" Only the costliest offerings were worthy of the star. These ranged from washable dresses for girls age seven to twelve, styled in accord with Shirley's latest movies, for $1.89 (twice the price of similar dresses in the same catalog without the Shirley Temple name) to a wool herringbone coat, leggings, and hat set for $10.95. Even for those who could not afford such clothes, the Sears, Roebuck catalog served as a "wish book," filled with goods to dream about.[48]

Shirley Temple similarly dominated doll industry sales. In 1934 Ideal Novelty and Toy Company's plight resembled that of Fox Film. The company's founder, Morris Michtom, a Russian Jewish immigrant, achieved his first great success with the famous Teddy bear, named in honor of Theodore Roosevelt. Using assembly-line techniques, Ideal became a leading manufacturer of composition dolls, notably its Flossie Flirt doll introduced in 1924. "Says Ma-Ma," one advertisement declared, "rolls her flirty eyes from side to side, winks and blinks mischievously and also closes her eyes in sleep." When sales slumped at the onset of the Great Depression, the company sought a new attraction. Watching the Educational Films movie short *Merrily Yours* late in 1933, Ideal's dress designer Mollye Goldman spotted an unknown child actor: Shirley Temple. Goldman anticipated Fox Film's Winfield Sheehan in sensing the five-year-old girl's

Shirley Temple doll with polka-dotted dress, 1934.
(Courtesy of The Strong,® Rochester, New York)

potential. Yet not until August 1934, when Shirley had indeed become a celebrity, did Ideal sign a contract with the Temple family and apply for a patent.[49]

In October 1934, just in time for the Christmas shopping season, Ideal breathlessly announced the introduction of its Shirley Temple doll in the toy industry trade magazine *Playthings*: "This newest Ideal doll will be an exact replica of 'Shirley Temple,' the sweetheart of America. She will come in an authentic Shirley Temple dress, packed in an unusually attractive Shirley Temple box and with a Shirley Temple button." The following month Ideal ran another advertisement in *Playthings*, this time reproducing a postcard supposedly from Shirley herself, in childish printing, "'I LOVE MY DOLL AND I PLAY WITH IT ALL THE TIME. IT IS JUST LIKE ME.'"[50] The look-alike doll would greatly intensify the process of imitation central to Shirley Temple's success.

The company's initial model, with loose strawberry-blond curls, open-and-shut hazel eyes, peaches-and-cream complexion, and rosy, dimpled cheeks, sported a red coin-dotted organdy dress like the one Shirley wore in her big dance number for *Stand Up and Cheer!*. The doll came in four sizes: 15 inches for $3, 18 inches for $5, 20 inches for $6, and 22 inches for $7. Even the smallest of these cost considerably more than many families could afford—$3 in 1934 was roughly the equivalent of $50 in 2013. The biggest, almost half the height of Shirley herself, was a distinct luxury. Nonetheless, all of these models proved enormously popular. To satisfy the rush of orders, Ideal hired additional workers and sold more than fifty thousand Shirley Temple dolls by Christmas.[51]

Ideal further stimulated demand by introducing a range of sizes and outfits keyed to each new Shirley Temple film. "Hitch your toy department to a star," Ideal urged in another *Playthings* advertisement. "Every Shirley Temple talkie is a Shirley Temple Doll promotion." Ultimately, the company offered Shirley Temple dolls in nine different sizes, ranging from 11 to 27 inches. The most lavish of them all, a 27-inch doll elaborately reproducing Shirley's outfit in *The Little Colonel*, had "Flirty" eyes that moved back and forth, a taffeta dress available in pink or yellow, cotton pantaloons and long skirt trimmed with lace and picoting, and a matching taffeta hat with a silk ribbon and feather. While slimming the face mold of Shirley Temple dolls, reportedly in response to Gertrude Temple's complaint that the original looked chubby, the company also introduced a Shirley Temple baby doll, depicting her as a two-year-old, available in models from 16 to 27 inches. Here was cuteness to fit every size, if not every purse.[52]

What remains astonishing is how many purses sprang open. Ideal's Shirley Temple dolls accounted for almost a third of all dolls sold in 1935. Sales continued to be robust in 1936, the last year in which Mollye Goldman designed the dresses. Customers with still smaller purses could buy dolls made by Ideal's various imitators and make their own outfits. Barred from using the child star's name, these look-alikes sold under such sobriquets as Bright Eyes, Miss Charming, Little Miss Movie, and the Movie Queen. Although they lacked Ideal's attention to detail, most of these were significantly less expensive, and they found ready buyers.[53]

Once purchased, often as a gift, Shirley Temple dolls entered deeply into the imaginations of young girls. Even a half century later, participants in an oral history project in Rochester, New York, spoke of such dolls as one of the highlights of their childhood. Six years old when she was given her doll around 1936, Ann Reebok remarked, "I guess the Shirley Temple Doll is the one that I thought I had to have forever." Her doll became an active companion: "I played house with her. I put her to bed, she had naps, she had company. We had parties. We probably had dances." Most of all, she combed Shirley's hair: "I combed her and curled her until she had no hair left." Similarly, Joanne Wasenske (born 1930) from Fairport, New York, said, "Shirley was very important to me. She went everywhere with me." Remarking on a photograph of herself as a girl with her Shirley Temple doll, she added, "We were on our way to the beach for a picnic. I had on my bathing suit so, of course, she had on hers." Lois Green-Stone (born in 1934), who grew up in Flushing, New York, imagined her "adorable" Shirley Temple doll as an extension of herself: "I related to Shirley Temple much the way I related to me. . . . I would get up and tap dance. I would imitate what I expected Shirley Temple was doing." Even an older girl, Esther Camelio Zannie (born 1925), who was given a Shirley Temple doll at age twelve, regarded it as "the main thing" in her childhood. Yet for her the doll was not a playmate but an icon: "I think she was too pretty to

Shirley plays with her look-alike doll: "I have such fun curling my dolly's hair. Now I can always keep her looking nice." (Photofest/Twentieth Century–Fox)

play with. I more or less just kept her on my dresser. . . . I kept her for years and years."[54]

Of course, in the grip of the Great Depression, many children and their families could not afford such dolls. Some entered contests, hoping to win a Shirley Temple doll by coloring a drawing of the child star or writing a short essay. In 1934 two hundred children wrote letters to the manager of the Republic theatre in Brooklyn, New York, saying why they would like to win a life-size Shirley Temple doll for Christmas. They poured out tributes to Shirley and vividly imagined themselves in her roles. "She is the littlest girl that can do the biggest things in the movies," one of the winning contestants wrote. Nine-year-old Amelia Ungolo, who won first prize, said, "Shirley acts so as to make everyone in the audience dance, sing and laugh in his seat. Shirley Temple has a beautiful smile. When I see her smile I can't help but smile back at her."[55]

Other young girls who could not afford a doll wrote directly to Eleanor Roosevelt, to whom they also felt a personal bond, cultivated by newsreels, radio, magazines, and newspapers, beseeching her help. In 1935 a Chicago girl wrote:

> Dear Mrs. Roosevelt,
>
> You have nieces and sons who were young and some still are wanted a thing very much but tried hard to get it and can't. I a girl from Chicago have tried so so hard to get five suscriptions to get a 22 inch Shirley Temple [doll] which the Daily Chicago Tribune is giving away. It is cheap for at 65 cents a month you get daily paper. You have millions of friends couldn't you please ask them to take for one year at 65 cents a month the Daily Chicago Tribune. I don't know how I'd ever thank you if you got them. I know one thing I'd pray with all my heart in Holy Mass and when receiving Holy Communion pray to God to bless you and all. Please please do help

me. Here is a picture of the Shirley Temple. [A cutout picture was enclosed.] If you do get them send them as soon as you can.

Yours truly,

[Signature][56]

A few months later, in spring 1936, a younger girl wrote Mrs. Roosevelt with a similar request:

> I am 6 years old this is my first year in school i am a little colored girl my name is B. J. R. I wish you wood please send me a Sherley temple Doll because my doll got broke i will take good care of the doll if you sen me one please Answer. My daddy helped me to writ you yours with lots of kisses XXXXXX
>
> B. J. R.[57]

In such ways the ache for consumer goods affected virtually all children in the Great Depression, whether they could afford them or not. A Shirley Temple doll was certainly not a physical necessity, but it could serve as a psychological comfort, a transitional object assisting the child's developing independence from her mother. In this respect, it may have been most needed by those most exposed to the insecurities of the Great Depression. Yet the transition led two ways: from the elemental comforts of family and toward the consumer comforts of the market economy. The letters also remind us that the obverse side of consumer pleasures in the 1930s, which Shirley Temple embodied, was the deep ache of consumer envy.[58]

Like her films and fashions, Shirley Temple dolls achieved international distribution. Ideal sold doll molds to companies in Canada, Australia, and Latin America. In some other countries, companies produced authorized Shirley Temple dolls from different materials: a cloth body and pressed felt face mask with painted features in Great Britain and France, two composition versions in Germany, a celluloid version with a mohair wig in Poland, and similar versions in Holland and elsewhere. Japanese manufactures made a number of unauthorized composition Shirley Temple dolls and exported them for the American market, underselling Ideal.[59]

Yet the biggest threat to Ideal's sales was not its domestic and foreign competitors but Shirley's waning luster. In 1937, as Shirley took on more dramatic roles in *Wee Willie Winkie* and *Heidi*, Ideal's doll sales slumped. Varying the Shirley Temple formula in dolls much as Darryl Zanuck was doing in her movies, Ideal allowed her to grow up slightly. The dolls acquired a higher forehead, slimmer, rosier cheeks, more defined eyebrows, darker lips, and a side-parted wig with less distinct curls. She also wore longer, more modest skirts. None of these innovations revived sales, however, and neither did lowered prices. By the late 1930s Ideal had other film stars in their stable of dolls, including Judy Garland, Deanna Durbin, Pinocchio, and Snow White. The company finally announced the Shirley Temple dolls' retirement in December 1940, half a year after the Temple family ended Shirley's contract with Twentieth Century–Fox. By this time the public had spent an estimated $45 million on Shirley Temple dolls. The most popular doll to that time in history took her final bow, not to return for almost twenty years.[60]

Shirley Temple's films, products, and endorsements collectively stimulated the American consumer economy at a crucial time, so much so that to some she appeared to be a relief program all by herself. With his tongue only partly in cheek, Frank Dillon, writing in the fan magazine *Modern Screen* in December 1935, recalled how "a year ago when things looked bleak and hopeless all over the country, when no conversation was ever concluded without a few groans over the depression, Washington held out helping hands in the form of the AAA [Agricultural Adjustment Administration], NRA [National Recovery Administration], SERA [State Emergency Relief Administration], and many other alphabetical combinations." Still, he observed, "one depression cure has made greater strides toward a complete mental and financial recovery than all the other remedies put together," and that was the TRA, a program originating in Hollywood rather than Washington, and one that the Supreme Court could not declare unconstitutional. The TRA, he explained with mock solemnity, stood for the Temple Recovery Act, led by Shirley Temple. "Not content with cheering up half the civilized population of the world," the writer continued, "she has done a man's size job of bringing about financial recovery for a great many people," from her coworkers in Hollywood to film distributors to the manufacturers of dolls, dresses, and other Shirley Temple products. Dillon did not attempt a comprehensive estimate of how many workers could trace at least a part of their jobs to Shirley Temple, for that would have been incalculable. Certainly within the United States alone they would have numbered in the tens of thousands. A grand parade of their legions would have easily dwarfed the extravagant parade of workers that ended Shirley's 1934 breakthrough film, *Stand Up and Cheer!* As is so often the case, life imitated and surpassed art.[61]

CHAPTER 5
KEEPING SHIRLEY'S
STAR ALOFT

When Shirley Temple's beaming smile and indomitable spirit first seized the public fancy in 1934, most film industry observers thought that she would be a shooting star, flaring briefly and then vanishing. When in 1935 she soared to the position of top American and international box-office attraction, they were astounded. That she retained this position for three more years, setting a record never equaled, confounded all expectations. Fox producers, distributors, and exhibitors worked energetically to keep her star aloft, but they were never sanguine they could do so. For them, the most exciting and suspenseful Shirley Temple story concerned how long her charmed life as a child star could last. They feared two things above all: the fickle nature of the moviegoing public and the perishable character of Shirley's cuteness. They tried to preserve both as long as possible.

In the golden age of the studio system, movie stars were popularly imagined as made in Hollywood, the "dream factory," as surely as American automobiles were made in Detroit.[1] Yet among Hollywood stars, far more than automobiles, there were thousands of potential models to choose from, and public response determined which would become most popular and profitable. Whether the studio strenuously prepared a potential star, changing her name, teeth, hair, makeup, wardrobe, place of birth, parentage, and life history, or, as in the case of Shirley Temple, left her for audiences to discover, they could only launch careers, not determine their course. Actors' images and personae circulated in a complex, multidirectional chain linking producers and publicists, distributors, exhibitors, journalists, retailers, and moviegoers in first-run and small, independent theaters, with numerous other interests all along the way. Stars might be conceived in Hollywood, but they were born in the collective responses of the moviegoing public.

That public was far from passive. Although it never spoke with one voice, it expressed its preferences powerfully. It did so most obviously in box-office receipts and more articulately (if less reliably) in praise and complaints to local movie exhibitors, opinion polls, fan mail, and the like. The challenge for the film industry, then, was both to follow that public and to lead it, to anticipate its desires, to satisfy its expectations, and to expand its dimensions. Sustaining Shirley Temple's place as a star thus involved continued negotiation between moviemakers and moviegoers as to what a Shirley Temple movie should be.

The two men most responsible for devising and perfecting the Shirley Temple formula were Winfield Sheehan, head of production at Fox until its merger with Twentieth Century Pictures in 1935, and Darryl Zanuck, who succeeded him. Both knew the necessity of keeping this public always in mind—and the impossibility of consistently satisfying it. By the time Sheehan met and signed a contract with Shirley Temple and her parents shortly before Christmas 1933, he had amassed considerable experience in gauging public sentiment. A former reporter for the *New York World*, he began working for William Fox in 1914 and quickly became his "right-hand man."[2] He played a significant role in expanding the Fox empire overseas, establishing Fox branches in forty-nine countries. In addition, as head of production for Fox studios beginning in 1926, he early sensed the potential of sound to transform the movie industry. From his first years at Fox, he helped to develop a veritable galaxy of stars, including Theda Bara (born Theodosia Goodman), Tom Mix, Will Rogers, Janet Gaynor, Paul Muni (born Meshilem Meier Weisenfreund), Alice Faye (born Alice Jeanne Leppert), and Warner Baxter.

Even though Sheehan had sensed Shirley's extraordinary film presence in making *Stand Up and Cheer!*, her spectacular success stunned him. After her breakthrough, he immediately lent Shirley to Paramount for *Little Miss Marker* and *Now and Forever* while he scrambled to find suitable vehicles for her talents. She starred in *Baby Take a Bow*, released on June 30, 1934, and then in *Bright Eyes*. Soon most of Fox's associate producers were wearing paths to his door with story ideas for his young star. Before Fox Film's merger with Twentieth Century Pictures in May 1935, three more Shirley Temple films followed: *The Little Colonel*, *Our Little Girl*, and *Curly Top*. *Our Little Girl*, which placed Shirley within a troubled marriage, played poorly, but the other two films pressed closely behind Will Rogers's *Steamboat Round the Bend* and *In Old Kentucky* as the studio's most profitable in the domestic market in 1935.[3]

When the two companies united as Twentieth Century–Fox, Sheehan formally retained his title—but within two months he was gone. Young Darryl F. Zanuck in effect shoved him aside and assumed the position of vice president and head of production. For the next five years, until August 1940, when Shirley's parents severed her contract, Zanuck closely supervised her movies for the studio and was the master wizard concocting the Shirley Temple formula.

Sheehan and Zanuck were a study in contrasts. Fat and jolly, with blue eyes, rosy cheeks, and a square jaw, Sheehan needed only a white beard to look like Santa Claus, Shirley Temple Black later wrote. Extravagant in both his professional and personal life (his Beverly Hills mansion included thirty-three servants), he spent lavishly on old-fashioned epics, allowed directors to consume film prodigally, and frequently exceeded his budgets. He regally presided over Fox's decentralized system of production, a common practice at Hollywood's major studios by the 1930s, and relied heavily on associate producers, such as Sol M. Wurtzel for *Bright Eyes*, Buddy DeSylva for *The Little Colonel*, and Edward Butcher for *Our Little Girl*. Among the films starring Shirley between *Stand Up and Cheer!* and the time of his ouster, Sheehan personally produced only the last, *Curly Top*.[4]

In an industry replete with scantily educated boy wonders, Darryl Zanuck was one of the most phenomenal. The *New Yorker* writer Alva Johnston described him as a bantamweight version of Theodore Roosevelt, with piercing blue eyes, curly hair, an unruly mustache, a mélange of protruding and missing teeth, and a swagger in his walk. More fancifully, the rival producer David O. Selznick said that the sandy-haired Zanuck looked like "an ear of corn only a maniac would eat." Still shy of his thirty-third birthday when he took command of Twentieth Century–Fox studios, and nineteen years Sheehan's junior, Zanuck had already established himself as one of the greatest producers in Hollywood's brief history. He had launched his career while still in his early twenties as a writer and adapter, and the lessons of this background informed all his later work. "Success in movies," he liked to say, "boiled down to three things: story, story, story."[5]

He worked on *The Jazz Singer* when he was twenty-five, then honed the cutting edge of tough, contemporary gangster films such as *The Doorway to Hell* (1930), *The Public Enemy* (1931), and *Little Caesar* (1931). He helped produce one of the most powerful of all early Depression films, *I Am a Fugitive from a Chain Gang* (1932), and contributed its chilling conclusion. There we see the protagonist James Allen, once an upright citizen, wrongly convicted and barbarously punished, reduced to a pathetically frightened figure constantly on the run. When his erstwhile fiancée meets him and asks how he lives, he replies as he shrinks again into the shadows, "I steal."

A similar sense of toughness and topicality infused Zanuck's production of the celebrated backstage musical *42nd Street* (1933). In addition, Zanuck vastly expanded the possibilities of movie biographies with such films as *The House of Rothschild* (1934) and *Young Mr. Lincoln* (1939). He also offered distinctly American interpretations of literary classics, such as *Les Misérables*, which he called "'I Am a Fugitive from a Chain Gang' in costume."[6] He would go on to make such acclaimed films as *The Grapes of Wrath* (1940), *How Green Was My Valley* (1941), and *Gentleman's Agreement* (1947). In the course of his career, he molded a series of Hollywood stars from Rin-Tin-Tin to Marilyn Monroe.

Pulsing with nervous energy, constantly chomping on cigars, Zanuck grabbed the reins of power at Twentieth Century–Fox and pulled hard. He immediately discarded twelve of Sheehan's film projects and halted another six already in production. Reversing the trend toward decentralized organization, Zanuck placed himself at the very center of all production as he expanded and thoroughly revamped the studio. He kept Dictaphones around his home, office, and projection room and poured all of his thoughts. Sweeping into the studio an hour or so before noon, he continued working long after others had left, at times until three or four the next morning. He selected story ideas from numerous book digests prepared for his perusal, immersed himself in script conferences, cast the roles, chose the production team, considered the music, sets, and costumes, and claimed many of the prerogatives of a director, from shooting instructions to film editing. He later said it was not simply the way he liked to work but "the only way I know how to produce."[7]

The two most lucrative actors in the Fox stable that Zanuck inherited were the comedian Will Rogers and Shirley Temple. With his winning folksy manner and vast productivity, Rogers stood at the summit of box-office popularity, although Shirley was already advancing rapidly. Yet within months of the merger, on August 15, 1935, Rogers was killed in a plane crash. The devastating loss meant that Zanuck needed to pay especially close attention to his precious young charge, who continued to be immensely profitable to the studio. Only modest expenditures on her films reaped glittering gross returns: $1 million to $1.5 million on their first runs and even more on subsequent runs.[8] Later, Zanuck increased her budgets substantially, beginning with John Ford's *Wee Willie Winkie*.

Although Zanuck clearly had no reluctance to break with precedents set by Sheehan, he nonetheless preserved much of the Shirley Temple formula concocted during her first year and a half at Fox. Beginning with *The Littlest Rebel* (released November 22, 1935), *Captain January* (released April 17, 1936), and *Poor Little Rich Girl* (the first of these three in production but released on July 24, 1936), he ultimately produced fourteen Shirley Temple films. Only one of these, *The Blue Bird*, was a commercial failure.

Quite early, Shirley Temple movies established their own genre, and soon, within the industry, they would be known simply as "Shirley Temples."[9] In April 1935, only a year after Shirley's breakthrough in *Stand Up and Cheer!*, a cartoon in *The New Yorker* paid backhanded tribute to the generic conventions. Pitching an idea in a script conference, a man declares: ". . . and here's the surprise ending that knocks 'em cold, Mr. Feinglass. Shirley Temple is the killer." As if she could ever be anything other than triumphantly virtuous! Indeed, Shirley had been foiling hardened criminals and converting soft-hearted ones as early as *Little Miss Marker*, and she continued her work as crime-stopper in *Baby Take a Bow* and *The Little Colonel*. All of these movies proved enormously popular, although some criticized the gangster elements as unsuitable for children, and *Baby Take a Bow* was banned for this reason in Nazi Germany. By the time Zanuck assumed control, such elements had been purged, although larcenous characters popped up occasionally.[10]

Yet Shirley stood for much more than virtuous innocence. Underlying the spirit of her films, the very essence of Shirley Temple's appeal, as Sheehan, Zanuck, and virtually everyone else in the film industry agreed, was the charm of childhood, a charm best captured by a word consistently used to describe her: cute. "Cute," as it came to be understood in the early twentieth century—as charming, adorable, and often diminutive—was an American linguistic and cultural innovation. Previously, "cute," deriving from "acute," meant shrewd, clever, often with an implication of deviousness. The shift in meaning signaled a new sentimental appreciation for figures and objects that combined the pert and the powerless: above all, small children and their accoutrements. Cuteness invited the beholder's responses on various levels: aesthetic delight, moral protection, and possessive desire. It powerfully combined elements of sentimental reform and the rise of modern commercial culture, especially as they conjoined in admiration and indulgence of childhood's innocence and wonder. From its inception around the turn of the twentieth century, this notion of the cute celebrated children's freedom from the besetting concerns of adulthood, so much so that a "normal" childhood came to be understood as defined by an absence of those concerns, including the need to work for a living, to worry about adequate food, shelter, love, and protection, or to know mature sexual desires and relations. Benign parents and other protectors could cherish children's eager imitations of adult life, even their play of work, marriage, and child rearing, safe in the belief in the boundary separating the realms of childhood and adulthood.[11]

Such a conception of cuteness depended on an economy of abundance, permitting childhood to be considered as a stage of life utterly distinct from maturity, one characterized by the pleasures of economic consumption rather than productive labor. To be sure, in the early twentieth century children still constituted an important sector of the labor market, despite attempts to pass meaningful child-labor legislation. At the same time, one of the defining aspects of American middle-class life came to be the enshrinement of children as objects of indulgent spending and the ability to protect them from working prematurely. Images of cute children were used from the turn of the twentieth century onward to advertise products specifically for children and also a wide variety of adult goods and services from radiators to life insurance, and even, as with Buster Brown endorsements, cigars and whiskey.[12] In the effort to stimulate consumer spending, moreover, cute children achieved special prominence in movies from Hal Roach's Our Gang series to *The Wizard of Oz* (1939), in radio serials and cartoon strips such as *Little Orphan Annie*, and in real life with the enormous fascination with the Dionne quintuplets, born in Ontario in May 1934, who costarred in two Hollywood feature films.

Although cuteness provided an obvious theatrical mode for staging Shirley Temple's talents, above all, her remarkable camera presence, it entailed important requirements. The first of these was for her to remain distinctly childlike in appearance, manner, and feeling as she interacted and even imitated adults and appealed to their— and viewers'—solicitude. To this end, Winfield Sheehan and Darryl Zanuck did everything they could to exaggerate Shirley's youth and diminutive stature. In addition to shaving a year off Shirley's age, the studio often depicted her as still younger in some of her movies, as with the five candles on her birthday cake in *Baby Take a Bow* (1934), seven on her cake in *Little Miss Broadway* (1938), and eight candles on another such cake in *The Little Princess*, released on March 10, 1939, shortly before she turned eleven.

In addition, Shirley Temple's juvenile appearance was consistently heightened to intensify her cuteness. All infant mammals share certain features: relatively large heads, prominent brows, large eyes, bulging cheeks, and short and thick limbs. As they mature, their snouts protrude, their bodies become larger with respect to their heads, and their limbs become larger with respect to their bodies. Adults innately recognize juvenile features and characteristically respond with solicitude and nurture. As an aesthetic, cuteness elaborates and extends this biological response from children to puppies,

Shirley in a characteristic expression of astonishment.
(Photofest/Twentieth Century–Fox)

kittens, and the like and also to dolls, stuffed toys, and other inanimate objects with similar proportions.[13] Shirley Temple was consistently presented so as to maximize her juvenile appearance and the responses that it prompted. The assiduously cultivated blond pin curls that her mother set each night perpetuated the baby ringlets that many infants (including Shirley) naturally outgrew. They also made her head seem especially large. Moreover, her broad brow and dimpled cheeks, small nose and chin, and plump, short torso and legs were all accentuated by costumes and camerawork. Frontal close-ups in her movies magnified her face to fill the screen and foreshortened her already tiny nose as she addressed viewers directly, often rounding her eyes in astonishment. Other close-ups locked her in embraces with adults—occasionally women but usually white male fatherly and grandfatherly protectors, their heads touching as she sat in their laps, scenes that further cued viewers' own solicitude. Careful lighting enhanced these effects. The brilliant cinematographer Arthur C. Miller, who worked on most of Shirley's films for Fox, later boasted, "I always lit her so she had an aureole of golden hair. I used a lamp on Shirley that made her whole damn image world famous."[14]

Shirley's outfits greatly reinforced her juvenile appearance. "Keep her skirts high," Darryl Zanuck ordered. "Have co-stars lift her up whenever possible to create the illusion now selling so well. Preserve babyhood." Reviewing photographs of her in proposed costumes when Shirley was about ten, he complained, "You've got her looking like Mae West. Give her a streamline. Minimize her, back there. What do they feed her, Hershey bars?"[15]

From *Little Miss Marker* in 1934 through *The Little Princess* in 1939, the very titles of seven Shirley Temple movies emphasized her diminutive stature. Moreover, in all of her movies, Shirley was made to look smaller (and implicitly, more powerless) by contrast with bigger-than-average adults, men especially. Three feet tall at the beginning of her movie career in the Baby Burlesks, she was forty-three inches

Victor McLaglen and Shirley wearing dress uniforms of the Seventh Highlanders in a production still for Wee Willie Winkie. *(Photofest/Twentieth Century–Fox)*

tall by summer 1934 according to one source, yet another reported her as only forty-one inches tall the following year and forty-nine inches tall in 1938. (She would ultimately grow to five foot two.)[16] Most of the leading men with whom she appeared were above medium height, and a conspicuous number were large, strapping figures. These began with Gary Cooper in *Now and Forever* and Joel McCrae in *Our Little Girl*, both of whom stood six foot three, and included barrel-chested John Boles in *Curly Top* and *The Littlest Rebel*, and six-foot-three Randolph Scott in *Rebecca of Sunnybrook Farm* and *Susannah of the Mounties*. Cesar Romero accentuated his six-foot-two height by wearing turbans in *Wee Willie Winkie* and *The Little Princess*. Two of her dance partners were slender men who towered roughly two and a half feet above her: six-foot-three Buddy Ebsen in *Captain January* and six-foot-four Arthur Treacher, who appeared in four of her films, although they danced together only in the last, *The Little Princess*.[17]

Such physical contrasts created numerous opportunities for humor, intensifying Shirley's cuteness. Especially when Shirley and an adult performed the same movements in tandem, whether in dances, calisthenics, or drill, her mimicry of her partner comically highlighted their contrasting bodies, age, status, and, frequently, gender. In *Wee Willie Winkie*, loosely based on a short story by Rudyard Kipling and set on British India's Afghan border in 1897, Shirley's character strives to earn the love of her crusty grandfather, the regiment commander, by learning to be a soldier under the demanding Sergeant MacDuff, played by Victor McLaglen. Of all the actors who appeared with Shirley Temple, McLaglen provided the greatest physical contrast. A circus strongman and boxer before he turned actor, he once fought an exhibition bout against heavyweight champion Jack Johnson— which he decisively lost. Nine years later, in 1918, McLaglen became heavyweight champion of the British Army. When he made *Wee Willie Winkie* he stood six foot three and weighed perhaps 250 pounds. As Sergeant MacDuff, he provides Shirley's character a miniature version of the dress uniform of the Seventh Highlanders and instructs her in the rigors of military drill. The disparity between her tiny body and movements and those of the husky sergeant and the men under his command prompt passing officers to explode in laughter.

Without further development, this mock-heroic effect would have made Shirley cute but inconsequential. To exploit the full potential of the contrast between her tiny body and great ambition, the makers of *Wee Willie Winkie* have her voluntarily join the men when they are ordered to drill for three more hours in the broiling sun. Like so many of Shirley Temple's films, *Wee Willie Winkie* exposes the similarity of sentiment beneath disparities of size, age, and status. Her character's demonstration of pluck testifies to the large soul in her tiny body, even as she reveals the soft boy's heart in the biggest and toughest of men, McLaglen's Sergeant MacDuff.

Nevertheless, the contrasts of scale produced an unexpected result: rumors that she was not a little girl at all but an adult dwarf. Such charges persisted in Europe as late as 1937, the year *Wee Willie Winkie* was released, sustained by her preternatural talents, including a gift for mimicking adults evident as early as the Baby Burlesks and fully displayed in two of her major films.[18] In the "You've Got to S-M-I-L-E" number of *Stowaway* (1936), she deftly imitated Al Jolson, Eddie Cantor, and the dancing couple Fred Astaire and Ginger Rogers. The "When I Grow Up" number in *Curly Top* (1935) demanded still more of her gifts. Here Shirley's character performs a rapid series of imitations of various stages of womanhood: first, sweet sixteen; next, marriage at age twenty-one; and finally old age and the pleasures of the rocking chair. The quavering voice and stiff, stooped movements with which she performs this last are so successful as to be uncanny.

Shirley Temple preserved much of this enchanting, toylike character while turning what might have been considered freakish attainments into talented set pieces. Both dwarf and child actors had enjoyed great popularity in the United States since the mid-nineteenth century, and both kinds of performers highlighted the boundaries—and ambiguities—between childhood and adulthood. Little People, particularly those with proportional dwarfism such as P. T. Barnum's celebrated attraction General Tom Thumb (Charles Stratton, 1838–83) specialized in adult impersonations. Beginning when little Charlie was still shy of his fifth birthday and was no bigger than he had been at six months (fifteen pounds and twenty-five inches tall), Barnum trained him as a performer who, dressed in elaborate costumes, sang, danced, quipped, and spoofed eminent figures. As with the characters in Shirley Temple's early Baby Burlesk shorts, his body seemed to contradict his adult roles.[19]

Although Shirley and other child actors frequently imitated adults, their principal task was to perform childhood—without calling too much attention to the fact that it was indeed a performance. In the opinion of many movie reviewers and exhibitors and countless millions of fans, Shirley did so very well. "The nation's best-liked babykins," a New York Times reviewer called her in summer 1934: "A miracle of spontaneity, Shirley successfully conceals the illusion of sideline coaching which, in the ordinary child genius, produces homicidal impulses in those old fussbudgets who lack the proper admiration for cute kiddies."[20] That her spontaneity and ease were to an extent an "illusion," the product of "sideline coaching," the reviewer took for granted, though millions of less sophisticated fans did not.

As Shirley grew older, the challenge of keeping her cute without arousing the ire of fussbudgets young and old mounted year by year. In a script conference for Dimples a few months after he thrust Sheehan aside, Darryl Zanuck insisted, "Be sure and put in a lot of pieces of business for Shirley—some cute things that Shirley could do."[21] The 1936 movie provides an illuminating instance of the Shirley Temple formula, its potential, and its perils. Like The Little Colonel and The Littlest Rebel of the previous year, the movie placed her in a historical setting, here New York City circa 1852. The plot rang a few new changes on an already familiar Shirley Temple pattern. Once again, she is an orphan, this time as Sylvia "Dimples" Appleby, living in lower Manhattan in a shabby apartment with her grandfather, "Professor" Eustace Appleby, a broken-down actor played by Frank Morgan. Unlike most of Shirley's film guardians, he is a larcenous if lovable scoundrel, full of fustian bombast and blandishments. From the outset, Dimples wishes both to believe in his goodness and to mend his ways. The movie clearly sought to exploit the sounds and color of old New York as early Shirley Temple films had exploited the moonlight and magnolias of the Old South. The script's original working title was *Under the Gaslight*, then *The Bowery Princess*, before the studio finally settled on *Dimples*, no doubt reasoning that the most important thing was to highlight Shirley Temple's smiling face and the spots where, as one man said, she had been "kissed by an angel."[22]

Early in the story the professor robs the furs of partygoers at the mansion of a rich widow, Mrs. Caroline Drew. Suspicion falls on the innocent Dimples, but the kindly host (played by Helen Westley) befriends and forgives her. The professor returns for Dimples, scattering the purloined furs outside and then pretending heroically to rout the thieves.

Quickly, then, the contending figures and issues are established. Should Dimples live with rich Mrs. Drew, who will love her and give her every advantage that money can buy? Or should she remain with her poor grandfather, who also loves her but can supply none of these advantages—and is an incorrigible rascal to boot?

Almost as quickly, a subplot emerges. Mrs. Drew's nephew, Allen, is smitten with the theater and is working on a new play—a stage rendition of Harriet Beecher Stowe's *Uncle Tom's Cabin*. Allen hires Dimples to play the role of Little Eva, and, after a long series of comic complications, her performance of Little Eva's deathbed scene leaves not a dry eye in the house. The movie ends with a blackface minstrel show, in which Shirley Temple, in white satin tails, plays the interlocutor to Stepin Fetchit's Mr. Bones.

Shirley Temple certainly had plenty of cute things to do in *Dimples*, including performing the most famous deathbed scene for a child actress in the history of the American theater. Yet her costar Frank Morgan in the role of the professor found many cute things to do as well, so that the two strenuously competed for viewers' attention. Shirley Temple Black later claimed to have understood the nature of this struggle and acknowledged she was a keen competitor. Nonetheless, she complained, Morgan used all of his tricks to divert the camera eye from Shirley during close-ups: flicking his handkerchief, jiggling his gloves and top hat, gesturing with his hands, and the like. Shirley felt powerless to stop him, short of nipping his fingers. A veteran character actor with a special talent for playing lovable hucksters (including the title character in *The Wizard of Oz*), Morgan adroitly used his ingratiating chuckle and winning smile, thus dueling Shirley with her chosen weapons.[23]

The struggle was evident to movie reviewers and presumably some moviegoers, although they did not necessarily see Morgan as the chief offender. Indeed, *Time* magazine cautioned Shirley for her methods: "She steals scenes from two old-time stage mimes [Morgan and Helen Westley], dances, sings, mugs shamelessly on Little Eva's death bed." The *New York Times*'s Frank Nugent, whose impish wit and critical sarcasm frequently sparkled in his columns, openly sympathized with Morgan's plight. Shirley's "Little Eva performance is shameless bathos," he declared, "and so is the love song she sings with her arms twined about the suffering neck of Mr. Morgan. If that episode had been done in Technicolor, I am quite sure we should have observed a blush at his collar line."[24]

Rejecting the Temple formula as a whole, Nugent delivered a sharply worded verdict: "'Dimples' is its apt title, apt because it is just another word for Little Miss Precocity and does not pretend to describe the story material it employs." He continued, "Why they bother with titles, or with plots either for that matter, is beyond us. The sensible thing would be to announce Shirley Temple in 'Shirley Temple' and let it go at that. Or to follow the example of the authors of children's books and call them 'Shirley Temple in Dixie,' 'Shirley Temple at Cape Cod' or 'Shirley Temple in Little Old New York.'"[25]

Variety agreed. "All that the production does is closely follow the pattern set from way back for the youngster, missing not a single trick, whether it comes to jerking tears, dancing, singing or bringing true love together." Even so, the trade paper thought movie exhibitors would not be disappointed with box-office returns. "Regardless of the soggy humor and the straining at human interest, the going of Shirley Temple with her fans won't be a bit undiminished [*sic*]."[26]

Yet some of the independent movie exhibitors who mingled most closely with Shirley Temple's fans expressed similar frustrations as they examined their disappointing receipts. "'Dimples' is poor entertainment," Ralph Cokain of the Indiana Theatre in Marion, Indiana, declared. "The plot is thin, the continuity is jumpy, and the whole thing leaves the impression that Darryl Zanuck must have said to associate producer Nunnally Johnson, 'Now, Nun, we've got to get this picture out to meet the release date. Rush everything. . . . It may not turn out to be the best Shirley Temple, but then it's a Temple, and that's all that matters.'" Another Indiana exhibitor added ominously, "While Shirley still draws above average business, we are beginning to hear some rumbles from the adult audience that these child prodigy pictures are all cut over the same pattern, and certainly there is nothing original about this. It is the same old gag. Feed all the lines to the prodigy and have her do a couple of songs and a dance or two. Shirley is cute and a good little actress, but is the same thing over again in all her pictures."[27]

Zanuck and Twentieth Century–Fox wrestled with this dilemma

for the next four years. If they continued to give the moviegoing public more of the same thing in which Shirley played Little Miss Fix-It, they could easily anticipate its bitter end in stale situations and a child star who outgrew her cute persona. Alternatively, they could place Shirley in more dramatic roles that would enable her to develop as an actress—but at the risk of violating fans' expectations. Either way, it was a high-stakes game.

In *Wee Willie Winkie* Zanuck gambled on the second approach—with mixed results. From the outset, he conceived of it as a distinctly new kind of Shirley Temple picture, one devoid of her usual "tricks." Although it was loosely based on a rather slight Kipling short story, and one necessitating that the title character be changed from a boy to a girl to fit Shirley Temple, Zanuck imagined a film comparable to the movie adaptations of *Little Women* (1933) and *David Copperfield* (1935), both directed by George Cukor. Always alert to story possibilities, on an early treatment outline for the movie, Zanuck scrawled excitedly with his orange pen: "Magnificent adventure as little child sets out to settle impending war on her own—Courageous—Glorious—walks into forbidden territory with childlike confidence that enemy will listen to her—and they do—You feel for her." Amid doodles, he added, "Wonderful possibilities . . . full of sentiment—tears—heart aches—child philosophy—very human and devoid of hoke or physical melodrama."[28]

In keeping with his determination to mount a new kind of Shirley Temple picture, Zanuck chose as director the brilliant but irascible John Ford, who had recently won an Academy Award for *The Informer*. Ford's explosive temper and antipathy to studio executives were notorious, and he loathed child actors. "I'm going to give you something to scream about," Zanuck told him. "I'm going to put you together with Shirley Temple."[29] To mollify Ford, Zanuck promised him a large budget and another chance to work with Victor McLaglen, who had won his own Academy Award for Best Actor in *The Informer*.

Although *Wee Willie Winkie* considerably varied the Shirley Temple formula, it retained its essence. Once again, Shirley plays a half-orphan, in this case Priscilla Williams; she and her mother are forced by poverty to leave their American home in 1897 and depend on the support of a stern, forbidding grandfather, Colonel Williams (played by the six-foot-four C. Aubrey Smith), commander of a British outpost near the Afghan border in colonial India. The colonel is locked in a struggle with a rebellious Afghan tribe, led by Khoda Khan (Cesar Romero). Rather like Shirley's characters in *The Little Colonel* and *The Littlest Rebel*, Priscilla plays the part of peacemaker as her character simultaneously wins the admiration and affection of her grandfather and the Afghan chief. Ultimately, through her simple childish innocence, she brings the warring leaders to reconciliation, thus saving untold lives.

Along the way, there are many of the familiar elements of the old formula, including Shirley's beaming smile and stifled tears, gift for mimicry and guileless trust, and longing for acceptance and for love. There are also a cute terrier puppy that is given limited exposure so as not to upstage Shirley's own cuteness, and an older drummer boy, earnest and unsympathetic, to provide a foil for her winning charm. Yet there are distinct departures from the formula as well. Shirley does not dance, and she sings her one song with notable simplicity (albeit with offscreen accompaniment). Most importantly, more is demanded of her as an actress.

In fact, as Shirley Temple Black described the making of *Wee Willie Winkie*, she appears unconsciously to have transposed a major theme of the movie—Priscilla's determination to learn to be a disciplined and courageous soldier and so win the affection and respect of her crusty grandfather—to her relationship as a child actress determined to win the respect and affection of crusty John Ford. Ford demanded much from his actors and gave little praise in return. Black later described how she thawed his icy facade and won his friendship and respect, culminating in her portrayal of the scene in which she visits Victor McLaglen, as the gentle giant Sergeant MacDuff, on his deathbed. Ford, whose dark glasses and gruff manner concealed a deeply sentimental streak, elicited the full measure of her tender affection without letting her fall into mawkishness. There had been numerous lullaby scenes in her films, but here she sings "Auld Lang Syne" straightforwardly to MacDuff. Told he is improving, she believes him to be merely falling asleep as he takes his last breaths and expires.[30]

Reviewers praised *Wee Willie Winkie* as a notable departure from Shirley Temple's usual films. *Time* magazine's critic wrote, "In the most exacting role of her astonishing career, Producer Darryl Zanuck has metamorphosed her from a collection of dimples into a self-conscious, capable child actress." Howard Barnes, a film critic for the *New York Herald Tribune* and one of Shirley Temple's most thoughtful and balanced reviewers, similarly remarked, "The small star is not permitted to take refuge in cute antics in this offering. . . . She creates a solid and engaging portrait of an American youngster adjusting herself to the curious routine of an Indian army post in 1897."[31]

Nonetheless, in their reports to *Motion Picture Herald* on the response of moviegoers to *Wee Willie Winkie*, independent movie theater exhibitors divided between cheers for the movie's innovations and chagrin over the disappointment of many Shirley Temple fans, especially children. The deeper and unmistakable question that consumed them was whether Shirley would remain box-office champion or fall into a slump—an anxiety that grew with every year. "Who said that Shirley Temple is slipping," wrote a theater manager from a working-class district in Detroit about her performance in *Wee Willie Winkie*, adding enthusiastically, "They did not leave it all to Shirley . . . a swell production and a fine supporting cast." "One of the best of the Temples," an exhibitor from Anamosa, Iowa, declared. "Has production, story value and cast." From Hazen, Arkansas, the manager of the Cozy Theatre exulted, "She is still the girl that will lift the mortgage."[32]

In contrast, other exhibitors grumbled over their meager returns from *Wee Willie Winkie*. "Lowest grosser of the Temple pictures," lamented L. A. Irwin from Penacook, New Hampshire. "Shirley is excellent in her part," the writer acknowledged, but "the fault lies in her part not being the sort of thing Temple fans expect of her. On its own, it's a fine picture, but as a Shirley Temple picture, it's a mistake and no fault of the star." An exhibitor from Sodus in upstate New York agreed that "this is not the type of picture that appeals to most of our Shirley Temple fans," even while observing "it pleased generally." The manager of the Owl Theatre in Lebanon, Kansas, wailed, "For the first time a Shirley Temple picture fell flat at the box office. . . . Not even the kiddies manifested any interest in this one. . . . It is not the type of picture they like to see Shirley in, and, well, they just did not come." "Why mix this wonderful star up with all these soldiers," demanded an exhibitor from Bengough, Saskatchewan. "The kids come to see her as well as the grownups, and they don't like shooting and too much of the military stuff." "Too bad they are killing this little star with such material," J. A. Fair of the Elite Theatre in Laurens, Iowa, wrote. An exhibitor in Westby, Wisconsin, similarly complained: "The story is not really suited to Miss Temple and [I] personally think it about the least entertaining of anything she has appeared in. At that, it is quite a show as compared to the rank and file of ordinary pictures."[33]

Zanuck might have liked to please Shirley's critics, but he had to ensure Shirley's hold on her fans. In subsequent movies, he placed her generally in either stories that had the prestige, if not always the substance, of childhood literary classics or else more contemporary song-and-dance situations in which she could play the plucky performer. To the extent possible, he did both at once.

From Kipling's "Wee Willie Winkie" he turned to Johanna Spyri's 1881 novel *Heidi*. The adaptation included more melodrama and also more slapstick, more picturesque fantasy, and notably far less emphasis on religious faith. As the director, Allan Dwan, recalled, "The whole idea was to keep it light, because it can get awfully sticky if you really make those kind of stories seriously."[34] The movie brightened Heidi's unquenchable optimism and darkened the souls of her scheming enemies: her selfish aunt Dete, who abducts her from her grandfather's Swiss Alpine hut and takes her to Frankfurt to serve as a companion to a crippled rich girl, Klara Sesemann; and Fraulein Rottenmeir, Herr Sesemann's housekeeper, who is transmogrified from a nervous martinet in the novel to a cruel and treacherous villain in the movie. As Herr Sesemann's butler, Andrews, Arthur Treacher continues in the vein that he had established in previous Shirley Temple films (and others of the period, such as *Thank You, Jeeves*), repeatedly exclaiming, "My word," just as he had in *Curly Top*.

Heidi gave Shirley Temple fans more of her dancing (a pleasure denied them in *Wee Willie Winkie*), although instead of the tap-dancing that had been her staple ever since her "Baby Take a Bow" number in *Stand Up and Cheer!*, it placed her in a sugar-plum fantasy. As her grandfather reads the sleepy Heidi a storybook, the camera dissolves through the page to a production number, "In My Little Wooden Shoes," that is thickly coated with cuteness. Shirley accentuates her own childish appearance in a folkloric Dutch song and dance, lisping shamelessly as she sings of taking "a twip wherever we choose." Then, as the scene shifts to an eighteenth-century court ball, she dances a minuet looking like a porcelain doll.

Heidi might be seen as a charming Old World fairy tale, but it nonetheless resonated powerfully with the fears and fantasies of Depression America. Both the Alpine pastoral simplicity and the luxuries of Herr Sesemann's household expressed longings prominent in the 1930s. In addition, the story of how Shirley's Heidi taught lame Klara Sesemann the courage to rise from her wheelchair and gradually to walk again (a recovery significantly different from that in the original novel) carried special meanings for a nation whose own president, they believed, had, through indomitable courage, overcome paralysis.

When *Heidi* was released in October 1937, the *New York Herald Tribune's* Howard Barnes observed, "It is no secret by now that Shirley Temple is being guided into and through a difficult transition period in her acting career. The tiny star is no longer a precocious infant with an extraordinary gift for snatches of make-believe, but a youngster rapidly approaching the conventional limits of child star popularity." Striving to be fair, Barnes delivered an ambiguous verdict. Her acting, he noted, "still lacks emotional power, but the Heidi she creates is more Heidi and less Shirley Temple than one might have expected."[35]

Most local exhibitors agreed, many calling *Heidi* Shirley's best picture in some time. A representative comment came from the Green Lantern Theatre in Claymont, Delaware: "This has been reported as her best to date, and I agree with this estimate of the picture. It has the elements that make pictures good—well acted, some comedy, action. What more can be asked for?" From the opposite side of the country in McMinnville, Oregon, came an echoing cheer. "Splendid," wrote the manager of the Lark Theatre. "Just what the cash customer want[s]. Real entertainment for old and young. A story that touches the heart and one that makes the exhibitor feel glad to show."[36]

Following *Heidi*, Zanuck plucked another children's classic off the shelf: Kate Douglas Wiggin's *Rebecca of Sunnybrook Farm* (1903), a much lighter, more humorous story of a winning bright-eyed girl's adventures with her spinster aunts, schoolmates, teachers, and a rich male benefactor, set in a Maine village in the late nineteenth century. From Zanuck's first story conferences, it is clear that he and his scriptwriters intended to strip the original novel of all but its cover and to turn it into a vehicle for the kinds of songs and dances that had made Shirley famous. Criticizing an early story outline, Zanuck said, "In order to be a musical, this has got to be funny." They planned to have Shirley play her usual role of trouper and Cupid, but precisely how she would do so developed more slowly. "She is now in no real jeopardy," Zanuck observed in another story conference, "and we need an exciting element to give us suspense and the feeling that Shirley is in danger." Zanuck and his team laced the story with the principal ingredient of so many Shirley Temple films: the competition among potential guardians to protect (or exploit) a priceless radio child star. Ultimately, Shirley's crass stepfather is foiled and her deserving aunt and grown-up cousin are each united with the man of her dreams. For good measure, Shirley brings together still a third pair of lovers—a record score in a Temple picture.[37]

In much of *Rebecca of Sunnybrook Farm*, the line between Rebecca's character and Shirley Temple's own career is intentionally blurred. Rebecca is portrayed as coolly professional, as much at ease in a radio studio as on a swing, as, according to countless testimonies, Shirley was in the film studio. In addition, Shirley had previously played a similar role of a radio child star ("America's Sweetheart of the Air"), with business rivals and potential guardians vying for her in *Poor Little Rich Girl*. Indeed, the distinction between Rebecca and Shirley's other roles drops when, as part of a supposed radio debut, Shirley sings a medley of her hit songs from previous films especially to her fans, "On the Good Ship Lollipop", "Animal Crackers in My Soup," "When I'm with You," "Oh My Goodness," and "Goodnight, My Love." The plot of the film as a whole implicitly defended Shirley Temple, her family, and the terms of her career (including the contract with Twentieth Century–Fox) from any charges of exploitation.

To preserve the full flavor of the Shirley Temple formula in *Rebecca*, Zanuck cast the roles as from a Temple stock company. Helen Westley, a veteran stage and movie actress who had appeared variously in warm-hearted, selfish, and malevolent guises in *Dimples*, *Stowaway*, and *Heidi*, played Aunt Miranda. Slim Summerville, Gloria Stuart, and Jack Haley had each appeared in an earlier Shirley Temple movie, and Franklin Pangborn, a newcomer to a Temple picture, would return in her next. For the leading male role, Zanuck again chose a tall, strapping hero, Randolph Scott, newly free from his contract with Paramount. Already a veteran of many movie westerns, Scott would again play opposite Shirley Temple the next year in *Susannah of the Mounties*.

Finally, the enormously popular Bill "Bojangles" Robinson made his third appearance with Shirley as Aunt Miranda's farm hand Aloysius. Wearing a straw hat and overalls, he waits good-naturedly through the action for his big dance number, "The March of the Wooden Soldiers," which, like a similar number in *Poor Little Rich Girl*, concludes the film. The dance might, with greater dramatic relevance, have appeared in several other Shirley Temple movies, for here the number is presumably unseen by its ostensible radio audience. But no matter, for, unlike John Ford's *Wee Willie Winkie*, which aimed for dramatic coherence, *Rebecca* was intended to provide an engaging story that could support songs, dances, and pratfalls wherever they might be most entertaining.

Yet one small variation in the formula signaled the growing division between Gertrude Temple and Darryl Zanuck. *Rebecca of Sunnybrook Farm* began and ended with Shirley wearing her iconic fifty-six curls, but when she went to stay with her aunt, Miranda immediately combed out her curls and tied her hair in two ribbons, one behind each ear. It was a concession to Gertrude Temple, who itched to change Shirley's screen persona in more major ways. "I'd like to see Shirley, just once anyway, in a role which was a complete reversal of things she had done before," Mrs. Temple told a reporter. "Let her get down and play in the mud—let her be human."[38]

Despite Gertrude Temple's qualms, this time the formula worked. Zanuck's radically transformed Shirley Temple version of *Rebecca of Sunnybrook Farm* pleased virtually all who consumed it, despite the misleading label of the Wiggin novel. "Why they name it 'Rebecca of Sunnybrook Farm' is one of those mysteries," *Variety* mused. "More fitting title would be 'Rebecca of Radio City.'" Frank Nugent of the *New York Times*, an early detractor of the Shirley Temple formula, marveled at her achievement, albeit somewhat ironically. Observing that the original character of Rebecca scarcely existed in Zanuck's version, he acknowledged that this radical departure was beside the point: "We had ceased to think of her as Rebecca, at all. She was just Shirley to us, and so far as we are concerned, Sunnybrook Farm could go peddle its produce." Waving aside the blithe disregard for Wiggin's treasured story, he declared, "Any actress who can dominate a Zanuck musical . . . with Jack Haley, Gloria Stuart, Phyllis Brooks, Helen Westley, Slim Summerville, Bill Robinson, et cetera, can dominate the world. We go even further: we venture to predict for Miss Temple a great future, and that includes singing, dancing, straight dramatic acting, or all three combined, if her fancy runs that way."[39]

Motion Picture Daily similarly applauded the movie as, above all, a vehicle for Shirley Temple's extraordinary talent: "Singing, dancing, mimicking, exercising her magic personality . . . she is the Shirley of old." The trade journal noted the enthusiasm of the preview audience. "Rattling in applause continuously and erupting into a roar at the conclusion, [it] gave emphatic evidence that Shirley's 'Rebecca' should take rank with the most successful in which she has been starred."[40]

Motion Picture Herald's William R. Weaver, perhaps attending the same preview, fervently joined in the applause for Shirley. Unlike earlier versions of *Rebecca of Sunnybrook Farm*, "tenderly sentimental works aimed at the cardiac and lachrymal reflexes," the Temple version "pointed at eye, ear and, in a sense, intellect. Rhythm and its uses, humor unrooted in precocity and, most of all, sheer professional ability to perform entertainingly, comprise the stuff with which this expert young lady demonstrates that she doesn't need curls, tears and Jean Hersholt [her grandfather in *Heidi*]—or anybody else—to put her over." Weaver confidently—and accurately—predicted that this box-office champion of 1935, 1936, and 1937 would win the title again in 1938. Far less accurately, he added, "There isn't the slightest reason for thinking she'll drop out of that top spot in the next ten or fifteen years."[41]

Despite such enthusiasm, *Time* magazine's critic refused to buy the Temple formula. He especially balked at her glib dismissal of the importance of money in the Samuel Pokrass and Jack Yellen song "Come and Get Your Happiness." When Shirley sang to her radio listeners, "with well-rehearsed and gleefully interpolated chuckles," of the riches pouring down on those in ragged trousers on which they paid no income tax, "they will see that this Rebecca is a $2,400-a-week Hollywood specialist with no mortgage to pay off" or any of the other obstacles that the original Rebecca faced in Wiggin's novel—and that millions still faced in the Great Depression.[42] It was a rude reminder to Twentieth Century–Fox that for the vast majority of Americans, unlike the Temple family, a high income tax bracket was not the most pressing problem.

Zanuck dispensed with even the pretext of a juvenile classic in Shirley's next two movies, dropping her squarely into Depression New York and contriving ways for her to put on a show. The first of these, *Little Miss Broadway*, threw in all of the most familiar Temple elements: girls in an orphanage, vaudeville veterans, a lovable uncle, a rich, imperious dowager, and a young romantic couple. The movie ends with Shirley and friends putting on a triumphant variety show and then leading her new mother and father to get a marriage license. Cupid has done her work once again. As the couple kiss, she exclaims what had become her signature line, "Oh my goodness!"

Although in one scene Shirley's character blows out seven candles on her birthday cake, she was in fact ten, and her cuteness could not last indefinitely. The opening scenes in the orphanage posed special perils: possible invidious comparisons between Shirley and the other girls. The talented and attractive jazz trio the Three Brian Sisters, with whom Shirley sang the perky song "Be Optimistic," presented the greatest risk. The eldest of the three, Betty, was five years older than Shirley, Doris only two years older, and Gwen exactly Shirley's age, although Shirley was shortest. Pitch-perfect and adept at close harmonies, they exposed the limitations of Shirley's pleasant but unremarkable voice. Ultimately, in the trio with Shirley, Betty wore glasses to make her appear studious, and Gwen was eliminated entirely. The sisters later attributed these decisions to Gertrude Temple's vigilant protection of her daughter against potential rivals. Yet even in early story conferences, Zanuck himself had warned against "writing *too* cute lines for the other children."[43]

Little Miss Broadway pleased those who liked their Shirley Temple straight up. As William Weaver wrote in *Motion Picture Herald*, "If Darryl Zanuck had set out to produce for the young lady's grandchildren one film which they could regard in reverent awe as the 'typical Shirley Temple picture' this would be it." The story, he observed, was a quintessential Temple vehicle: "She is a cheerful, tearful tot in an orphanage. She is the precocious idol of a theatrical boarding house. She is persecuted by a rich old spinster in black alpaca. She cajoles a judge on the bench and she fixes things for a romantic couple. And she sings a lot and dances a lot and spends all her screen time being just Shirley Temple."[44]

Yet was "just being Shirley Temple" still enough? A number of the local movie theater exhibitors who wrote to *Motion Picture Herald* did not think so. A faithful contributor, A. E. Hancock of the Columbia Theatre in Columbia City, Indiana, declared, "I'll tell Fox and the whole world that they will have to come better than this one to keep Shirley on top. The scenario is trite and has not a new idea in it. All had been done before, the little orphan, the cruel aunt who breaks down finally under the winsome Shirley. . . . Too bad," he concluded. "She has been a wonder but she is growing up."[45]

L. A. Irwin of the Palace Theatre in Penacook, New Hampshire, still believed in Shirley's talent but lamented the fare that Twentieth Century–Fox was giving her: "There sure is a gosh awful lot of orphans to scribble about. If Shirley does a story about each and every one of them, folks sure will get mighty sick of this type of story and most of our patrons are feeling that way about this routine plot already."[46]

"Sorry, Shirley," wrote an exhibitor from the Ritz Theatre in Stafford, Kansas, "but you can't get them in any more. Since 'Curly Top' you have been steadily losing ground until now you can't even get average Sunday business for me." A man from the Paramount Theatre in Schroon Lake, New York, added the ominous report, "Many a time during the run of the picture I heard the remark, 'She isn't as cute as she used to be.'"[47]

For the moment Zanuck could shrug off such complaints. *Little Miss Broadway* finished among Twentieth Century–Fox's most popular movies in the domestic market in 1938, closely followed by two other Temple films, so that Shirley retained her title of box-office champion for the fourth year in a row.[48] No one else had ever come close to such success. Still, local exhibitors and Hollywood moguls agreed that her luster was fading fast.

For Shirley's last film of 1938, instead of devising fresh innovations, Zanuck redoubled his bet on familiar situations, characterizations, songs, and dances, as if to cash in on Shirley's popularity while it lasted. Originally titled *All American Dad*, it was variously known as *Lucky Penny*, *Little Lady*, and *Sunny Side Up* until Zanuck and the studio finally settled on *Just around the Corner*—a reference to the predicted return of prosperity popularly attributed to Herbert Hoover.[49] In what would be Shirley's last movie set entirely in the Great Depression, she has a broken-hearted widowed father for whom to find a new wife, another frozen-hearted tycoon to melt, and, in a mild twist, a spoiled rich mamma's boy to turn into an all-American kid. Shirley's character, Penny Hale, earnestly seeks to understand her architect father's and the country's economic plight. When he shows her a political cartoon, in which various figures—farmer, businessman, laborer, and housewife—all pull on Uncle Sam's legs and demand, "Help me first," she asks, "Why doesn't somebody try to help Uncle Sam instead of pulling on him?" The plot ends in a ringing reaffirmation of "that good old American spirit" of confidence. Once again, Shirley lifts the country out of the Great Depression, just as she had in *Stand Up and Cheer!*

Like *Little Miss Broadway, Just around the Corner* provided numerous opportunities for Shirley to sing and dance, including numbers with Bert Lahr, Joan Davis, and, most notably, Bill Robinson, in what would be their final pairing. Yet in the rush to keep the running time to seventy minutes, such interludes were brief.

By now the cheerleaders and detractors of such fare were predictable. William Weaver of *Motion Picture Herald*, who certainly needed no Uncle Sam to stoke his optimism, marveled, "This Shirley Temple matter is getting out of hand. All the rules say she's overdue for a flop. . . . This film proves the signs mean nothing. . . . [It] is as near an approach to perfect box office as it is reasonable for any showman or customer to expect to lay eye upon."[50]

By contrast, the *New York Times*'s Frank Nugent seethed with exasperation, a sign of the widening divide between film critics and Shirley's diehard fans. "Certainly nothing so aggravating as this has come along before, nothing so arch, so dripping with treacle, so palpably an affront to the good taste or intelligence of the unwary beholder," he sputtered. After sardonically recounting the film's plot and situations, he concluded, "Shirley is not responsible, of course. No child could conceive so diabolic a form of torture. There must be an adult mind in back of it all—way, way in back of it all."[51]

Less irritated, the *New York Herald Tribune*'s Howard Barnes still reluctantly agreed. Although he praised Shirley as "the most talented acting tot of our time," he lamented the unimaginative material that Twentieth Century–Fox furnished her. Granting the "extraordinary assurance and virtuosity" of her performance, he added, "The trouble is that we have seen all of Miss Temple's tricks and pirouettes so many times before that they are apt to seem a bit monotonous in so dull a framework as this. . . . The new Shirley Temple picture," he concluded, "is little more than a reprint of her previous song-and-dance successes" and so "a very ordinary entertainment."[52]

Even an ordinary Shirley Temple film enjoyed box-office success, although *Just around the Corner* trailed previous Temple pictures in sales. The experiences of local movie exhibitors inevitably varied, but many filed reports similar to Sam Schiwetz of the Rialto Theatre in Three Rivers, Texas: "A good Shirley Temple picture that failed to draw. Business falling off with every Temple picture. Fox better give Shirley something different or she will be a has-been within a year."[53]

Perhaps foremost among those worried about typecasting Shirley in predictable stories was her mother, Gertrude Temple. Publicly restless about Shirley's material as early as *Rebecca of Sunnybrook Farm* and alarmed by what she regarded as the thin substance and weak casting of *Just around the Corner*, she demanded a meeting with Zanuck. As Shirley Temple Black later recounted their interview, Zanuck listened patiently to her concerns but defended the formulaic character of Shirley's films as necessitated by the star system. The business of the studio was not principally to develop Shirley's growth as an actress, much as Gertrude Temple might wish it. Rather, it needed to capture or produce a personality for as long as it suited popular taste. "Now she's lovable. The less she changes, the longer she lasts." "You can't create a public fad," he insisted to Mrs. Temple. "Once you have a fad, leave it alone."[54]

The year 1939 remains Hollywood's annus mirabilis, with high movie attendance and an exceptional number of excellent films, including *Beau Geste, Dark Victory, Destry Rides Again, Drums along the Mohawk, Gone with the Wind, Young Mr. Lincoln, Gunga Din, The Hunchback of Notre Dame, Love Affair, Mr. Smith Goes to Washington, Ninotchka, Of Mice and Men, Only Angels Have Wings, Stagecoach, The Wizard of Oz, The Women, Wuthering Heights*, and *Goodbye, Mr. Chips*. Although

Louis B. Mayer, head of production at MGM Studios, at one point had discussed with Zanuck the possibility of trading Shirley to play the part of Dorothy Gale in *The Wizard of Oz*, no serious negotiations ever followed. Given Judy Garland's consummate performance in the role, only the most ardent Shirley Temple fans can regret this outcome. Still, Zanuck did respond to the increased emphasis on lavish color productions, of which *The Wizard of Oz* and *Gone with the Wind* were the most celebrated, with two full-length color feature films starring Shirley Temple. The first, *The Little Princess*, which offered a deluxe version of the formula he had established, achieved Shirley's last financial and critical success for Twentieth Century–Fox.

For *The Little Princess* Zanuck cut up another children's classic to fit Shirley. Frances Hodgson Burnett had published the original novella, *Sara Crewe; or, What Happened at Miss Minchin's Boarding School*, in 1888. She later turned the story into a play and, in 1905, expanded it into a full-length novel. Mary Pickford had starred in a silent film version in 1917, the same year she made two other movies that Shirley would rework, *The Poor Little Rich Girl* and *Rebecca of Sunnybrook Farm*. For Zanuck and his scriptwriters, the nub of the story proved irresistible. A young motherless girl, Sara Crewe, who has been raised in India by her rich and adoring father, is left at a fashionable London boarding school run by the imperious Miss Minchin. At first she leads a pampered existence as the school's "show pupil." Then, when her father dies and his fortune is apparently lost, Miss Minchin cruelly compels Sara to serve as a scullery maid and lodge in a cramped garret. Endowed with an indomitable imagination, Sara pretends that she lives in a room of rare splendor. An invalid gentleman and his Indian servant, living next door, contrive to make her dream come true. The gentleman proves to be her father's friend and partner, and he becomes a second father to her, doubling her lost fortune and enfolding her into his own affectionate household.

Such a melodramatic plot of luxury and privation, of fortunes,

Shirley works as a scullery maid in a production still for The Little Princess. *(Photofest/Twentieth Century–Fox)*

affection, and fathers lost and restored, clearly provided much to appeal to a movie audience in the Great Depression and especially to Shirley Temple fans. After discarding several earlier treatments of the screenplay, Zanuck and writers Ethel Hill and Walter Ferris included what had become requisite elements for a Temple picture: a young couple for which Shirley could play Cupid and a partner (Arthur Treacher) with whom to perform a music-hall-inspired song-and-dance number, as well as a dream ballet. (Shirley performed expertly in the former but, a ballet novice, she was the only ballerina in the fantasy sequence not on pointe.) To intensify the drama, in what was sure to appeal to British audiences, the film's creators moved the story forward a decade to 1899 and the Second Boer War, in which Sara's father is reported to have died at the Siege of Mafeking. Sara refuses to believe that he is dead, however, and repeatedly searches for him at the nearby hospital. Finally, pursued through the hospital corridors by Miss Minchin and assisted by no less a personage than Queen Victoria, Sara at last finds her wounded, amnesic father and restores his mind, memory, and spirit. Joyfully reunited, father and daughter stand at attention as the aging Victoria leaves the hospital and the band plays "God Save the Queen."

In addition to talented character actors, several veterans of Shirley Temple films among them, the cast included South African–born Sybil Jason as Becky, the cockney scullery maid at Miss Minchin's who becomes Sara's devoted friend. Almost exactly Shirley's age and height, she delighted the film crew with her accomplished cockney speech. Shirley, who did not attempt to alter her American accent, apart from her rendition with Arthur Treacher of the music-hall song "Knocked 'Em in the Old Kent Road," later confessed jealousy at Sybil's appeal. Shirley effectively channeled this envy to another target in the memorably naughty scene—unusual in her roles—in which she is goaded beyond endurance by the spiteful taunts of a snobbish schoolmate and dumps a scuttle of coal ashes on her head.[55]

The Little Princess had a running time of ninety-one minutes, longer than any previous Shirley Temple film except *Wee Willie Winkie*. Lavishly produced and luminously filmed in Technicolor, it was Shirley's most expensive vehicle to that time. At its release, Zanuck led the ballyhoo, calling it "the finest picture with which I have ever been associated."[56]

No critic went this far, but Nelson Bell in the *Washington Post* proclaimed *The Little Princess* "Shirley Temple's best picture to date." He applauded the rich color, the dream ballet, the supporting cast, and Shirley's own performance. Yet he could not resist deriding "the attempt to make the prodigious Miss Temple, with her round face and plump little body, serve as the symbol of persecution and the victim of deprivation that verges close to the borders of starvation." Mae Tinee of the *Chicago Daily Tribune* expressed similar delight. "They say she's at the awkward age," she noted. "Nonsense. Shirley Temple will never have an awkward age!"[57]

Despite the success of *The Little Princess*, Gertrude Temple continued to chafe at the roles in which Zanuck cast her daughter. "No more backstairs waifs," she insisted. The time had come for Shirley to portray the "everyday problems of a child." Instead of settling for mediocre ratings, Shirley would either regain her place at the "top of the heap" or make "a graceful exit."[58] Zanuck ignored these demands, placing Shirley in another familiar situation, as the difference between his and the Temple family's conceptions of Shirley's career widened to a chasm.

In *Susannah of the Mounties*, Shirley continued the work of healing on behalf of imperial Britain begun in *Wee Willie Winkie* and pursued in *The Little Princess*, this time on Canada's western frontier. Once again, she is already an orphan as the story begins, the sole survivor of a Blackfoot Indian attack. Scooped up by a handsome Mountie (Randolph Scott), she becomes the pet of the men on a military post. Like a B western, the movie included a young Indian boy, a noble Indian chief (played by the former Yiddish-theater actor Maurice Moscovitch in redface), and treacherous Indians and settlers in roughly equal measure, who together propel events to the point in which Randolph Scott would have been burned at the stake had not Shirley saved him in the nick of time.

Critics did not attempt to conceal their disappointment. "Heap big eyewash as cinema entertainment," *Time* magazine grunted. "Strictly for the juvenile trade," wrote *Variety*, adding ominously, "Youngster is growing up fast, and is losing some [of] that sparkle displayed as a tot." Frank Nugent of the *New York Times* added sardonically, "The early Canadian Northwest Mounted Police certainly wore tricky uniforms. . . . Except for the fact that they are on the screen, people at the Roxy might almost mistake them for ushers."[59]

The independent small-town exhibitors who wrote to *Motion Picture Herald* echoed such laments, and many felt that Shirley's star was waning at last. "Fox's darling is going the way of all child stars," wrote A. E. Hancock of Columbia City, Indiana. "Each picture she slips a little more." A woman from Konawa, Oklahoma, sadly agreed: "I believe Shirley Temple is outgrowing her popularity." A man from the Plaza Theatre in Lyons, Nebraska, chimed in: "Shirley will have to make different and better picture[s] or she will be completely washed up."[60]

By this time virtually everyone, including Zanuck and his subordinates at Twentieth Century–Fox, Gertrude and George Temple, film distributors and exhibitors, reporters, and fans, sensed—and feared—that Shirley was at a crucial point in her career. The illusion of childhood could not last forever. What had been extraordinary was how long Zanuck had been able to sustain it. Perhaps he reasoned that, if Louis B. Mayer could bind and corset sixteen-year-old Judy Garland's breasts in order for her to play Dorothy in *The Wizard of Oz*, he could certainly preserve the illusion of Shirley's prepubescent girlhood for at least another year or so. Yet, no matter how much her age was trimmed in scripts and her costumes designed to deny any hint of maturity, signs of puberty could not be wholly disguised. (Her menarche occurred on her eleventh birthday, in April 1939.)[61]

Yet, for the first time since Shirley's spectacular breakthrough in *Stand Up and Cheer!* five years earlier, no new film project immediately followed *Susannah of the Mounties*. Instead, Shirley and her parents waited an agonizing six months for the next assignment from Zanuck. "Shirley has been merely cute long enough," he declared in a widely circulated interview in late July 1939. Proudly calling her the "greatest theatrical attraction since Valentino" and the "outstanding child star of all time," he added, "Shirley is more beautiful than ever, and she is certainly a much better actress than she was a few years ago."[62]

Nonetheless, Zanuck acknowledged, the revenues from her films had not kept pace with their rising costs. "A slight apathy toward her pictures is becoming apparent in remarks from her fans and in letters, which they still write in very large numbers. They say they think there isn't much to the Temple pictures any more, but they admit they still like to see this precocious 10-year-old [sic] perform." It was her fans who made her a star and kept her aloft, and Zanuck clearly took their reactions seriously. "We arrived at the conclusion [that] to retain their interest we must do something absolutely new and different. She can be cute and still 'do something.'"[63]

Yet he admitted that finding the proper material was difficult. "She is a specialist, limited to a very few types of things. Specialists never last long, but Shirley is the exception to the rule." In the search for "more definite characterizations, more meat to her stories," the studio had invested close to $200,000 in potential material for her that year. Discarded projects included *Little Diplomat*, in which Shirley would extricate her companions from various European troubles, a mystery, a film with Al Jolson, and a costume drama called *Lady Jane*. Zanuck had even announced a contest with a prize of $25,000 for an acceptable story idea.[64]

One of the stories that Zanuck had purchased with Shirley in mind, outbidding Walt Disney, was the sound film rights to the 1908 allegorical play *The Blue Bird* by the Belgian author and Nobel Prize winner Maurice Maeterlinck. Regarded as a symbolist masterpiece, it would be Zanuck's answer to MGM's *Wizard of Oz*. In the play a boy, Tyltyl, and his sister, Mytyl, two woodcutter's children reminiscent of Hansel and Gretel, go on a quest, led by the figure of Light, for the blue bird of happiness. Their search takes them to various realms, ending with the Kingdom of the Future, with the souls of children awaiting the hour of their births and preparing to bring inventions, agricultural improvements, ideas, and reforms, even one destined to conquer death itself. There they meet their future younger brother, who is also bringing the disease that will kill him, and two child lovers, fated to be born at different times and so be separated forever. Finally, Tyltyl and Mytyl return to their parents' simple cottage, and, waking from their dream, discover the blue bird and happiness all about them.[65]

By the time that Zanuck was steering *The Blue Bird* through various story treatments and into production, his relations with Gertrude and George Temple had sunk to such a point that they communicated only in writing, following a circuitous route through the Temples' attorney, Loyd Wright, to Twentieth Century–Fox chairman Joseph Schenck and from him to Zanuck. Shirley Temple Black reported that her mother pressed Zanuck through every script revision to make Shirley's character "impish, spoiled, and naughty." (In Maeterlinck's

Shirley and Johnny Russell in a production still for The Blue Bird.
(Photofest/ Twentieth Century–Fox)

play the children are naive rather than nasty.) If Shirley's performance in rehearsal made the film crew hiss, Gertrude Temple wrote, her daughter would be "in seventh heaven." Shirley's character did indeed darken in successive drafts, and Gertrude Temple claimed victory. Shirley could have been "even meaner," she later told reporters. Her daughter was bored with her monotonous goody-two-shoes roles, and Gertrude clearly felt that moviegoers were growing tired of them as well.[66]

Because Zanuck's *The Blue Bird* was to be, first and foremost, a Shirley Temple vehicle, Shirley's Mytyl became the dominant sibling, and Tyltyl was demoted to the position of her younger brother. Even so, to retain Tyltyl as a character at all represented a significant innovation in the Shirley Temple formula. Never before had another child been paired with her throughout the story, and the boy assigned to the role of Tyltyl, six-year-old Johnny Russell, was notably talented and cute. Gertrude Temple, who always warily eyed potential rivals for Shirley's limelight, tried to have him replaced. Through the elaborate chain of communication she argued that Shirley needed someone her own age. "Ridiculous," Zanuck replied, maintaining that a boy the same age would naturally be the leader. As her younger brother, he would naturally rely on her guidance and example.[67]

Gertrude and George Temple lodged other objections as well. Although Shirley was the movie's star, they protested, no one reading the script would guess so. They invidiously compared her part to Judy Garland's in *The Wizard of Oz*, the film that cast its shadow over the entire undertaking. With asperity, Zanuck replied that Shirley's part was larger than any other character's in the movie—much bigger than Dorothy's in the *Wizard of Oz*. Observing that Twentieth Century–Fox had paid $100,000 for story rights and had consulted Maeterlinck when preparing the script, he insisted that Shirley clearly had won the starring role. He shook his head in bewilderment at their complaints: "I cannot accept your reasoning."[68]

The unborn children in the Kingdom of the Future also concerned the Temples. Gertrude Temple especially disliked the idea of Mytyl and Tyltyl's younger sibling, whose early death was foretold. (The character was retained.) George Temple objected to the boy who would be the future Abraham Lincoln because his talk of national honor and the necessity of war might provoke sectional bitterness and also encourage American intervention in the looming European conflict. To George Temple's Republican ears, the boy sounded suspiciously like Franklin Roosevelt: "Were it not for our good isolationist Congress, we would already be at war." Zanuck replied that he would "think it over." A somber, long-faced older boy in the film speaks of ending slavery and injustice and predicts the people will destroy him, but he avoids the inflammatory references that troubled Shirley's father.[69]

The Wizard of Oz famously presented Dorothy Gale's Kansas in sepia tones and then bursts into color in the Land of Oz. The contrast captured the spirit of L. Frank Baum's original novel and also the physical and emotional gulf separating the bleak dust-bowl landscapes of the 1930s from a land without cares "somewhere over the rainbow."

Twentieth Century–Fox's *The Blue Bird* also opened and concluded in sepia tones. Unlike Dorothy in spare, windblown Kansas, however, Mytyl and Tyltyl live near a lush forest in a picturesque Tyrolean village around the beginning of the nineteenth century. They reside with their parents in a simple home in which the only true concern is the possibility of war with Napoleon. (The analogous specter of war with Nazi Germany would have been unmistakable for American moviegoers.) Nonetheless, Mytyl is selfish and unhappy: envious of the rich, ungenerous to an invalid girl, discontented with her lot, and disobedient and ungrateful to her pious, hardworking parents. Her misery is in sharp contrast to the spirit of virtually every previous Shirley Temple character, whose cheer and pluck invariably rise to the occasion and who repeatedly sings advice to those about her of the joys of the simple life, wherein anyone can "come and get your happiness." Depression seems to have overtaken her, not in the economic sense, for her family enjoys ample sufficiency, but emotionally. For the first time in any Shirley Temple movie, her character has nothing to teach the adults about her, morally or spiritually, and everything to learn.

Overnight Mytyl and her little brother launch on their dream-quest for the blue bird of happiness—the thing that in previous films Shirley has possessed from the start. As they do so, like Dorothy in the Land of Oz, they leave the gray world of everyday for a marvelous Technicolor realm, filled with strange and wondrous beings, some beautiful and virtuous, others ridiculous and comic, still others treacherous and malignant. Accompanying the children on their quest are their faithful dog Tylo (metamorphosed into a man and played by Eddie Collins in a performance redolent of Bert Lahr's Cowardly Lion in *The Wizard of Oz*) and treacherous cat-turned-woman Tylette (Gale Sondergaard, who had originally been cast as the wicked witch in *Wizard of Oz* but withdrew).

The film condensed the figures and adventures of the original play but left it recognizable. It included one musical number for Shirley, "Lay-De-O," in which she yodels a happy tune and dances with the great vaudeville comedian Al Shean. By Zanuck's standards and those of Hollywood in general, this was a reasonably faithful adaptation. Yet what the film found more elusive was the tone of Maeterlinck's play: at once playful and philosophic, witty and austere, humane and detached.

Zanuck did not attempt to rival *The Wizard of Oz*'s tremendous budget, which soared to more than $2,750,000, although he did invest considerable sums into the production, particularly in the lavish Palace of Luxury and the forest fire sequence. He had originally intended *The Blue Bird* to open in first-run theaters before Christmas 1939, and, like previous Shirley Temple movies extending back to *Bright Eyes*, the story ended on a Christmas scene. Instead, Twentieth Century–

Fox officials decided to delay the formal premiere to January and to promote the movie in select markets, saturating them with publicity, while holding back the general release of the picture until March 1940.[70] With such advance preparation, they must have hoped, comparisons with *The Wizard of Oz* would have run their course and audiences would eagerly flock to the film.

Nonetheless, critical reception, instead of propelling *The Blue Bird*'s flight, weighed it down. To be sure, some California newspapers close to the film industry cheered lustily. The *Los Angeles Times* critic Edwin Schallert called the film a "masterpiece": "Rare imagination is conjured out of the clouds once again in 'The Blue Bird,' which adheres to the spirit of fantasy created in 'The Wizard of Oz,' yet touches deeper wells of sentiment." The movie, he asserted, was much more than merely a Shirley Temple vehicle, and he especially praised the use of color and the spectacular storm scene. "Women will be dissolved in tears over the final episode of the Kingdom of the Future with its children who are waiting to come into the world," he predicted.[71]

Similarly, knowing how crucial *The Blue Bird*'s success was to Shirley Temple's future, *Motion Picture Herald*'s William R. Weaver emerged from a preview gasping with relief: "The film is a delight to the eye, the ear and the intellect, adult or juvenile, and the manner of its making, the keen professional judgment displayed in every aspect of its composition and in the Zanuck decision to produce it just this way at just this time with just this star, is something to make you Ladies and Gentlemen of Show Business glad."[72]

Other critics were disappointed, however. Howard Barnes found the film "ornately literal where it should have been magically suggestive. It has some sequences which have the irresistible illusion of a fairy tale," he wrote, "but for the most part, it is a pretentiously dull rendition of a classic." Barnes did not blame Shirley herself, noting that "she plays with all of the grave charm and assurance which the role demanded." Nonetheless, he concluded, she could not rescue this "singularly maladroit transcription of a notable stage fantasy." As for the episode in the Kingdom of the Future with the unborn children, which had so impressed Edwin Schallert, Barnes called it, "almost, but not quite, bad enough to be funny."[73]

Frank Nugent, who had suffered through many a Shirley Temple vehicle, admired the forest fire episode but for the most part watched the movie "stoically and even with Spartan resignation." No fan of the original play, which he called "complete twaddle," he found it still "more earthbound in the manner of its screen translation." Six months earlier, he had pronounced *The Wizard of Oz* a "delightful piece of wonder-working." Damning *The Blue Bird* with the faintest praise, he concluded, "It is edifyingly moral and moralistic and not too frightening."[74]

Small-town independent movie exhibitors generally echoed the verdicts of big-city critics. Although some expressed their appreciation for *Blue Bird*'s splendid scenes, sorrowfully, they reported how Shirley had lost many of her fans, adults especially. From Dewey, Oklahoma, the Paramount Theatre wrote, "This little fairy tale is okay for the kiddies, but the adults won't go for it in a small town. Shirley is about through." A spokesman for the Uptown Theatre in Pueblo, Colorado, mordantly agreed: "A beautiful fairy tale that kept the adults away in droves." Floyd Jacobs of the New Theatre in Sardinia, Ohio, crisply summarized his experience: "It was beautiful, [but] no story, and no rural patronage. They walked out on it." Most damning of all, John Stafford wrote from the Royal Theatre in Leonardville, Kansas, "Many came thinking it was Shirley's last picture and went away hoping that it was."[75]

Even while making *The Blue Bird*, on October 19, 1939, in his characteristic manner Zanuck excitedly dictated an idea for another Shirley Temple film. The problem nagging him had been Shirley's emerging adolescence and with it, he feared, the end of her career as a child star. He had done everything possible to disguise that transformation, giving her short dresses and tall costars, but at the rate she was growing, he might well have thought, the rest of the company would soon have to walk on stilts. Suddenly, he saw how to turn the problem into the ultimate Shirley Temple picture: instead of concealing her growing body and stuffing her into little girl's clothes, he could dramatize her transformation from tot to incipient teenager. "Last night I looked at the musical numbers that Shirley Temple did in her old pictures made three, four, five and five and a half years ago," he reported. "In viewing these pictures, I realized that Shirley has almost tripled in size since her first pictures and it would be sensational if we could see her actually grow up in front of an audience from a little kid who could hardly walk, to the young lady she is at the present time. If we could get a story of this kind, we would have a sure-fire hit for her."[76]

"Story, story, story" had always been Zanuck's credo. Now he enthusiastically spun out his idea for a new one, in all likelihood smoking a cigar and pacing his office as he did so. The movie would open on a husband-and-wife vaudeville act, so as to establish "that the little girl, who is to become Shirley Temple, is reared in backstage dressing-rooms of cheap vaudeville houses." Then, "when the child is about three and a half years old, or the age that Shirley was at the time she made her [screen] debut," she joins the act and improves it. Zanuck imagined incorporating film footage of Shirley's early numbers, showing her gradually growing older until the family stood at the summit of vaudeville success, the Palace Theatre in New York. They retire and settle down on a farm, but soon weary of farm life and return to the theater, only to discover that vaudeville has been eclipsed by radio and movies. "This gives us the marvelous situation of a girl who has been a star in the theatre finding herself, at ten, in a position of having to practically start all over again and beg for opportunities," Zanuck declared. "At the end, of course, she will make a sensational comeback in some way—on the radio, in a musical show, or in the movies." His temporary title was *The Comeback* or *The Girl Who Came Back*.[77]

Zanuck's story idea, of course, steered Shirley away from the self-consciously allegorical *Blue Bird* and back to the familiar adventures of a little trouper who loved nothing more than to sing and dance, smile and cheer. He did not say that she would also be an orphan who is adopted by the hoofing couple—probably because he took that for granted. As he and writers Edwin Blum and Don Ettlinger developed the screenplay, it fleshed out Zanuck's initial idea in a story of how an adopted baby named Wendy joins a hoofing couple to become the Three Ballantines. The film did indeed incorporate early footage of Shirley Temple performing a hula dance (using footage cut from *Captain January*) as well as her breakthrough number, "Baby Take a Bow" from *Stand Up and Cheer!*

Once the Ballantine family retires to a New England farm, they are met with scorn and suspicion by much of the local population, led by the town matriarch. As Democrats and innovators among rock-ribbed Republicans, defenders of youthful ambition against repressive killjoys, the Ballantines find themselves stymied at every turn. Climaxing a series of rebuffs, the jazzy, mildly impudent vaudeville show that they organize for Wendy's schoolmates turns into a fiasco in which disapproving parents drag off their charges. As the Ballantines sadly prepare to move away, a hurricane roars through the community, and Wendy's father heroically rescues a group of children. Afterward, the townspeople have a dramatic change of heart. They now cherish the Ballantines and their dynamic spirit and embrace them as first citizens of the community.

The story contained many of the stock contrasts of Shirley Temple films: between good-hearted show people and their pretentious detractors, progressive visionaries and hidebound conservatives, young lovers (encouraged by Shirley) and an old spinster aunt. Above all, it allowed Shirley to return to song-and-dance numbers with a popular flavor, but no longer obliged to wear short dresses.

Zanuck's story outline was also a kind of dream-work, of the Hollywood rather than Freudian variety. He took the fear that Shirley's own career as a child performer had run its course and that she might soon retire from movies, attend school rather than be tutored at the studio, and lead a normal childhood and converted it into a nostalgic tribute to vaudeville and an encore to her association with Twentieth Century–Fox. Certainly Zanuck knew by this time the depths of Gertrude and George Temple's dissatisfaction. And, as he watched Shirley slide from top box-office champion from 1935 through 1938 to fifth place in 1939, he clearly feared that her success could not last. His temporary title of *The Girl Who Came Back* expressed a hope that Shirley could recover her Midas touch. If not, the movie could still make money and also serve as a kind of parting gold watch, a pink slip cut into a valentine.

The film to blossom from Zanuck's seed was *Young People*. Filming finally began in late March 1940, the time of *The Blue Bird*'s general release, and was finished by early May. By this point Gertrude Temple's long-simmering frustrations had boiled over: "I'm just waiting here for Shirley's contract to be over," she declared in an interview. Twentieth Century–Fox might be content with repeating the Shirley of old, but her mother was not. Gertrude ached for her daughter to tackle more challenging and realistic roles. Starting to attend school at the age of eleven and a half (like her character Wendy Ballantine in the screenplay) and no doubt swayed by her parents' opposition to the studio, Shirley herself fabricated an illness as shooting began. Zanuck saw right through her and permitted no excuses.[78]

Almost all of the cast of *Young People* joined Shirley Temple for the first time (Mae Marsh was the exception), but they played familiar roles: affable Jack Oakie as Shirley's adoptive father; tall, long-legged Charlotte Greenwood, the "only woman in the world who could kick a giraffe in the face," as Shirley's adoptive mother; and Kathleen Howard as the formidable pillar of prim conservatism, who could roll her *r*'s so as to make a word such as "thrift" spin like a top.[79] Shirley herself gets a chance to act more her age while still playing the emotional scales from hearty cheer to loving devotion, as well as occasional tears of rejection and gratitude. Allan Dwan, whose long film career dated back to Douglas Fairbanks and Mary Pickford, directed, making this his third Shirley Temple film. The songs, with lyrics by Shirley Temple veteran Mack Gordon, now joined by composer Harry Warren, returned to the upbeat ditties and lullaby tributes of old. The movie's finale marveled at the "merry world" all around us and urged people once again to smile through the rainstorms, knowing that the stars would shine again.

Maybe not. Immediately after making *Young People* and starkly exposing the difference between life and art, happy endings and bitter divides, on May 11, 1940, Gertrude Temple announced that Shirley would end "her screen career for the present and will retire to the life of a normal child." In an "amicable settlement" with Twentieth Century–Fox Studios, the Temples canceled the remaining fourteen months of Shirley's contract. Gertrude Temple reiterated her dissatisfaction with Shirley's story material but stressed that the Temples chiefly desired to have Shirley regularly mingle with other children. During the past five years, the United Press news service reported, she had earned $20 million for the studio and had accumulated $3 million in her own right. However brief Shirley's "retirement" would prove, the years with Zanuck were over.[80]

Thus, the release of *Young People* three months later, in August 1940, assumed special poignancy to Shirley's fans. Gertrude Temple must have found bitter satisfaction from those reviews that castigated the screenplay Zanuck had inspired. Howard Barnes dismissed the film as "a hodgepodge of variety turns, precocious antics and overly sentimental drama, with a hurricane thrown in for good measure. The little veteran has had some bad deals on story material in the past, but [this] . . . offering establishes a new low." Despite lobbing these rotten tomatoes, Barnes threw his own bouquet to Shirley: "Being one of those who always found her extremely attractive, unself-conscious and artful, I am sorry that she has decided to retire before reaching adolescence." Richard Coe delivered a similar verdict in the *Washington Post*: "In 'Young People' Shirley is called upon to deliver New England to the New Deal. Although she saved the Empire in Queen Victoria's glorious days, the job is pretty tough with no help whatever from a script department which obviously pulled the lines out of an old box."[81]

Yet Bosley Crowther, who had replaced Frank Nugent at the *New York Times*, regarded the movie more indulgently. "As usual in Temple pictures, 'Young People' goes heavy on sweetness and light," he conceded. "But perhaps because it is a modest production, because the budget prohibited excessive splash, it keeps within reasonable bounds. For patrons who can take so much precocity, it should be one of the more charming of the miracle child's films."[82]

A few independent exhibitors agreed with Crowther. "Oh, why wait till Shirley's last picture to give her a story," sighed one from Brooksville, Kentucky. "Good picture and story. . . . Too bad they did not give her better stories in the past," an exhibitor from Roaring Spring, Pennsylvania, lamented. Nonetheless, most exhibitors reported poor business.[83]

Zanuck's formula for a good Shirley Temple movie, which he had inherited from Winfield Sheehan, was fashioned in response to the demands of movie audiences in the midst of the Great Depression. For five years it sustained Shirley Temple's unprecedented popularity, buoying up spirits of children, women, and men in the United States and worldwide at a time when cheer and the promise of happiness were badly needed. That it finally lost its appeal is hardly surprising. What is most remarkable is its immense staying power. Unquestionably, it confined Shirley to a relatively narrow series of roles, but it might equally well be argued that it gave her special talents extraordinary prominence. Several factors conspired to bring her reign as a child star to an end: the onset of her adolescence, the exhaustion of the formula, and the changing context of the emotional needs and desires of the moviegoing public. By 1940 war had erupted in Europe, the international movie market had contracted significantly, action and adventure movies had gained new popularity, and even family audiences hungered for different fare, such as Charlie Chaplin's *The Great Dictator*. The abundance of young child actors, so prominent in Hollywood films of the early 1930s when Shirley achieved her break-through, lost the spotlight to a formidably talented group of adolescent stars, including Mickey Rooney, Judy Garland, and Deanna Durbin.

Twentieth Century–Fox, too, had arisen from the financial disarray that surrounded its union to an impressive stature, measured both in profits and also in its best films, including a much more searing examination of the Great Depression than any Shirley Temple movie, *The Grapes of Wrath*, released in January 1940. By this time the little girl had burst into adolescence, President Roosevelt was increasingly preoccupied by the looming war, and neither the studio nor the nation needed saving by her cute ways and adorable smile.

CHAPTER 6
WHAT'S A PRIVATE LIFE?

Onscreen, Shirley triumphed fundamentally as a personality. Many admirers believed that she was simply portraying herself. Still, they wished to authenticate the shadow on the screen with testimonials to the flesh-and-blood little girl. For the success of Shirley's career, this reassurance was fundamental. For Darryl Zanuck, film reviewers, and small-town movie exhibiters, a pressing question throughout the 1930s remained: how long could Shirley's box-office magic last? For many of her fans, however, the most urgent and abiding question that they combed fan magazines and newspaper articles to answer was, would success spoil Shirley Temple?

The image of the spoiled child—pampered, willful, unfeeling—remained a prominent concern for parents, and the abnormal terms of child actors' lives appeared to place them at special risk. Suspicions about the emotional perils of the professional child actor, a charged issue earlier in the century, still lingered in the 1930s. Acting might encourage artifice, success breed self-importance, studio and public pressures lead to a warped personality. Child-rearing experts in the 1920s and 1930s enshrined the concept of the normal child and stressed parents' responsibility for that development.[1] Many parents were themselves torn between older values of thrift, self-control, and deferred gratification and the rising consumer values of self-expression and indulgence. In addition, many middle-class parents and child experts worried about the seductive pleasures of commercial amusements, movies especially, that pulled children away from the home. Shirley embodied many of those pleasures. She helped to transform merchandising to children. She influenced the ways that little girls dressed, wore their hair, and shopped with their families, and the dolls, toys, and games they played with, as well as the films that they watched. Still more profoundly, she shaped their own personalities, desires, and dreams, and those that their mothers and often fathers had for them. The question of whether Shirley was spoiled, then, held enormous stakes. She represented the ideal child. How did she, her family, and the film industry in which she worked—or played, as her mother always insisted—manage to balance her acting career and her private life, her integral participation in the media that transfixed children and her own moral development as a child? If she was spoiled, might others also be tainted? If she was not, what could others learn from her example? Was she abnormal? Unique as was her situation, the answer to such questions contained important implications for millions. If Shirley was truly as good as gold, if she could pass reporters' acid tests and not expose base metal, then the consumer market in which she was so deeply enmeshed might be safe for all children and their families.

The boundaries between public and private life have always been porous, but beginning around the turn of the twentieth century, the pressures of an emerging celebrity culture eroded them considerably. In fact, the right of personal privacy as a modern legal concept was first formulated to protect individuals from the prying intrusions of celebrity-chasing journalists. It was famously articulated in an 1890 article by Samuel Warren and his law partner the future United States Supreme Court justice Louis Brandeis as "the right to be let alone." Warren had married into the socially and politically prominent Bayard family, whose weddings, funerals, and social doings attracted persistent press coverage, and so his complaint had a personal dimension.[2] "Instantaneous photographs and newspaper enterprise have invaded the sacred precincts of private and domestic life," he and Brandeis wrote, "and numerous mechanical devices threaten to make good the prediction that 'what is whispered in the closet shall be proclaimed from the house-tops.' . . . Gossip . . . has become a trade," they lamented, "which can only be procured by intrusion upon the domestic circle." Warren and Brandeis argued that this breach was not only a domestic intrusion but an act fundamentally at odds with American law. They conceived of the "right to privacy" as "a part of the more general right to the immunity of the person,—the right to one's personality" shielded from public exposure.[3]

Thus, two understandings of "personality" emerged around the turn of the twentieth century in dialectical tension with one another, and the contest between them held momentous implications for modern life. The legal assertion of privacy defended the "personality rights" of individuals to pursue their personal lives and domestic arrangements free from intrusive regulation or exposure. A quite different understanding of personality, however, emerged at the same time as part of a new concept of self in modern consumer culture. Here personality meant the personal qualities that distinguish an individual from the crowd, such as charm, poise, magnetism, charisma. These were the qualities of a performer, and the supreme exemplars of such performers were movie stars.[4]

More than any other child star of the Great Depression, perhaps more than any other Hollywood star of the twentieth century, Shirley Temple carried this performative notion of personality into the private lives of many families. Yet the public fascination with her personality meant that her own family's private life was rocked as well. This was the ironic outcome of Gertrude Temple's ambitions for her daughter. Mrs. Temple could not have imagined the scale of Shirley's ultimate celebrity when she groomed her as a child performer, for the magnitude of that success was unprecedented. Nor could genial

George Temple have anticipated that his daughter would become the family business, turning his own role as breadwinner topsy-turvy.

It was her fans, not Fox Film, that initially made Shirley a star, and she depended on her fans to keep that star brightly shining. Yet the nature of fan culture and of the movie industry in the golden age of the Hollywood studio system made it especially difficult to place limits on admirers' desire to pierce beyond the shadows on the screen and encounter the "real" Shirley Temple, as much as the Temples strove to maintain a wall of privacy. Fame required that the line between public and private life be minimized. In an interview with a fan magazine writer, Shirley supposedly asked, "What's a private life?" The interviewer replied, "When you're not acting" and "just having fun." "Dimples dawned at the corners of her mouth. 'I'm just having fun when I'm acting too,' she chuckled. 'So I guess my whole life's a private life.'"[5]

Film publicists kindled the flames of fans' fascination with the stars and did everything they could to keep them burning. Indeed, the origins of movie fandom may be dated to a publicity stunt. In March 1910 Carl Laemmle's Independent Moving Pictures Company (IMP) leaked a story that their leading actress, "the IMP Girl," previously known as the Biograph Girl for her work with that studio, was in fact Florence Lawrence and that she had been killed in a streetcar accident. A few days later, IMP piously protested that Lawrence's death was a lie perpetrated by a rival studio and that "very shortly some of her best work in her career" would be released. It was the kind of hoax to make P. T. Barnum wink in his grave, and it launched an endless succession of Hollywood stunts intended to tantalize fans' appetites for news of movie actors' offscreen lives. Yet the stunt triggered a genuine threat to Florence Lawrence's safety—one that was also a portent of future threats to other stars. When Lawrence appeared in St. Louis to reassure admirers that she was alive and unharmed, she was nearly crushed by a mob, consisting mainly of women and children, "that swept toward her . . . like an avalanche."[6]

Henceforth, movie fans persisted in delving into stars' private lives, and occasionally other mob scenes erupted. When in 1920 two of Hollywood's most celebrated stars, Mary Pickford and Douglas Fairbanks, celebrated their honeymoon in London, a frenzied horde almost pulled Pickford out of a moving convertible and nearly crushed her at a garden party. As the New York drama critic Alexander Woollcott wrote, "The public passion was to see, in the flesh, these two mimes whose dancing shadows had played so large a part in the humbler public's festivities for many years—to see (if possible to touch) Douglas Fairbanks and more especially to see, touch, and kiss Miss Pickford. The intention was amiable and the process may sound agreeable; but when, on the way from the station to your rooms, ten thousand people approach you with beaming countenances but a none-the-less grim determination to pet and fondle you or die in the attempt, it is a trifle dismaying."[7]

Similar mob scenes, teetering on the edge of riot, came to represent the ultimate seal of popular approval at movie palace openings and film premieres. The opening of Sid Grauman's Metropolitan Theatre in Los Angeles in 1923 earned this dubious accolade. As the *Los Angeles Times* reported, the police were joined by militia forces armed with rifles, who at times "struggled for the possession of the guns" with unruly fans. "The police had to be continually on guard to keep the crowd from storming the theater so great was the spectators' desire to obtain a glimpse of the stars and of the interior of the house."[8] Premieres of such films as *Rosita*, with Mary Pickford (1923), *The Thief of Bagdad,* starring Douglas Fairbanks (1924), and *The Trespasser*, in which Gloria Swanson had her first talking role (1929), sparked similar crowd frenzy.

In 1927 in New York City still larger crowds of women, men, and children pushed and shoved one another as they pressed toward the Broadway funeral home where the matinee idol Rudolph Valentino lay in his silver-bronze coffin. On several occasions the crowd surged forward, breaking large plate-glass windows and trampling onlookers. When the funeral home flung open its doors, the throng swept up even the mounted police in its tide, and officers repeatedly charged into the mass to break it up. Ultimately, over a hundred people suffered injuries, and the street was littered with torn hats, shoes, umbrellas, and other personal belongings.[9]

During the Great Depression unruly crowds continued to swell movie premieres in Los Angeles, New York, and other cities for films such as *Little Caesar* (1931) and Charlie Chaplin's *Modern Times* (1936). The 1937 Los Angeles premiere of one Shirley Temple film, *Wee Willie Winkie*, nearly erupted in riot. On that occasion an estimated five thousand fans paid fifty cents apiece to perch on backless seats for up to eight hours, eagerly awaiting a glimpse of the diminutive star. Another five thousand standees joined the throng. The appearances of stars such as Eddie Cantor, Tyrone Power, Sonja Henie, and Sophie Tucker merely whetted their appetites. Then, just as the Temple family arrived, many of the luminaries and their parties turned stargazers themselves, forming a wall that eclipsed Shirley's appearance from the view of the multitude. The outraged roar of the crowd could be heard for miles, as frustrated spectators surged against the ropes. It took fifty police to restore order.[10]

Less menacingly, waves of fan mail also poured over Hollywood stars. Such letters began with the advent of the star system, and the flow quickly became a torrent. In 1920, at the peak of her career, Clara Bow received forty-five thousand letters a week. Some stars hired their own secretaries. Mary Pickford's mail became so voluminous that the Los Angeles post office asked her to cancel her own stamps. Hollywood studios also organized fan mail departments to respond to the intense demands. In 1928, on the eve of the Great Depression, some 32,250,000 letters flooded the Hollywood film studios, which spent over $2 million dealing with them.[11]

Despite the need to pinch every penny in the Great Depression, ordinary citizens wrote public figures—politicians, entertainers, journalists, and others—in greater numbers than ever. They often claimed a personal relationship with these celebrities, confiding their own stories and difficulties. In addressing movie and radio actors, they frequently assumed continuity between the fictional characters such actors portrayed and the performers' own personalities. Shirley Temple's fan mail began pouring in immediately after her success in *Stand Up and Cheer!* in 1934. At first, she and her two older brothers enjoyed the novelty of slitting open the envelopes, but the correspondence quickly amounted to a deluge. By early 1935 her mail was reported as four thousand letters a week, demanding a full-time secretary to handle it.[12]

None of these letters appears to have been preserved, but a few that were published at the time suggest the range of correspondents as well as the diversity of their attraction to Shirley. They included messages from girls and boys, women and men, seeing in her an adored sister, friend, sweetheart, or daughter. "I think you are very cute," a seven-year-old girl wrote, "and I'd like to be like you. You dance so much better than I do." A grade school boy mixed adulation with a dash of caution (shared by many, as we shall see) that Shirley might lose her unaffected innocence: "I think you're swell and when I grow up I'm going to marry you if you haven't been spoiled by then." Mothers often included photographs of their daughters, nominally asking Shirley but really Gertrude Temple to confirm the striking likeness of their offspring and wondering how to get into the movie business. (Rarely did Gertrude Temple see any resemblance to Shirley.)[13]

Shirley herself never read these letters, but other attentions could hardly escape her notice. Much as Gertrude Temple had worked to achieve her daughter's success, the intrusions on their family life that immediately followed Shirley's sudden celebrity overwhelmed them. "Overnight, we, who had lived an inconspicuous and very modest life in our bungalow at Santa Monica, found ourselves in the floodlight of motion-picture publicity," Mrs. Temple said. In addition to the torrent of mail and unsolicited gifts, "people knocked at our doors. Bolder ones pressed their faces against our windows. The telephone rang from morning till night. It simply was too much for us, not to speak of the child, who was tugged at, fondled, gushed over, and followed." One evening as the Temple family sat at dinner, the doorbell rang and eight tourists rushed into the dining room. "We're from Pennsylvania," they explained, "and we just had to see Shirley before we went back home."[14]

When strangers recognized Shirley in public, they often flocked around her. As early as the summer of 1934, only months after she had become a celebrity, the Temple family discovered that they could no longer enjoy the beach near their home in Santa Monica, as in previous years. "We expected to stay at the beach all summer, but it is impossible," George Temple told a reporter. "People came swarming down here like a cloud of locusts. I believe youngsters came from a hundred miles around to play with Shirley and she can't play with so many at one time. We have been besieged by tourists, salesmen, autograph collectors and people who were just plain curious so we have to move." By August 1934, less than four months after Shirley's breakthrough, the Temples were making plans to leave their Santa Monica bungalow for a house in Hollywood or Beverly Hills, surrounded by a high wall or hedge. "We have to have that," George Temple said, "to protect our little girl."[15]

Even in shopping for a new house, the Temples found themselves pestered by real estate salesmen—from "subdivision promoters to depression millionaires who would sacrifice their Bel-Air mansion for a paltry $50,000," as one fan magazine reported. California Bank, where George Temple had risen from teller to assistant branch manager prior to Shirley's breakthrough, quickly discovered that employing the father of a child star was excellent publicity. The bank displayed life-size photographs of Shirley handing her paycheck to her father

Wearing her jacket from Stand Up and Cheer!, Shirley hands her paycheck to her father, George Temple, to deposit at the California Bank, where he worked. (Culver Pictures, Inc.)

around its numerous branches in the Los Angeles area and made him manager of a branch in the heart of the neighborhood where major motion picture companies maintained distributing offices. With no secretary to act as a buffer, he sat prominently at a desk and shook hands with dozens of new customers eager to meet the father of the adorable child star. Within a few months, the bank's receipts had risen a reported 20 percent. Still, not only did salesmen besiege him here, but "even my own bank picked on me!" he said with rueful amusement. "The trust department tried to sell me one of the Hollywood show places—with about 10 bedrooms, 6 garages, and at least a dozen baths. It was too much for me. I'm not going in for that kind of thing."[16]

Soon the Temple family moved several blocks in Santa Monica into a larger, more secluded red-tiled bungalow. Still modest by

Hollywood standards, it nonetheless reflected Shirley's new importance within her family. She had a bedroom with a Bo Peep mural, a playroom with space for her doll collection, and accommodations for a housekeeper. Shirley could also play outside shielded from gaping strangers in an enclosed patio and fenced-in backyard, complete with a playhouse. She had always been her mother's special delight, eclipsing her brothers. By now they were largely absent: Jack, twenty, at Santa Monica Community College (he would soon transfer to Stanford); and Sonny, four years his junior, at New Mexico Military Institute—opportunities made possible by Shirley's earnings. In permitting journalists to chronicle their domestic arrangements, George and Gertrude Temple—and the Fox publicists who monitored them— tried to preserve a balance between family privacy and public curiosity, as well as between comfort and circumspection. A reporter for the fan magazine *Screenland* declared appreciatively, "Such a home befits the manager of a bank rather than an ostentatious movie star." Gertrude Temple struck a still more egalitarian note: "I suppose we live exactly like most of the families in American small towns."[17]

Yet a year later the Temple family moved again, exchanging their more elaborate bungalow for a fashionable fortress fully befitting the adored child star. On a wooded four-acre lot along the rim of North Rockingham Avenue in Brentwood, with views of the Pacific Ocean, the Temples built a two-story, shingle-roofed house designed by John Byers and Edla Muir in an eclectic mixture of English and Norman styles. The showplace that they had earlier resisted was now theirs. Extending to more than five thousand square feet, it boasted a two-story circular entryway, a living room with an impressive fireplace and vaulted wood-beamed ceiling, and four bedrooms, including one for Shirley with adjoining dressing room and playroom. Beside well-tended gardens and terraces, Shirley could skip along flagstone paths to the swimming pool, guest cottage, carousel, badminton court, and stable with a riding ring for her ponies. The address placed them snugly among a constellation of Hollywood celebrities, including the British actors Charles Laughton and Nigel Bruce and the director Henry Hathaway, as well as ZaSu Pitts, with whom Shirley had performed a bit part in *Out All Night* (1933), and Mary Nash, who portrayed the formidable villainesses Fraulein Rottenmeier in *Heidi* and Miss Minchin in *The Little Princess*.[18]

The new house testified not only to the Temple family's new social standing among the Hollywood elite but also to their effort to protect their daughter from benign and sinister attention. An eight-foot-tall chain fence ringed the property on three sides, and a massive fieldstone wall faced the street, allowing admission only through an imposing iron gate that was electrically operated from the house.[19] A photoelectric eye monitored Shirley's bedroom door, and electric alarms linked every window of the house to the local police station. Armed security guards patrolled the property at night, and if one failed to reach any of a series of keyed time clocks on schedule, the police were automatically summoned.

The large house staff included Shirley's personal bodyguard and chauffeur, burly John Griffith. He had saved Darryl Zanuck from drowning when he was a boy, and Zanuck depended on the former carnival roustabout to keep his precious charge safe. "Watch the kid like a hawk," Zanuck told Griffith. "If anything happens to her, this studio might as well close up." The portly, mustached bodyguard was true to his charge. He hovered near Shirley, squinting suspiciously at all and sundry, his holstered .38 caliber pistol bulging under his armpit, a pair of folded handcuffs at the ready. On most days Griffith drove Shirley and her mother to the studio in a shiny Cadillac—the modest family cars were now a thing of the past. With his wife, Mabel, who worked as Gertrude Temple's maid, he lived in an attached apartment with the Temple family.[20]

The new Temple house immediately became a major tourist attraction. Hollywood sightseeing buses hourly disgorged eager passengers, who clustered at the gate, taking photographs, as well as pebbles, twigs, and leaves as souvenirs, while the driver described the site and its famous resident through a megaphone. She was also becoming a ripe target for kidnappers and extortionists. Kidnappings of rich and socially prominent figures rose considerably during the Great Depression, and they riveted the attention of government officials and popular media. The famous insurance company Lloyd's of London offered Americans ransom insurance, and Hollywood celebrities Bing Crosby and Marlene Dietrich bought policies. Yet what made the prospect of kidnapping especially dreadful was the most notorious child kidnapping case of the century, one indelibly seared on the minds of Gertrude and George Temple, and millions of other parents.[21]

Beginning in 1932, two years before Shirley's meteoric rise to fame, the fate of another blond curly-haired child, twenty-month-old Charles Lindbergh Jr., held the public spellbound. The boy's tall, handsome father had himself vaulted from obscurity to the greatest of American heroes in 1927 with his solo flight from New York to Paris. The reserved Lindbergh had always been uneasy with his celebrity, and it proved to be a curse of tragic proportions. Immense as was the public acclaim for his stupendous flight, such publicity paled in comparison to the media frenzy that followed the abduction of his son. Even before the kidnapping, Colonel Lindbergh had attempted to shield his family against persistent media intrusion. As a part of this effort, he and his wife, Anne Morrow Lindbergh, an aviator in her own right and a future author, had recently moved into Highfields, a new, rambling French-provincial-style farmhouse on four hundred acres near Hopewell, New Jersey. Despite their seclusion, right under the noses of the Lindberghs and their servants, their infant son disappeared from his nursery crib on the evening of March 1, 1932. The abduction and its aftermath became the greatest human interest story of the decade. When the child's badly decayed and mutilated corpse was discovered ten weeks later, newspaper circulation surpassed that

Charles Lindbergh Jr., in a photo that was widely circulated
after his kidnapping on March 1, 1932. (© Bettmann/Corbis)

following the 1918 Armistice that ended the Great War. The search for the child's murderer transfixed public attention for more than two years, and the fate of the man charged with the brutal killing, Bruno Richard Hauptmann, further gripped the public from September 1934, when he was arrested, through his trial and conviction to his execution in the electric chair in April 1936. Meanwhile, to escape the incessant publicity and possible further threats, in December 1935 the Lindberghs and their second son sailed under assumed names to England to live for a time in self-exile in a village in Kent.[22]

In his tragic death and media afterlife, the Lindbergh baby became—despite his parents' efforts—a macabre child celebrity.

Reportage of the kidnapping case established a new low in the commercial exploitation of childhood, and its dreadful details transformed the lives of children and their families across the country. The future writer and illustrator of children's books Maurice Sendak, born only a few weeks after Shirley Temple in 1928 to working-class immigrant Jewish parents, experienced the ordeal as "a personal torment." "I remember everything," he later said. "I couldn't read, but the radio was always on. I remember Mrs. Lindbergh's cheerful voice, where she was allowed to speak on radio to say that the baby had a cold and would the man or men or women who took him rub camphor on his chest. It was a slight cold, but she didn't want it to get any worse." Sendak wondered, "If that fair-haired, blue-eyed princeling could not be kept safe, what certain peril lay in store for him, little Murray Sendak, in his humble apartment in Bensonhurst?"[23]

The Lindbergh kidnapping and other sensational extortionist child abductions in the 1930s, such as that of six-year-old June Robles in 1934, nine-year-old George Weyerhaeuser in 1935, ten-year-old Charles Matson in 1937, and twelve-year-old Peter David Levine and five-year-old James Bailey Cash in 1938, pointed to another paradox in the role of media publicity in the private lives of children and their families. Child kidnappings represented the ultimate violation of the sanctity of the family and the despoliation of the innocent. In responding to extortionist demands for ransom, families were forced to participate in a criminal market, in order to redeem what was most sacred and priceless. They were compelled to participate in a media market as well, one that compounded the plunder of the lost child. The child's appearance and distinctive traits were repeatedly described, and if the child was ultimately found dead, the assault on the body was obsessively detailed. In such ways the child became "public property," in the words of the father of Charley Ross, the four-year-old victim of the most celebrated nineteenth-century American extortionist child-kidnapping plot. In addition, the process sharply exposed the vulnerability of the most powerful families and converted intimate details of their lives into serialized Gothic thrillers. Images of family members, servants, and strangers, together with layouts of households and neighborhoods, flooded the media. Every newspaper reader and radio listener could ponder clues and join the search for suspects. Inevitably, false leads abounded. Suspicions often whirled wildly, alighting on a hapless servant, a mysterious outsider, the lost child's very parent. All the while, each sensationalized case intensified millions of families' anxious concern for their own children, creating the conditions for further threats, abductions, and extortions.[24]

Crime stories and courtroom dramas fueled many Hollywood movie plots in the 1930s, so that the sensationalized coverage of kidnapping and murder trials, especially the Lindbergh case, assumed the character of a thrilling entertainment. Reporting the opening day of the Hauptmann trial, the novelist Kathleen Norris wrote, "We have been regaled by so many prison pictures, so many crime and detective and district attorney pictures, that as the day dawdles on and one would-be juror after another is questioned, challenged, rejected, it begins to seem like a picture. Presently the reel will end, and Minnie Mouse and her white shoes take the screen."[25]

The menace of child kidnapping even loomed at the edges of several of Shirley Temple's films in the mid-1930s, when public attention on Hauptmann was at its height. In *Baby Take a Bow* Shirley's character is held hostage by a hardened criminal, in *Our Little Girl* police suspect a tramp's intentions toward her, and in *Poor Little Rich Girl* a sinister man stalks her and tries to lead her away with him.[26] More importantly, the broader drama of the popular fascination with child abduction—the longing to see the beloved child restored to devoted parents or protectors in a safe, secure home—remained crucial to almost all of her movies.

Meanwhile, Shirley Temple and other child stars were targets of real-life kidnapping plots and extortionist threats. In 1936 alone, the year that the Temple family moved into their Brentwood retreat, such threats were made not only against Shirley but also against Jane Withers, who catapulted to fame in her supporting role as the brattish girl in *Bright Eyes*, and Freddie Bartholomew, famous for his performances in adaptations of literary classics such as *David Copperfield*, *Little Lord Fauntleroy*, *Captains Courageous*, and *Kidnapped*.[27]

On May 2, 1936, a "gangling" sixteen-year-old high school student, Sterling Powell, from a farm on the high plains near Grant, Nebraska, wrote a letter to Shirley's father. It demanded that Mr. Temple charter an airplane and drop an envelope containing $25,000 near where the boy lived. Unless Mr. Temple complied with these demands, the letter warned, "Shirley will encounter dire results." The letter was turned over to the Federal Bureau of Investigation, and the boy arrested three months later as he was plowing the family farm. He "didn't mean to go through with it," he told the local sheriff, and sent the letter on an impulse. A voracious reader of film and detective magazines and an avid moviegoer, Powell attended a movie with a kidnapping plot one night and, as he later told his bewildered father, "got the idea of the letter from the show." He returned home, wrote the letter and mailed it, and then, after a sleepless night, "forgot all about it."[28]

That same summer another letter arrived in the bundles directed to the Temple family, this one addressed to Shirley's mother. It demanded that $25,000 be sent to a grocery store in Atlanta, Georgia, saying, "Get the money if you want to keep Shirley." The FBI traced the letter to another sixteen-year-old movie-struck boy. Frank Stephens had spent six years of his young life in reform school and worked part-time in an Atlanta grocery store. The "undergrown" lad with slicked-down hair and a taste for gaudy neckties conceived of his kidnapping plot while watching a movie with his girlfriend, even adopting the name of one of the film's characters as a pseudonym. He planned to use the money to entertain his sweetheart. Asked why he targeted Shirley Temple's family for the extortion threat, Stephens said with a knowing air, "Because they [movie people] pay off better than any-body else."[29]

Feeble as such threats proved to be, they considerably alarmed Shirley's parents and Twentieth Century–Fox studio officials. As the FBI pursued the culprits, George Temple bought a Colt revolver and anxiously patrolled the house at night whenever he heard a strange noise. During this time, while traveling in the car with her bodyguard, Shirley had to crouch under a lap robe on the backseat.[30]

Yet the most serious threats to Shirley came not from movie-struck teenage boys but from the crush of crowds—and a demented woman. The throngs of tourists and fans that had flocked around Shirley beginning in summer 1934 later swelled to as many as twenty thousand. They swarmed about her not only at film premieres but on private Temple family excursions, well publicized by Twentieth Century–Fox, and trampled the boundary between public and private appearances. When the Temple family took a vacation in Honolulu in August 1935, one such crowd broke through rope barriers and shoved aside police, National Guardsmen, and a hundred Boy Scouts as it stormed toward Shirley. Retreating to the balcony of the Iolani Palace, she sang "On the Good Ship Lollipop" to mollify the throng. These were not truly vacations, as undoubtedly Gertrude and George Temple understood and Shirley came to realize, but another aspect of her work.[31]

In Boston three years later during another much-publicized family vacation, Shirley found herself in still greater danger. A frenzied crowd, the *Boston Globe* reported, "swept into a tumultuous fight to touch her, get close to her, shout hello to her or catch her eye long enough to have her return its smiles." It took seventy-five police-men, eight of them on horseback, to clear a path across the street, and she was borne aloft on the shoulders of her father and then of a detective. "At first she was slightly taken back by the excess enthusi-asm," the newspaper reported. "But soon she was in the spirit of the occasion, laughing back at the sea of faces, raising first one hand and

Fans greet Shirley and her parents in Honolulu, August 7, 1935.
(© Bettmann/Corbis)

then the other in greeting and turning ever in the direction of the greatest noise." Yet Shirley remembered the event with considerable unease. "What happened to the kids and shorter people," she wondered, "when the crowd broke in its hysterical rush? Handclapping was one thing, but why did they tug at my shoes, hold on to my legs, and shout so unintelligibly?" "It's because you make them happy," her mother reassured her, trying to preserve her innocence while fulfilling the desires of Twentieth Century–Fox publicists. Yet to Shirley the crowd seemed not happy but devouring.[32]

Even as her luster as a child star was waning, during a 1939 Christmas Eve *Screen Guild Theater* radio broadcast in Los Angeles, Shirley became the target of irrational rage. As she sang a song promoting *The Blue Bird*, a scowling, frumpy woman, seated in the front row, took a small handgun from her purse, stood up, and aimed directly at Shirley. Two local FBI agents, alerted to the presence of a suspicious person, seized her and bore her silently away as Shirley continued a very nervous performance. It emerged that the woman had given birth to a baby girl several hours before Shirley's reported birth, and the infant had died at the moment when Shirley was believed to be born. She blamed Shirley for stealing her daughter's soul and determined to avenge the theft with a bullet. In the sort of garish irony in which Hollywood specialized, the change of her birth year, intended to lengthen her film career, set in motion a mad psychological thriller that came within a hair's breadth of ending both career and life with a shot.[33]

In addition to the people who pressed toward Shirley individually or in crowds, millions tried to peer into her and her family's private life by reading articles and interviews. Some titillated readers with the prospect of shocking revelations. Articles bore such titles as "The Story behind Shirley Temple's Amazing Career," "The Real Miss Temple," "The Life and Loves of Shirley Temple," and "The Private Life of Shirley Temple."[34] Yet, with rare exceptions, these writers collaborated with studio publicists to present a portrait of the child star as meticulously constructed as the thousands of close-ups for which Shirley expertly posed.

Normality was an ideal enshrined by child-rearing experts in the 1920s and 1930s, so that it was essential to portray Shirley's personal— and even, as far as possible, her professional—development within its sturdy frame. There were obvious difficulties in this effort. After all, she seemed to enjoy little that was private, given the demands of her career. She had started performing in motion pictures around age three and had been signed by Fox when she was five and a half. Thereafter Shirley worked a six-day week, almost entirely with adults, that included spending long hours on the set, cramming three hours' worth of school lessons into short work breaks, and ending at bed-time with her mother coaching her on her scenes for the next day and curling her hair. In 1934 child actors in Hollywood between ages two and six were supposedly limited to six hours on the studio grounds, including three on the set. Once over six, they could work eight hours on the lot, four of these on the set. School instruction needed to be provided, but this restriction was lifted on Saturdays, school holidays, and vacations. Shooting schedules for Shirley's films generally ran six to seven weeks, and she made four movies a year through most of the decade. Between films, she was still obliged to work at the studio for six to seven hours a day to be fitted for costumes, give interviews, and pose for publicity photographs, which appeared in newspapers, maga-zines, and advertisements at an estimated rate of twenty a day. Even her vacations with her family amounted to publicity tours.[35]

Then there was the stigma of precocity. Her camera sense unnerved some of the greatest actors of the day. "This child frightens me," Adolphe Menjou said when making *Little Miss Marker*. "She knows all the tricks." Shirley would back him out of the camera, step on his lines, and steal his laughs. "She's making a stooge out of me. . . . If she were forty years old . . . she wouldn't have had time to learn all she knows about acting. . . . She's an Ethel Barrymore at four [sic]." Making *Now and Forever* the same year with Gary Cooper, the six-year-old per-formed most of her own scenes in a single take, and when he needed three takes to complete one scene, she asked, "Mr. Cooper, I did mine in one. Why can't you?" The publicity photographer George Hurrell, who began working with Shirley when she was seven, later marveled, "Shirley Temple had the photographic sense of someone four times her age." How in the world could this demanding routine and uncanny professionalism be made the stuff of a normal, carefree childhood?[36]

Certainly, to preserve the image of a normal private life within the Temple household, Gertrude Temple's dreams of a film career for her daughter and Shirley's early dance instruction had to be minimized. Accounts of stars' accidental discoveries, such as that of fifteen-year-old Lana Turner while sipping a Coke, were a staple of movie fan magazines. If Shirley's film career sprang from a lucky break rather than years of preparation and knocking on studio doors, then she ducked the charge of being merely a parental puppet or a hothouse plant. A 1935 Fox publicity profile stressed that she did not come from "a theatrical family" and that "the baby star came into the film industry by accident." While "dancing with a group of children," the release said blandly, she "was selected for a small part in pictures."[37]

Gertrude Temple learned to stick faithfully to this story. Shirley's movie career, she frequently explained, emerged from the unforced development of natural gifts. "From the time Shirley started to talk she carried on imaginative play-acting," and she danced "almost from the time she began to walk." Mrs. Temple sent her infant daughter to a neighborhood dancing school simply because Shirley so enjoyed dancing and music. There scouts for Educational Films noticed her and asked permission to give her a screen test. "We thought it would be amusing," Gertrude Temple said. "The tests were good, and what we had thought might be a novelty in Shirley's life—facing a movie camera—suddenly became a problem for us to solve." Santa Monica might be only twelve miles from Hollywood, but Mrs. Temple affirmed the values of the American heartland: "We didn't want Shirley spoiled, didn't want her made artificial, didn't want her to lose her childhood, regardless of what screen fame meant otherwise. . . . So at first we were a bit doubtful about a screen career." When she once slipped and mentioned in an interview Miss Meglin's dance studio, well known for its training of child stage and screen performers and thus a dead giveaway of her intense ambitions for her daughter, she demanded that the published article speak vaguely of a neighborhood "dancing school" instead.[38]

Similarly, at each step of Shirley's career, the goal was to emphasize the extreme solicitude of everyone around her, the film studio and her parents especially. Her personal welfare came first. This solicitude was supposedly enshrined in the contract that the Temple family negotiated with Fox on Shirley's behalf in summer 1934. The agreement that irretrievably transformed Shirley into a commodity was celebrated as safeguarding her childhood. As reported in "The Private Life of Shirley Temple, Wonder Child of the Screen," some of that contract's provisions (the full text was never publicly disclosed) were protections that any parent might applaud and delights any child might envy. She was provided with her own cottage on the studio lot. (Its previous tenant, Gloria Swanson, and her steamy affair with actor Herbert Marshall were discreetly unmentioned.) A bulwark of privacy, it had a bedroom where she could rest, a schoolroom in which she had lessons from a private tutor, and a dining room with kitchenette, where she could take her meals, prepared by the studio chef according to her dietary needs, free from distractions or the fuss of coworkers. Decorated with pictures and furnished with toys and games, the cottage amply fulfilled Fox's contractual obligation to "keep her as much as possible in the atmosphere of childhood." Shirley appeared on the set only during shooting of her own scenes and, again under her contract, purportedly never for more than an hour a day—although directors and producers were notorious for overriding such restrictions. All coaching on her lines was to take place in her cottage, often by her mother, who drew a salary for her services. Fox provided medical supervision to ensure Shirley's healthy development. Her regimen included a nutritious diet, ample exercise and relaxation, and plenty of sleep—all detailed in publicity materials for the instruction of others. Perhaps the most notable difference between Shirley's life and the lives of her fans was that she was forbidden to go to the movies at night. Studio officials aimed to keep her from imitating other performers and also from realizing her own importance. A preening little moppet would be box-office poison. In this last goal, public relations and self-interest converged. "She can't get spoiled," Winfield Sheehan warned Gertrude Temple. "She gets spoiled, it shows in the eyes."[39]

Articles on Shirley presented her life on the set as thoroughly normal, supremely educational, and more fun than a circus. William Seiter, who directed Shirley in four films, declared, "It makes me laugh to hear people ask: 'But aren't stage children cheated out of their childhood?' Shirley has a grander time than any kid I know—with her school work *and* her movie work." The atmosphere on the set was light and joyous. "Everything's a game with Shirley. . . . She likes to clown and tease, she likes to peep through a door before she comes in. Then, when she's played enough, you say: 'O. K. Shirley'—and, whatever's to be done, she goes to work and does it." Between shots, Shirley mastered her lessons at her own pace, faster than in a conventional schoolroom. Her mind was unusually retentive, readers were told, and she reportedly had an IQ of 155. Yet, as a piece in *Ladies' Home Journal* reported, "she conforms to the pattern from which the little girl next door is cut. She makes mud pies and plays jacks."[40] Movie magazines bulged with photographs of her in energetically normal activities: feeding fish, swinging on a gate, riding a bike, twirling a lariat, and the like, or, in another, proceeding through a day in her life from breakfast to bedtime prayers. Even her height and weight, which might have been seen as sensitive points, were presented as close to the average for a girl of her presumed age.[41]

Such depictions placed Shirley within the comfortable larger narrative of "egalitarian distinction," in which movie stars much resembled their fans in their personal tastes and private pleasures. The qualities that stars and fans shared far outnumbered those that differentiated them, such stories stressed, and, indeed, the essence of a star's distinctive gift was characteristically indefinable. A special "something" had by a stroke of luck grabbed the attention of Hollywood producers, for whom it was as mysterious and compelling as it was to fans. But was it luck or destiny? In a tradition of success stories stretching back through Horatio Alger novels to Puritan narratives, the star's elevation from the multitude represented both a seal of merit and a sign of grace. A deserving star would prove worthy of such favor by seizing the opportunity that Hollywood extended without losing the common touch. Public acclaim would not alter the star's private self.[42]

When Shirley Temple rose to stardom, her mother was elevated to the position of a child-rearing expert, repeatedly telling the story of "How I Raised Shirley Temple" to reporters, mothers, and movie fans in the United States and abroad. Middle-class parents read such articles avidly, although no one seemed the least interested in how she raised her two sons. They were irrelevant to what millions considered the central drama of the Temple household, one all the more compelling because it was set in the midst of the Great Depression. That drama concerned how to enjoy Shirley's success to the utmost while insulating her from its excesses and preserving her private life. A plethora of experts could give instruction on how to raise normal children, but none of them could speak from personal experience about how to raise this golden child who could transform entire industries, achieve worldwide fame, and earn a fortune while remaining a delightful and dutiful daughter. How could Shirley remain at once so powerful and so innocent? What was Mrs. Temple's secret?[43]

Although Gertrude Temple undoubtedly downplayed her desire to see her daughter in movies, her determination to keep Shirley unspoiled appears genuine. From the moment that Shirley became famous, she received what her mother called "a constant flow of flattering, petting, and attention." As one journalist described Shirley's predicament, "Strangers seeing her on the studio lot, or in those unavoidable moments when she would go from the Temple car into a shop or a restaurant, would cry out with little gasps of ecstasy, would instantly cut off any escape, would grasp her chin and turn her small face up to be stared at and commented upon in extravagant language, which included eulogies also upon her cleverness and charm, her adorable eyes, her wonderful curls!" Gertrude Temple's challenge was to muffle that attention whenever possible so as to keep Shirley's fame from overwhelming her personal development. "Mommy, why do people always want to touch me and ask questions?" her daughter asked. "Shirley," her mother replied, "haven't you ever noticed that everybody loves little kittens and rabbits and baby birds? Don't you love them? You're just like a little kitten—a little rabbit. And you're a happy child, too. People like happiness." Shirley accepted this explanation, and her mother sighed in relief. Yet her dread persisted: "I was afraid it was dawning upon her that those people adored her image and her acting. I was afraid she would begin to act for me." She added, "I want her to be natural, innocent, sweet. If she ceases to be that, I shall have lost her—and motion pictures will have lost her, too."[44]

On the set and off, Gertrude became Shirley's watchdog, fiercely defending her daughter's interests but also shielding her from the pressures of moviemaking. Contending as she did that "making movies is chiefly play-acting and make-believe to Shirley," she declared, "I make it my job to keep it that way, to smooth away any feeling of tension or excitement." She also shielded her from effusive praise, believing "no one is pleasant with a superiority complex."[45]

Yet inevitably, in extending the emotional ties between mother and daughter from the privacy of home to the glare of the studio, they became intricately braided. Emotions are the stuff of acting, and the simulation and evocation of emotional effects is a key job of the child actor. In preparing Shirley at bedtime for a role, Gertrude meticulously rehearsed the script, acting out all of the parts, feeding Shirley her individual cue lines, and then having Shirley recite her lines for the next day's shooting while Gertrude played the other roles. In this fashion they ran through the script three times before kissing each other good night. Although Shirley Temple Black maintained that her mother entrusted to her minor refinements, Gertrude mapped the emotional terrain of each film, drilled Shirley in her role, and also communicated her emotional investment in her daughter's success.[46]

On at least one occasion, a director yanked the emotional ties between mother and daughter for the sake of a dramatic effect. When Alexander Hall needed Shirley to cry in a scene for *Little Miss Marker*, he told her, "I want you to think that you'll never see your mother again. Think hard, she's gone, gone for good. She'll never, never, never come back." Gertrude Temple was furious, not only at the emotional manipulation but also because she considered her daughter an accomplished crier.[47]

Beyond all the emotional demands involved in satisfying directors and others on the set, Shirley sought to satisfy her mother. Stage and screen mothers are notorious for living through their children, their daughters especially, and the most fiercely determined of them from the mid-nineteenth to the mid-twentieth century make a formidable roll call: Mary Ann Crabtree, mother of Lotta; Jennie Cockrell Bierbower (later Janis), mother of Elsie Janis; Charlotte Smith, mother of Mary Pickford; Rose Hovick, mother of June Havoc and Gypsy Rose Lee; Lela Rogers, mother of Ginger; Ethel Gumm, mother of Judy Garland. Gertrude Temple was never as ruthless and controlling as some in this list, but she was proudly and single-mindedly devoted to her daughter and keenly jealous of any rival for her success. Virtually every substantial description of their relationship emphasized Mrs. Temple's stern protectiveness, and the emotional control she demanded from her offspring. Gertrude's pet name for her daughter was "Presh," short for Precious, and the last words of Shirley Temple Black's memoir *Child Star*, published a decade after her mother's death in 1977 and dedicated to her, are "Thanks, Mom." Yet she also observed that her mother was "no namby-pamby. . . . Always inside that velvet glove was a hard hand," demanding obedience. Less affectionately, director Allan Dwan, who worked with Shirley on *Heidi*, *Rebecca of*

Sunnybrook Farm, and *Young People*, observed, "Shirley was the product of her mother . . . the instrument on which her mother played."[48]

Her daughter's success, Gertrude admitted to reporters, transformed her life almost as much as Shirley's. Previously, she followed
a "pleasant routine" that included household duties, bridge games,
women's clubs, lectures, and frequent evenings out with her husband.
All that changed overnight. "I must be with Shirley all day at the studio, and at night I go over her lines with her for the next day's work.
Although she is in bed early I hate to leave her alone with the boys
and the housekeeper. George goes out alone sometimes now to the
pictures, but I am usually too tired for that, anyway."[49]

Despite Shirley's celebrity, her mother insisted, by no means was
her child permitted to run the Temple household. Mrs. Temple did not
shrink from the task of disciplinarian. The consensus of the burgeon-
ing advice on child rearing in the 1920s and 1930s discouraged or condemned punishment. "A punishment never has the effect to correct
or improve," declared the psychiatrist Benzion Liber in *The Child and
the Home*. "Usually it has the contrary effect, leaving, besides, a more
or less pronounced feeling of rancor or hatred against the physically
stronger person who orders or executes the punishment." Gertrude
Temple disagreed. Some child psychologists frowned on corporal
punishment, she acknowledged, "but it works." In *How I Raised Shirley
Temple*, she stated, "I believe firmly in the old maxim, 'spare the rod
and you spoil the child.' I think a child must feel that you are will-
ing to back up your demands with force if necessary. This conviction
gives you moral support as far as the child's thoughts are concerned.
And I do not believe a spoiled child is ever a happy one." "Discipline is
enforced relentlessly by her mother," a reporter declared approvingly.
Ordinarily, a word sufficed, but "on at least two known occasions a
more solid punishment under the dainty lingerie was administered."
When in 1936 *Time* magazine published an admiring story on Shir-

ley, its cover bore not a beaming portrait of the child star but a candid photograph of Mrs. Temple disciplining her child on the film set. Clearly, the dominant concern was not that Shirley was treated too harshly but too leniently.[50]

At least one observer testified to Mrs. Temple's firm hand. George Hurrell, who conducted a number of photographic sessions with Shirley at the studio and at her home, always in her mother's presence, later observed, "Shirley was often sharply disciplined. I tried to intervene once—and only once, because Mrs. Temple snapped, 'Tend to your photography, Mr. Hurrell, and I'll attend to my daughter!'"[51]

In the eyes of the public, the vindication of Mrs. Temple's method was Shirley's personality. Both male and female journalists repeatedly marveled over her poise, charm, serenity, good humor, and docility—qualities especially prized in a little girl. Scrutinizing her in 1936, a reporter could find no hint of affectation: "The sunniness she radiates on the screen belongs not to 'Bright Eyes' nor 'Curly Top' nor 'Little Miss Marker,' but lies deep in the disposition of Shirley Temple." "She has been described widely as a precocious youngster," a reporter for the *Boston Globe* added in 1938, "and yet there is nothing of the precocious about her. In spite of her accomplishments and the intense consideration that surrounds her, she is still just a little girl, fond of dolls, exactly like a number of pretty and attractive 9-year-olds in any neighborhood in every respect save one. She has an ability to understand and get along with grown-ups. She does exactly what she is told, and she does it with a smile and without resentment, even when she is tired and would probably much prefer to be doing something else." In such praise, reporters enshrined a more tractable little girl than she often played in her films. She might fling mud at her grandfather in *The Little Colonel*, shove the building manager into the swimming pool in *Just around the Corner*, or dump coal ashes on her tormentor in *The Little Princess*, but this assertive spirit was less prized off the screen.[52]

Such testimonies to Shirley's unspoiled character also had precedents. The most famous film child star prior to Shirley Temple had been Jackie Coogan, and he too had been acclaimed as a thoroughly natural and unspoiled child. Here too his mother was given the lion's share of the credit. Still, the boyish qualities that she prized in him marked a significant contrast with those that Gertrude Temple and reporters praised in Shirley: "Jackie is all alive—and all boy. . . . I don't want my son to be a Little Lord Fauntleroy. I want him to be the sort of a child that he portrays on the screen—robust and appealing and muddy—and if necessary, a little bad."[53]

Shirley too could be bad on occasion, but in her case everyone contrived to overlook the matter. Even Eleanor Roosevelt did so, portraying Shirley as a model child in her syndicated newspaper column chronicling the Temple family's 1938 visit to Hyde Park. Meeting Shirley in Hollywood the previous spring, Mrs. Roosevelt declared, she had been impressed with Shirley's "natural simplicity and charm" and applauded Mrs. Temple's achievement: "She had kept her a child in spite of having to make her mature in so many ways." In fact, Shirley could be officious, and she was especially so about the Shirley Temple badges that she bestowed on visitors. She had given two to Mrs. Roosevelt for her grandchildren when they met in Hollywood with instructions that they should wear them on all occasions or pay a fine. Now, as Mrs. Roosevelt and her grandchildren hosted a cookout in Shirley's honor, she demanded that the children produce the badges or pay the penalty. When they simply laughed and ran away, she felt thwarted and blamed their grandmother. As Mrs. Roosevelt bent over in her cooking at the grill, Shirley extracted a slingshot from her purse. Then, reprising a scene from *The Littlest Rebel*, she fired a pebble into the rump of the most admired woman in the world. Not only did Mrs. Roosevelt placidly ignore the offense, but she concluded her column, "A well brought-up charming child is a joy to all who meet her." One examines this sentence for a hint of irony, but there is none. Yet Gertrude Temple saw everything. When the Temples returned to their hotel in New York, she immediately gave her daughter a sharp spank. Staunch Republican that she was, she would not brook such insolence. "Brattish," she exclaimed. "See how *you* like it."[54]

Shirley herself admitted this particular bit of brattishness, albeit fifty years later. Yet an incident that was potentially far more damning to her image as a sunny, unspoiled child was related by the popular-song composer Jule Styne, who, at the beginning of his own illustrious career, worked in the late 1930s as a voice coach to Shirley and other stars for Twentieth Century–Fox. While directors lauded Shirley's cheerful professionalism and reporters marveled at her modesty, Styne regarded her warily. "Shirley Temple?" he later said. "Listen, I was afraid of that kid. I didn't want to get in the middle with her. From Schenck and Zanuck on down, everyone humored her." Her moods changed unpredictably, he remarked, and the shrieks of her temper tantrums in her studio cottage pierced the lot. When the studio dispatched Styne to the Temple home to rehearse songs with her, Shirley demanded that they play badminton first. Styne chased about the court till he almost dropped. "She was tough as nails, stamina of a steam engine," he recalled. At last Styne suggested to Shirley's father that they get down to business. "Honey," George Temple said, "you have to stop playing now and start rehearsing." Her reply shattered the image of the unspoiled child: "She screamed at him, 'Look, I earn all the money in this family. Don't tell me what to do.'"[55]

Shirley's colossal income fundamentally transformed the Temple family and George Temple's position in it. Before her career took off, he could feel proud of his accomplishments. Despite his eighth-grade education, he had pushed through the ranks of white-collar workers in Los Angeles to branch manager. His appearance and personality fit well with such a position. He had an open face, hearty manner, twinkling eye, and ready laugh. Yet this affability hid a proud temperament. Easily offended by a slight or a suspicion, he had twice quit previous jobs. He knew that his chief qualification as branch manager was the business that he attracted as Shirley's father. When the bright gleam of that reflected celebrity tarnished in time, his supervisor charged him with complacency, and George Temple resigned. His salary had been ninety dollars a week, a comfortable income in the 1930s and a considerable increase over his wages a few years earlier. Still, asked how he felt as his daughter made a thousand dollars a week, a sum that did not include her enormous licensing income, George Temple replied, "Very foolish." His sense of foolishness was undoubtedly intensified by the knowledge that his wife's salary from Twentieth Century–Fox for her services as Shirley's assistant and hairdresser was roughly three times his own.[56]

George Temple could justify his departure from the bank by thinking that he had more important business to handle. According to the terms of Shirley's contract with Twentieth Century–Fox, he could not formally serve as Shirley's agent, but he could oversee her investments. With a banking associate he formed Temple-Thomason, Inc., which would manage investments for film personalities. His daughter became their first client. Try as he might to preserve his role as the pilot of the family fortune, from the age of six onward, Shirley had become its driving engine.[57]

Shirley felt close to her father as well as her mother, recalling that they "had long been secret best friends." He relished their time together in evenings at home and on neighborhood excursions. Like a character in one of her films, he would take her on his lap and croon a love song, the only one he knew, "You Are the Ideal of My Dreams." Yet Shirley's success inevitably diminished him. Whether or not the outburst that Jule Styne claimed to have witnessed was characteristic, he knew its stinging truth: she made all the money, and he was an accessory. What the former child star "Baby Peggy" Montgomery wrote about both her own and Jackie Coogan's fathers describes George Temple's position as well: "In the restrictive arena where the child star's father moved, there were no personal business triumphs, no million-dollar deals of his own to be celebrated. Without even real-izing it, [such] men . . . increasingly strove to keep the approval and affection of their wives by the only means left to them—furthering their child's career. Tragically, however, every financial victory for the child signified yet another moral defeat for the father. No matter how they tried to rationalize it, only the breadwinner earned the respect, and self-respect, proper to that role."[58]

Although the importance of Shirley's earnings was an open secret, like the parents of other child film stars, the Temples tried to keep Shirley innocent of her financial power and the degree to which they had become hostages to her career. Again, there were ample prece-dents. "We seldom refer to money before him," Jackie Coogan's father told reporters. "He has almost no appreciation of the fortune he has earned." Indeed, as a child his financial naiveté appeared to have been total. After his parents signed a million-dollar contract on his behalf, a family friend jokingly asked him what he would trade for it. "Will you give me a dollar and a quarter in cash?" Jackie replied earnestly. "I need that to get a new pair of roller skates."[59]

Shirley never appeared quite so clueless, yet fan magazines smiled at her indifference to wealth and how she took as much delight in the gift of a dime-store balloon as a diamond charm bracelet.[60] As a ten-year-old in fall 1938 she proudly reported that she received an allow-ance of five dollars every two weeks and had accrued a savings of $105, which she kept in a strongbox.[61] To poor children at the time, even this might have seemed to be a fortune, though it placed her reassur-ingly among the middle class. Among families of all classes, children's allowances had grown increasingly popular in the first decades of the twentieth century. Such payments acknowledged the historic trans-formation in the place of the child from a vital economic contributor to a helpful household member and fledgling consumer. Like the parents of such child stars as Jackie Coogan and Jane Withers, George and Gertrude Temple participated in this practice designed to teach how to save, spend, and give wisely. In this way, they sought to normalize their child's stupendous income and to neutralize its immensely transformative effects on their family, even as other children saved their pennies for Shirley Temple movies and products.[62]

By rights stretching back to British common law, as the parent of a minor under their roof, the Temples were entitled to every penny that Shirley made, but that situation was about to change. Precipitating that change were two spectacular instances of mercenary parents and relatives who plundered child stars' earnings for their own use. Freddie Bartholomew was the target of the first. His aunt, who had raised him from infancy, brought the ten-year-old English actor to America in 1934, signed with MGM for him to play the title role in *David Copperfield*, and had herself named his legal guardian. Over the next five years, while Freddie's film career and earning power soared, his mother, father, and grandparents all testified to how deeply they treasured the boy and how rightly they deserved a share of his earnings. Further suits for a portion of his earnings pursued him until 1943. Consequently, Freddie appeared in court only slightly less frequently than he did before the cameras. By the time he was fifteen, he had been the subject of twenty-seven legal suits among contending relations, and the legal fees squandered his fortune.[63]

In 1938, while disputes over Freddie Bartholomew's earnings dragged wearily onward, another sensational legal dispute erupted. Three years earlier, five months before his twenty-first birthday, Jackie Coogan narrowly escaped death in a car crash in which his father and two other passengers died. Soon afterward, his mother married his business manager, Arthur Bernstein, and the couple lived luxuriously while he remained virtually penniless. He sued them for the money he had made as a minor, an estimated $4 million. In a bitterly contentious trial, his mother tearfully testified, "Jackie was a bad boy, a very, very bad 20-year-old boy" who "couldn't handle money." Less tenderly, she insisted, "He isn't entitled to that money.

It belongs to us." Coogan reported that she told him firmly, "You will never get a cent."[64] As a result of the suit, Coogan gained support for a new principle that a child actor deserved a portion of his earnings. It was a largely pyrrhic victory, however, as he recovered only a fraction of his fortune. The dispute prompted the California state legislature in 1939 to pass the Child Actors Bill, the so-called Coogan Act, which required parents or legal guardians to put at least half a child actor's gross earnings in a court-approved fund or savings plan until the child turned twenty-one, though the law contained loopholes that considerably weakened its protection.

The Temple family did not seem to need the Coogan Act to remind them of their obligations to their child. They said they had established a court-approved trust fund for her as early as 1934 and repeatedly emphasized from that time onward that they placed her earnings in "sound securities." "All the money Shirley has earned has been invested for her," Shirley's fans were reassured again in 1939 in the aftermath of the Coogan case. "The Temples live on George's and Gertrude's salaries. So don't think Shirley is being taken advantage of, financially. She isn't."[65]

At this time Gertrude Temple passionately reaffirmed their selfless devotion to Shirley: "There is nothing, nothing that can hurt me so much, nothing that can make me so angry as to have it said that I am a 'money-grabbing woman making that poor child work so hard.'" She placed her confidence in her husband as an experienced banker and head of the household to manage Shirley's money prudently. As for herself, "I haven't the slightest idea in the world how much we have, how much money Shirley has. I know that her money is well and wisely invested for her, in Government bonds, mostly, and in insurance annuities which will mature at different ages." By ensuring that Shirley would never receive all of her money at once, this arrangement protected her against fortune hunters. "Beyond this certainty that all is safe for Shirley, as safe as anything can be in our times, I have not concerned myself. Mr. Temple keeps enough in my personal checking account to provide for my household and personal expenses and I let it go at that."[66]

Throughout the 1930s fan magazines and interviews with the Temple family celebrated their ability to retain a normal family life, little different in its essentials from the lives of millions of middle-class families. Yet the nature of private life was changing fundamentally, most obviously for the Temple family but also for all of those whose lives she touched. Shirley Temple's stardom marked dramatic changes in the interrelated cultures of celebrity, consumption, and the commodification of childhood. In important respects, these changes came not simply despite but because of the Great Depression. Eager to see faces of cheer and fables of optimism, adults and children alike responded intensely to Hollywood personalities whose smiles could fill the screen and lift their hearts. They wished to believe that such entertainments were created in the same spirit of play in which they were consumed and that the winning little girl's performances expressed a private life of perpetual happy-ending.

Yet the irreducible fact is that Shirley Temple worked hard. Children had done so for centuries, of course, but she saw herself not as a child laborer but as a professional. She made this point repeatedly in her memoir of her career as a child star. Far from bewailing her situation, she proudly insisted on her interest in the craft of film acting and pride in doing it well. Even so, as labor, Shirley's work made a variety of demands on her, physical and emotional. It was not as physically punishing as most forms of child labor, although it consumed long hours and included physical risks. Its emotional requirements extended far beyond the set, however. In addition to the work of acting, Shirley assumed the fraught position of becoming the financial and emotional center of her family's life. She possessed tremendous power not only in the universe of the global public but also, and more momentous to her own development, in her family's world.

While FDR sought to curtail or eliminate many of the most egregious forms of child labor, emotional labor nonetheless flourished in the Great Depression, most obviously on stage and screen, less so in the paid demands on children in service positions and the unpaid demands of cheering their families. As the service economy developed in subsequent decades, emotional labor became an essential element of many jobs performed by older children and adults in the workforce and also in more private and domestic settings. Yet service with a smile can take its toll. Just as workers can grow alienated from the goods that they produce in an industrial economy, the sociologist Arlie Russell Hochschild has observed, so too they can become alienated from the services that they provide in a service economy. From the hospitality industry to the growing care sector, such emotional alienation has become a prominent condition of much of modern work.[67] Children are usually considered the objects of adults' emotional labor, but they have often become the providers as well: from the trophy child who is constantly pressured to win new markers of achievement for the gratification of the parents to the emotionally abused child struggling to keep the remnants of family together. To be sure, children have always been centers of immense emotional expectations as well as economic ones. What has changed is the extent to which these expectations are now enmeshed in a consumer culture that idealizes childhood as blissfully carefree even as that ideal and the everyday lives of children and their families grow increasingly commodified.

In carrying the double burden of professional and familial expectations, child actors have been especially vulnerable to emotional alienation. The actor and comedian Milton Berle, who began performing at the age of five, later wrote, "I guess I thought my childhood was fun while I was living it. Looking back, I can feel in my gut that it was lousy." He added, "You don't take on grownup responsibilities while living inside a kid's body without paying a price for it." The child actor

Ted Donaldson, five years Shirley's junior, reflected, "It can be a wonderful life, but I think for it to be good you need parents who have their own lives, who are not trying to live your successes or not trying to be successes through you."[68] Shirley Temple may have escaped such a fate, but it was her greatest occupational risk.

In the face of such risk, child actors served as the canaries in the mine shaft of modern consumer culture. The carefully constructed image of Shirley's private life was cherished precisely because she seemed so impervious to the immense consumer markets in which her image circulated. Offscreen as well as in her films, in scores of articles and interviews during the Great Depression, the overarching narrative of Shirley Temple was of an irrepressibly sunny, good-hearted, emotionally direct, and delightfully unaffected child. Showered like a fairy princess with adulation, wealth, and luxuries, she seemed supremely uncontaminated by them.

As she assumed the position of a fairy princess, however, those most directly propelling her into the consumer market—her directors, producers, publicists, and parents—worked like alchemists to turn her ebullient child-spirit into gold while leaving her innocent and unchanged. They implicitly testified to their sense of the high risks of the endeavor with each reassurance that she remained unaffected, despite the myriad potential profanations of the markets in which she was a prime mover. Magnetic as Shirley Temple was to moviegoers and the larger industry of products attached to her name, she would break the spell if ever she awoke to a full realization of her immense economic importance. Those around her spoke repeatedly of her unspoiled nature, which they prized as the emotional and moral capital that children uniquely possessed, even as they sought to exploit that capital for its maximum financial return. They proved themselves to be both calculating capitalists and credulous sentimentalists. The separation of the child from the world of market relations in the twentieth century was increasingly a myth, but it was a useful one, not only in the self-serving way it consoled people such as film producers Winfield Sheehan and Darryl Zanuck and parents such as Gertrude and George Temple, but also for the reassurance it provided for the emerging consumer culture as a whole. It allowed both merchants of the child commodity market and parents of consuming children to sleep better at night.

EPILOGUE
SHIRLEY VISITS ANOTHER PRESIDENT

After the Temples broke with Darryl Zanuck and Twentieth Century–Fox in 1940, Shirley and her family sought to place her movie career on a new footing. George Temple erected an independent production company to give her family greater control of her film projects, but it collapsed like a sand castle. Then Gertrude Temple pressed for artistic control of her daughter's films in contract negotiations with Metro-Goldwyn-Mayer but got nowhere. Gertrude Temple blamed poor stories for Shirley's decline in 1939 and 1940, but the new ones were weaker still. Following Shirley's brief contract with MGM, for which she made another movie about a motherless poor little rich girl, *Kathleen,* and an independently produced remake of an old Mary Pickford property, *Miss Annie Rooney* (distributed by United Artists), the Temples eagerly signed on Shirley's behalf with producer David O. Selznick's Vanguard Films. Fresh from his triumphs in *Gone with the Wind* and *Rebecca,* Selznick sparkled as Hollywood's finest independent producer. Gertrude Temple felt that at last her daughter's career was in safe hands.[1]

Altogether between 1941 and 1949 Shirley made thirteen movies, less than half the pace that she had set in the 1930s but a considerable output nonetheless. These included some critical and commercial successes, notably in *Since You Went Away, Fort Apache,* and *The Bachelor and the Bobby-Soxer,* but increasingly in supporting roles in which other actors carried the pictures.[2] For a time she retained her popularity among core fans, but she landed some embarrassing flops.

The former adorable child now frequently played a perky, headstrong teenager (a word newly coined in this decade), spouting slang and brimming with puppy love, beginning with *Miss Annie Rooney* (1942). The *New York Times*'s Theodore Strauss called it "the kind of show that makes indulgent souls feel much less kind toward children. . . . Couldn't Miss Temple be kept in school for just a little while?" he asked.[3] The *Times*'s Bosley Crowther, who praised some of Shirley's performances, including her "superb" acting in the domestic farce *Kiss and Tell* (1945), shook his head in dismay at her last movies. By this time, David Selznick's production company was shaky, and his own attention distracted by his infatuation with the actress Jennifer Jones. Lending Shirley and other stars to various studios, he gave them little personal attention. Reviewing *Honeymoon*, in May 1947, Crowther sighed, "The friends of Shirley Temple must be getting a little bit tired of seeing this buxom young lady still acting as though she were a kid." Five months later, appraising the feeble melodrama *That Hagen Girl* (in which she costarred with Ronald Reagan), he wrote, "She acts with the mopish dejection of a school-child who has just been robbed of a two-scoop ice cream cone." Crowther went on to link Shirley with a political crisis quite different than that of the Great Depression. The House Committee on Un-American Activities was then embroiled in hearings on alleged Communist infiltration of Hollywood. Friendly witnesses before the committee included Ronald Reagan, then president of the Screen Actors Guild, and two of Shirley's former costars, Adolphe Menjou and Gary Cooper. Crowther, who would become an outspoken critic of such red-baiting, concluded his review, tongue in cheek, protesting her dreadful role and performance in the film and tweaking her costars in the process: "They shouldn't do such things to Shirley. It's downright un-American!"[4]

Shirley's movie career ended with a whimper. Of *Adventure in Baltimore* (1949) Crowther groaned wearily, "Whatever strides toward maturity Shirley Temple may have made in her two to three recent pictures are completely reversed by this job."[5] Significantly, neither he nor anyone else at the *New York Times* reviewed her last movie, *A Kiss for Corliss*, a thin and brittle sequel to *Kiss and Tell*.

As Shirley's professional life spiraled downward, her personal life did as well. Fulfilling a teenage ambition to beat her classmates at Westlake School to the altar, she became engaged to Army Air Corps sergeant John Agar when she was only sixteen. Six foot one with a lean, muscled body, he was seven years her senior. Their wedding in September 1945, immediately after the end of the Second World War, resembled a movie premiere, and it was indeed substantially produced by Selznick, who selected the massive Wilshire Methodist Church in Los Angeles, oversaw the arrangements, and paid the piper. In addition to Selznick, the five hundred guests included Darryl Zanuck and California governor Earl Warren. For every guest, outside the church there surged ten excited onlookers, five thousand in all, and despite the presence of forty-five restraining police, many broke through rope barriers to demand Shirley's autograph and to tear the bridesmaids' dresses for souvenir scraps.[6]

Newsweek titled its story of the nuptials "And They Lived Happily." But not so. By Shirley Temple's account, Agar's drinking and flirtations made their marriage rocky from the start. The couple lived on Shirley's allowance in her remodeled playhouse (her mother's idea), only yards away from George and Gertrude. As Shirley pursued her film career, her husband sulked in her shadow. His own contract with Selznick and roles in two of her films did not revive the marriage but only made him a ripe target for taunts as "Mr. Temple." A year after the birth of their daughter, Linda Susan, they separated.[7]

While awaiting her divorce on a Hawaiian vacation with her parents and baby daughter, Shirley met Charles Alden Black, a tall, tanned, handsome, thirty-year-old businessman with a smile to match her own. He did not recognize her, had never seen one of her movies, and was not the least awed by her fame. Son of the president and later chairman of the board of the giant utility company Pacific Gas and Electric, Charlie Black had breezed through the Hotchkiss School, Stanford University, and Harvard Business School, later returning to Stanford to complete his master's in business administration. During the Second World War he served on Gen. Douglas MacArthur's staff as an intelligence officer and, as a scout behind enemy lines in Indonesia, conducted over a hundred PT boat patrols and earned a Silver Star for valor. An expert sailor and surfer, he exuded vigor and competence. If she ached for an escape from Hollywood's celebrity, he offered it. Immediately smitten by him, Shirley (who had not befriended J. Edgar Hoover for nothing) had her friends in the FBI check his background to make sure this golden boy was not merely brass. The couple was married in a small private ceremony, far away from reporters and onlookers, in December 1950.[8]

Up to this time Shirley had remained blissfully ignorant of her finances. Although twenty-two, she still received an allowance from her father and knew nothing of the size of the nest egg that he had supposedly guarded so vigilantly throughout her movie career. Her first husband had acceded to these arrangements, but businessman Charles Black was less passive. At his urging, she finally insisted on examining her financial records. Only then did she discover how disastrously her father and his business partner had squandered her earnings from her films, licenses, and royalties. Of the $3,207,666 in earnings her family had received in her name, only $44,000 remained in her trust account, in addition to ownership of her former playhouse, a wedding present from her parents in 1945. Leaving the house aside, for every dollar she had made, only a fraction more than a penny was left. Poring over the thick bound volume containing the complicated and depressing account of income, investments, and expenditures, she found how much her innocence had been exploited. With her earnings, her father had indulged his penchant for expensive cars and her mother her taste for fashion. She had bankrolled her father's speculative gambles, which he consistently lost, and her mother's racetrack bets. She paid her brothers' school and college bills and the salaries of a large household staff. Other beneficiaries of her unknowing largess included her difficult grandmother and two paternal uncles, as well as numerous friends of George and Gertrude, to whom they freely gave loans and handouts, rarely repaid. Keeping more of Shirley's money in her parents' names, George muttered weakly to Shirley, was intended to save her substantial income taxes. Now it was gone. Through all of the dizzying records, she concluded bitterly, one theme beat clearly: "Keep dancing, kid, or the rickety card house collapses."[9]

Not only had her earnings been prodigally mismanaged, her father had also simply ignored the California Superior Court orders governing her 1941 MGM contract and seven-year contract with David Selznick's Vanguard Films mandating that half of her net earnings be placed in trust for her. Shirley's gross earnings during these nine years after leaving Twentieth Century–Fox amounted to $891,067. George Temple had evidently treated all of this money as if it were his own. She later likened her father to Mr. Micawber of Charles Dickens's *David Copperfield*, the jauntily optimistic, improvident man who always believed something would turn up. In a final twist of roles, she protected her father from the humiliation of his colossal ineptitude and, for the rest of her parents' lives, kept her discovery private.[10]

By the time of Shirley Temple's second marriage, the Hollywood studio system was rapidly crumbling, battered by antitrust actions and the television industry. Selznick himself stopped producing films for nine years. In addition, simmering tensions in Korea had burst into open conflict, and Charles Black was summoned back to active duty in naval intelligence. Shutting the door on her film career, Shirley moved with her husband and daughter to Washington, D.C., and took up life as a housewife and mother.

In 1953, fifteen years after Shirley Temple and her parents called

Shirley Temple Black with husband Charles Black and daughter Linda Susan at the White House for a visit with President Eisenhower, May 14, 1953. (© Bettmann/Corbis)

on Franklin Roosevelt and nineteen years after attaching her screen persona to FDR's coattails in *Stand Up and Cheer!*, she returned to the White House, this time with her husband and her own daughter to shake hands with President Dwight Eisenhower as her family prepared to return to California. Like FDR, Ike had a hearty laugh, an infectious grin, and an air of cheerful optimism. But the political, economic, and emotional contexts of their smiles were vastly different. FDR's smile sustained millions during the darkest days of the Great Depression. Ike's grin shone on a country more prosperous than ever before. Certainly, anxieties remained. The Cold War raged, the nuclear arms race mounted, and Wisconsin senator Joseph McCarthy inveighed against Communist conspirators at every level of government and the military. Yet long after McCarthy's self-serving charges collapsed in ignominy, the ideal of the private consumer, rooted in the middle-class family and the suburban landscape, dominated postwar politics and the economy to such an extent that John Updike famously wrote in a short story, "America is a vast conspiracy to make you happy." Shirley Temple had played an important part in launching this conspiracy, in 1930s movies that patched up romantic misunderstandings and family quarrels, bolstered people's spirits, and got folks spending again. New child actors flooded television, but none could ever attain the cultural centrality or economic significance that Shirley had achieved. America's model child and model consumer in the Great Depression, she prepared the way for the culture of postwar abundance, in which the smile, once a determined emblem of hope, became an obligatory expression. "The American must smile," the sociologist Philip Rieff observed in 1957, "or risk challenging the sacramental bond that unites him in one overpoweringly friendly people. In that wide, ever-ready smile the material abundance of America may be said to be transubstantiated into the personality of the American."[11]

Shirley Temple Black was not content either to bask in her former celebrity or to retreat into the shadows like Mary Pickford. She devoted herself to numerous charitable activities, political efforts for Republican candidates, and diplomatic duties, including ambassadorships to Ghana and Czechoslovakia. The former child star who once celebrated the end of the Great Depression, sat on President Lincoln's lap, and brokered peace on the India-Afghanistan border in her film roles could not claim to have ended the Cold War. But when East and West Germans celebrated the fall of the Berlin Wall in 1989, she watched them not from a suburban California living room but from her ambassadorial quarters in Prague.

ACKNOWLEDGMENTS AND PERMISSIONS

Many individuals and institutions helped to make this book possible. The University of North Carolina at Chapel Hill, my professional home for more than forty years, provided support of numerous kinds, including a Spray-Randleigh Fellowship, research and travel funds, library services, and encouraging colleagues in the Departments of History and American Studies, especially Lloyd Kramer. I advanced this project considerably at the National Humanities Center in Research Triangle Park, North Carolina, supported in part by a John Medlin Jr. Senior Fellowship and a National Endowment for the Humanities Fellowship. For scholars, the center is, quite simply, the happiest place on earth, made especially so because of its immensely helpful staff and stimulating fellows. To enumerate all of their individual contributions would be impossible, so let me simply express my profound gratitude to each and every one.

In conducting research for this book, I benefited greatly from the help of Michael Beck, Sara Bush, Angelica Castillo, Jennifer Donnally, Joey Fink, Rosalie Genova, Elizabeth Gritter, Rachel Hynson, Greg Kaliss, Jason Kauffman, Kimberly Kutz, Pamella Lach, Elizabeth Lundeen, Blake Sloanecker, Sarah Thomson Vierra, and Jessica Wilkerson. Rachel Hynson also translated Spanish-language articles, and Emily Taylor translated Japanese newspapers. Alison Robins gave me the benefit of her dance scholar's eye in analyzing Bill Robinson's numbers with Shirley Temple. Wanda Wallace lent me her cache of Shirley Temple films, and Charlene Regester called my attention to other films and essays. For other kindnesses and suggestions, I am indebted to James W. Cook, Kathryn Fuller-Seeley, Lawrence Glickman, Elliott Gorn, Karen Halttunen, Michael Hornblow, John Howard, Mary Kelley, Lary May, Michael O'Malley, Sharon O'Brien, Joel Pfister, and Charles Weinrab.

ACKNOWLEDGMENTS AND PERMISSIONS

I wish also to thank the crucial aid of archivists at the Franklin D. Roosevelt Library, the Harvard Theatre Collection, the Lilly Library at Indiana University, the Margaret Herrick Library of the Academy of Motion Picture Arts and Sciences, the National Portrait Gallery, the Stanford University Library, the State Library of New South Wales, The Strong, and the Cinema Arts Library Special Collections at the University of Southern California, where Ned Comstock was especially obliging. The staffs at Corbis Images, Culver Pictures, and Photofest considerably eased the process of obtaining illustrations.

This project began as an essay in honor of Lawrence W. Levine, and his memory and example have propelled me along the way. At every opportunity I have pelted audiences with the fruits of my research, and, instead of flinging back fruit of their own, they have consistently responded with thoughtful questions. Such generous listeners include faculty and students at American Studies Association annual meetings, the College of William and Mary, Doshisha University, Indiana University, the John F. Kennedy Institute for North American Studies at the Free University of Berlin, King's College London, the National University of Singapore, the University of North Carolina at Chapel Hill, the University of Sydney, the University of Ulster, Virginia Tech, and public audiences in Raleigh, Durham, and Chapel Hill, North Carolina.

I contributed early versions of portions of this book as essays in "Behind Shirley Temple's Smile: Children, Emotional Labor, and the Great Depression," in James W. Cook, Lawrence Glickman, and Michael O'Malley, eds., *The Cultural Turn in U.S. History: Past, Present, and Future* (©2008 by the University of Chicago, all rights reserved) and "Shirley Temple's Paradoxical Smile," *American Art* 25, no. 3 (Fall 2011): 16–19 (©2011, Smithsonian Institution). I am grateful for permission from the University of Chicago Press and the Smithsonian Institution to republish them here.

As I drafted this book, several people gave me their discerning criticism, including my good friends William Leuchtenburg, a prodigious scholar of twentieth-century political history, and Peter Filene, a sensitive historian, novelist, and photographer. My brilliant editor at W. W. Norton, Alane Salierno Mason, vastly improved the book by her many discerning suggestions. As editorial assistant, Anna Mageras guided the process from manuscript to book. My meticulous copy editor, India Cooper, saved me from numerous slips and stumbles, as well as a few pratfalls. Another good friend, Richard Hendel, devised the book's spirited design. My daughter, Laura, first brought Shirley Temple movies into my life, and as adults both she and my son, Peter, have cheered me onward. My wife, Joy S. Kasson, helped most of all, from her initial idea that I write about Shirley Temple through numerous archives, many drafts, and much handwringing to the very end. I cannot imagine writing this book—or, indeed, so much of my life—without her. Needless to say, the imperfections that remain are all my own.

NOTES

INTRODUCTION

1 "Peewee's Progress," *Time*, April 27, 1936, 36–38; "Gabriel Washington [Pseud. for Gabriel Meyers]," interview by Charles A. Von Ohsen, February 22, 1939, and John and Lizzie Pierce, interview by I.L.M., September 23, 1938, *American Life Histories: Manuscripts from the Federal Writers' Project, 1936–1940*, Library of Congress, Manuscript Division, WPA Federal Writers' Project Collection, Washington, DC; Blake Stimson, "Andy Warhol's Red Beard," *Art Bulletin* 83, no. 3 (September 2001): 528–29; Ovid Demaris, *The Director: An Oral Biography of J. Edgar Hoover* (New York: Harper's Magazine Press, 1975), 47; Shane White et al., *Playing the Numbers: Gambling in Harlem between the Wars* (Cambridge, MA: Harvard University Press, 2010), 170; Stacey Morris, "Ghosts of Prinsengracht: A Tour of the Anne Frank House," *Jewish Daily Forward*, April 13, 2007, http://forward.com/articles/10481/ghosts-of-prinsengra.

2 Arlie Russell Hochschild, *The Commercialization of Intimate Life: Notes from Home and Work* (Berkeley and Los Angeles: University of California Press, 2003), 83.

3 "Greeting to Shirley," *Variety*, April 29, 1936, 26; "Shirley Temple Contest Engineered by Ed Hart," *Motion Picture Herald*, August 11, 1934, 60; Louis A. Pérez Jr., *On Becoming Cuban: Identity, Nationality, and Culture* (Chapel Hill: University of North Carolina Press, 2007), 300–301; "Gaitou de Hirotta Wasei Tenpuru-jou" (Discovered on the Street: The Japanese Shirley Temple), *Asahi Shimbun*, Tokyo, March 26, 1938, evening ed., 4; "Peewee's Progress," 38.

CHAPTER ONE: SMILE LIKE ROOSEVELT

1 For material on George and Gertrude Temple's courtship in this and the following paragraph, see Shirley Temple Black, *Child Star: An Autobiography* (New York: McGraw-Hill, 1988), 1–2, 96.

2 Material in this and the following paragraphs on George and Gertrude Temple and their families comes from the 1900, 1910, 1920, and 1930 federal census and city directories of Los Angeles and Santa Monica, California, accessed through *Ancestry.com*.

3 Greg Hise, "Industry and Imaginative Geographies," in *Metropolis in the Making: Los Angeles in the 1920s*, ed. Tom Sitton and William Deverell (Berkeley and Los Angeles: University of California Press, 2001), 18; Kevin Starr, *Material Dreams: Southern California through the 1920's* (New York: Oxford University Press, 1990), 70, 84–85; Bruce Bliven, "Los Angeles: The City That Is Bacchanalian—in a Nice Way," *New Republic*, July 13, 1927, 197.

4 Black, *Child Star*, 15. Among other future stage and screen mothers who began coaching their children *in utero* were Jennie Cockrell Bierbower (later Janis) and Lela Rogers. See Diana Serra Cary, *Hollywood's Children: An Inside Account of the Child Star Era* (Dallas: Southern Methodist University Press, 1997), 22, 164. Jane Withers's mother similarly planned her daughter's career long before conception. See Tom Goldrup and Jim Goldrup, *Growing Up on the Set: Interviews with 39 Former Child Actors of Classic Film and Television* (Jefferson, NC: McFarland, 2002), 33.

5 Theodore G. Joslin, *Hoover off the Record* (Garden City, NY: Doubleday, Doran, 1934), 14; Joan Hoff, *Herbert Hoover, Forgotten Progressive* (Boston: Little, Brown, 1975), 118, 121. The last quotation is from Sherwood Anderson's 1927 interview with Hoover.

6 Herbert Hoover, August 11, 1928, *Containing the Public Messages, Speeches, and Statements of the President, March 4 to December 31, 1929*, Public Papers of the Presidents of the United States (Washington, DC: United States Government Printing Office, 1974), 503.

7 State of the Union Address, December 3, 1929, in Hoover, *Containing Public Messages*, 411–13; Lester V. Chandler, *America's Greatest Depression, 1929–1941* (New York: Harper & Row, 1970), 20.

8 "Employment Gains Cited by Hoover," *Wall Street Journal*, March 8, 1930, 1, 12; "Worst of Depression Over, Says Hoover," *New York Times*, May 2, 1930, 1.

9 Arthur M. Schlesinger Jr., *The Crisis of the Old Order, 1919–1933* (Boston: Houghton Mifflin, 1957), 231; Chandler, *America's Greatest Depression*, 11.

10 "Text of President Hoover's Address before American Bankers' Convention in Cleveland," *Chicago Daily Tribune*, October 3, 1930, 6. On February 12, 1931, Rogers added in the same vein: "Starving isn't so bad, it's getting used to it that is tough. The first three years of a Republican Administration is the hardest. By the end of that time you are used to living on predictions." Donald Day, ed., *The Autobiography of Will Rogers* (Boston: Houghton Mifflin, 1949), 241.

11 David M. Kennedy, *Freedom from Fear: The American People in Depression and War, 1929–1945* (New York: Oxford University Press, 1999), 66–67; Chandler, *America's Greatest Depression*, 21, 34.

12 *New York World*, October 15, 1930, as quoted in Edward Angly, *Oh Yeah?* (New York: Viking Press, 1931), 27.

13 Joslin, *Hoover off the Record*, 33.

14 Annual Message to the Congress on the State of the Union, December 8, 1931, in Herbert Hoover, *Containing the Public Messages, Speeches, and Statements of the President, January 1 to December 31, 1931*, Public Papers of the Presidents of the United States (Washington, DC: United States Government Printing Office, 1976), 583–84; Basil Rauch, ed., *The Roosevelt Reader: Selected Speeches, Messages, Press Conferences, and Letters of Franklin D. Roosevelt* (New York: Rinehart, 1957), 66.

15 Hoover in conversation with Bryan Price, as quoted in Hoff, *Herbert Hoover*, 163.

16 "Hoover's Silent Partner," *Literary Digest*, September 8, 1917, 52; William

Allen White, *The Autobiography of William Allen White* (New York: Macmillan, 1946), 515; Grace Tully, *F.D.R., My Boss* (New York: C. Scribner's Sons, 1949), 60.

17 Joslin, *Hoover off the Record*, 163, 170, 218, 306, 318, 324; Irwin Hood Hoover, *Forty-Two Years in the White House* (Boston: Houghton Mifflin, 1934), 218, 184.

18 Donald R. Richberg, *My Hero: The Indiscreet Memoirs of an Eventful but Unheroic Life* (New York: Putnam, 1954), 149; Henry L. Stimson and McGeorge Bundy, *On Active Service in Peace and War* (New York: Harper & Brothers, 1948), 205.

19 Louis Liebovich, *Bylines in Despair: Herbert Hoover, the Great Depression, and the U.S. News Media* (Westport, CT: Praeger, 1994), 146; Roy Victor Peel and Thomas C. Donnelly, *The 1932 Campaign: An Analysis* (1935; rpt. New York: Da Capo Press, 1973), 181; Joslin diary entry, August 8, 1932, as quoted in Liebovich, *Bylines in Despair*, 146.

20 Joslin, *Hoover off the Record*, 3; David Burner, *Herbert Hoover: The Public Life* (New York: Knopf, 1978), 314.

21 Liebovich, *Bylines in Despair*, 135; Joslin, *Hoover off the Record*, 315.

22 Hoff, *Herbert Hoover*, 140. The estimate of apple vendors appears in William E. Leuchtenburg, *Herbert Hoover* (New York: Times Books, 2009), 109; Herbert Hoover, *Memoirs* (New York: Macmillan, 1951), 3:195.

23 Hoover, interview by Raymond Clapper, February 27, 1931, in Olive Ewing Clapper, *Washington Tapestry* (New York: Whittlesey House, div. of McGraw-Hill, 1946), 4; "The Presidency: Opener," *Time*, October 10, 1932, 223; Day, *Autobiography of Will Rogers*, 275.

24 Hoover, interview by Raymond Clapper, February 27, 1931, in O. E. Clapper, *Washington Tapestry*, 4; Guido van Rijn, *Roosevelt's Blues: African-American Blues and Gospel Songs on FDR* (Jackson: University Press of Mississippi, 1997), 25.

25 On "bulldog gravy," see Kennedy, *Freedom from Fear*, 169; [Archibald MacLeish], "'No One Has Starved,'" *Fortune*, September 1932, 28.

26 Jonathan Alter, *The Defining Moment: FDR's Hundred Days and the Tri-

umph of Hope (New York: Simon & Schuster, 2006), 120; "Candidature," *Time*, January 25, 1932, 9.

27 Peel and Donnelly, *1932 Campaign*, 51; Burner, *Herbert Hoover*, 316.

28 Chandler, *America's Greatest Depression*, 3, 6; Herbert Hoover, *Containing the Public Messages, Speeches, and Statements of the President, January 1, 1932 to March 4, 1933*, Public Papers of the Presidents of the United States (Washington, DC: United States Government Printing Office, 1977), 569; Herbert Hoover, *Campaign Speeches of 1932* (Garden City, NY: Doubleday, Doran, 1933), 227.

29 Burner, *Herbert Hoover*, 315–17; Hoff, *Herbert Hoover*, 167.

30 "Election Results: President Reject," *Time*, November 14, 1932, 26.

31 John Gray, review of *Payback: Debt and the Shadow Side of Wealth*, by Margaret Atwood, *New York Review of Books*, April 9, 2009, 46.

32 Frances Perkins, *The Roosevelt I Knew* (New York: Viking Press, 1946), 166.

33 Gladstone Williams, "Smiles of Franklin D. Roosevelt Will End Decade of Dourness," *Atlanta Constitution*, November 25, 1932, 6.

34 Geoffrey C. Ward, *A First-Class Temperament: The Emergence of Franklin Roosevelt* (New York: Harper & Row, 1989), 91. On Roosevelt's childhood, see Geoffrey C. Ward, *Before the Trumpet: Young Franklin Roosevelt, 1882–1905* (New York: Harper & Row, 1985).

35 Perkins, *Roosevelt I Knew*, 11.

36 Ward, *Before the Trumpet*, 253; Ward, *First-Class Temperament*, 509.

37 Ward, *Before the Trumpet*, 315; Ward, *First-Class Temperament*, 86. FDR fulfilled TR's example even to the point of having six children, though one of FDR's sons died in infancy.

38 On Roosevelt's bout with polio, see especially Hugh Gregory Gallagher, *FDR's Splendid Deception* (New York: Dodd, Mead, 1985); Ward, *First-Class Temperament*, 576–648 and passim; and Garry Wills, "The Power of Impotence," *New York Review of Books*, November 23, 1989, 3–4.

39 Gallagher, *FDR's Splendid Deception*, 17; Ward, *First-Class Temperament*, 623, 647.

40 Sara Roosevelt to Frederic Delano, as quoted in Frank Freidel, *Franklin D. Roosevelt*, vol. 2, *The Ordeal* (Boston: Little, Brown, 1954), 100.

41 James Roosevelt and Sidney Shalett, *Affectionately, F.D.R.: A Son's Story of a Lonely Man* (New York: Hearst, 1959), 143.

42 On FDR's skillful and ultimately unconscious diversions from his handicap, see Rexford G. Tugwell, *The Brains Trust* (New York: Viking Press, 1968), 22.

43 "Republicans: Dutch Take Holland," *Time*, June 27, 1932, 11; James O'Donnell Bennett, "Boos Give Way to Victory Song as Tide Turns," *Chicago Daily Tribune*, July 2, 1932, 4; "Learns 'Happy Days,'" *New York Times*, July 10, 1932, 12; "Roosevelt's Theme Song," *Washington Post*, July 10, 1932, M6; Peel and Donnelly, *1932 Campaign*, 147.

44 Clinton L. Mosher, as quoted in Frank Freidel, *Franklin D. Roosevelt*, vol. 3, *The Triumph* (Boston: Little, Brown, 1956), 358; Peel and Donnelly, *1932 Campaign*, 170.

45 Chandler, *America's Greatest Depression*, 35, 40.

46 Tully, *F.D.R., My Boss*, 68; Stephen Hess and Sandy Northrop, *Drawn & Quartered: The History of American Political Cartoons* (Montgomery, AL: Elliott & Clark, 1996), 94.

47 Gallagher, *FDR's Splendid Deception*, esp. 93–97, 65; Ward, *First-Class Temperament*, 651, 780–84.

48 Samuel I. Rosenman, ed., *The Public Papers and Addresses of Franklin D. Roosevelt with a Special Introduction and Explanatory Notes by President Roosevelt*, vol. 2, *The Year of Crisis, 1933* (New York: Random House: 1938), 11, 12, 15. Although FDR had drafted much of the inaugural address with the aid of Raymond Moley, the famous phrase "The only thing we have to fear is fear itself" was contributed by his longtime aide Louis Howe. Davis W. Houck, *FDR and Fear Itself: The First Inaugural Address* (College Station: Texas A&M University Press, 2002), 120. On the enthusiastic response to FDR's possible use of broad executive power, see Alter, *Defining Moment*, 219.

49 "500,000 in Streets Cheer Roosevelt," *New York Times*, March 5, 1933,

1; Gish quoted in Sally Stein, "The President's Two Bodies: Staging and Restagings of FDR and the New Deal Body Politic," *American Art* 18, no. 1 (Spring 2004): 37.

50 For analysis of Roosevelt's Hundred Days, see William E. Leuchtenburg, *Franklin D. Roosevelt and the New Deal, 1932–1940* (New York: Harper & Row, 1963), 41–62; Kennedy, *Freedom from Fear*, 131–59; Anthony J. Badger, *FDR: The First Hundred Days* (New York: Hill and Wang, 2008); and Thomas J. Sugrue, "The Hundred Days War: Histories of the New Deal," *Nation*, April 27, 2009, 25–28.

51 Hiram Johnson to Katherine Edson, April 20, 1933, as quoted in Leuchtenburg, *Franklin D. Roosevelt and the New Deal*, 62 n. 54; William E. Leuchtenburg, *The FDR Years: On Roosevelt and His Legacy* (New York: Columbia University Press, 1995), 7.

52 Leo C. Rosten, *The Washington Correspondents* (New York: Harcourt, 1937), 39–53, esp. 49–50; Leuchtenburg, *FDR Years*, 11–13; "Roosevelt at Ease in Chat with Press," *New York Times*, March 9, 1933, 3; see also Alter, *Defining Moment*, 253–58.

53 The U.S. Census Bureau reported the proportion of families with radios rose from roughly 46 percent in 1930 to 81 percent in 1940. See table Dg117–130, "Radio and television—stations, sets produced, and households with sets: 1921–2000," in Susan B. Carter et al. eds., *Historical Statistics of the United States: Earliest Times to the Present*, Millennial ed. (New York, NY: Cambridge University Press, 2006), 4:4-1027. Obviously, many people also listened to the radio outside their own homes.

54 Bruce Lenthall, *Radio's America: The Great Depression and the Rise of Modern Mass Culture* (Chicago: University of Chicago Press, 2007), esp. 53–114.

55 Ira R. T. Smith with Joe Alex Morris, "Dear Mr. President . . .": *The Story of Fifty Years in the White House Mail Room* (New York: J. Messner, 1949), 12, 216.

56 Helen S. Brown to FDR; Laurence L. Prince to FDR; Frank J. Reveley

to FDR, President's Personal File 200B, Public Reaction, March 4, 1933, Hyde Park, New York (hereafter FDR Library).

57 Dow D. Burch to FDR, President's Personal File 200B, Public Reaction, March 4, 1933, FDR Library; Cleveland correspondent, quoted in Houck, *FDR and Fear Itself*, 10.

58 Mrs. John H. Quigley to FDR; Mae Barnie to FDR, President's Personal File 200B, Public Reaction, March 4, 1933, FDR Library.

59 William F. Purdy to FDR; Charlotte Reeve Conover to FDR, President's Personal File 200B, Public Reaction, March 4, 1933, FDR Library.

60 F. W. Clements to FDR (emphasis in original); James A. Peers to FDR, President's Personal File 200B, Public Reaction, March 4, 1933, FDR Library.

61 The description of FDR's conception of a chat around the fireside comes from his press secretary, Stephen T. Early, as quoted in Lenthall, *Radio's America*, 88–89. The Washington bureau chief for Columbia Broadcasting System (CBS), Harry Butcher, popularized the phrase "fireside chat." See Betty Houchin Winfield, *FDR and the News Media* (Urbana: University of Illinois Press, 1990), 104.

62 Lawrence Levine and Cornelia Levine observe that FDR usually spoke at not more than 100 to 120 words per minute, a pace 30 percent less than was commonly used on the radio and a decided contrast with the rapid-fire styles of the columnist Walter Winchell and Louisiana senator Huey Long. Lawrence W. Levine and Cornelia R. Levine, eds., *The People and the President: America's Conversation with FDR* (Boston: Beacon Press, 2002), 16.

63 Radio address, March 12, 1933, in Russell D. Buhite and David W. Levy, *FDR's Fireside Chats* (Norman: University of Oklahoma Press, 1992), 12–17.

64 F. W. Meyers to FDR; Florence M. Betts to FDR, President's Personal File 200B, Public Reaction, March 13, 1933, FDR Library.

65 Charles L. Kimmel to FDR, President's Personal File 200B, Public Reaction, March 13, 1933, FDR Library.

66 Frank J. Cregg to FDR; Ruth Liebermann to FDR, as quoted in Levine and Levine, *People and the President*, 37, 22.

67 Walker S. Duel, "Landslide Victory Held Tribute to Roosevelt's Courage, Character," *Atlanta Constitution*, November 7, 1936, 2; Levine and Levine, *People and the President*, 17.

68 Virginia Miller to FDR; Etta A. Buckley to FDR; Mrs. A. J. Bell to FDR, President's Personal File 200B, Public Reaction, March 13, 1933, FDR Library.

69 Paul H. Russell to FDR; Chester E. Bruns to FDR, in Levine and Levine, *People and the President*, 48, 42; Will Rogers, "Roosevelt Illiterate— Rogers," *Miami News*, January 26, 1936, 11; "Common Words Keynote of Roosevelt's Talks," *New York Times*, May 16, 1937, 174.

70 Perkins, *Roosevelt I Knew*, 72.

71 Eleanor Roosevelt, as quoted in Levine and Levine, *People and the President*, 18; FDR to C. Leffingwell, March 16, 1942, in Elliott Roosevelt, ed., *F.D.R.: His Personal Letters* (New York: Duell, Sloan and Pearce, 1950), 4:1298.

72 Melvyn Douglas, "Number One Movie Fan," *New Republic*, April 15, 1946, 543.

73 Of course, FDR's opponents did not applaud such appearances. One of Peter Arno's most famous cartoons depicted a patrician-looking group in evening dress inviting friends on an outing. It was captioned, "Come along. We're going to the Trans-Lux [a Manhattan newsreel theater] to hiss Roosevelt." *The New Yorker*, September 19, 1936, 16.

74 Douglas, "Number One Movie Fan," 543. The journalist Marquis Childs observed that FDR was a "man who could be photographed . . . always with just the perfect camera angle." Ward, *First-Class Temperament*, 552.

75 James MacGregor Burns, *Roosevelt: The Lion and the Fox* (New York: Harcourt, 1956), 447; Leuchtenburg, *FDR Years*, 13.

76 Samuel I. Rosenman, ed., *The Public Papers and Addresses of Franklin D. Roosevelt* (New York: Random House, 1938), 7: 615.

77 Conrad Black, *Franklin Delano Roosevelt: Champion of Freedom* (New York: Public Affairs, 2003), 316; Douglas, "Number One Movie Fan," 542.

78 "Smile like Roosevelt," *New York Times*, August 21, 1933, 11; "Roosevelt Canvas Approved by Wife," *New York Times*, March 2, 1934, 25; "A Laughing Cavalier," *Vanity Fair*, October 1933, 15. On portraits of FDR, see Stein, "President's Two Bodies," 32–57; and David Meschutt, "Portraits of Franklin Delano Roosevelt," *American Art Journal* 18, no. 4 (1986): 3–50.

79 I. Hoover, *Forty-Two Years in the White House*, 233; Fulton Oursler, *Behold This Dreamer! An Autobiography* (Boston: Little, Brown, 1964), 419; Ward, *First-Class Temperament*, 711.

80 Joseph W. Martin and Robert J. Donovan, *My First Fifty Years in Politics* (New York: McGraw-Hill, 1960), 73.

81 Graham J. White, *FDR and the Press* (Chicago: University of Chicago Press, 1979), 36.

82 H. L. Mencken, *On Politics: A Carnival of Buncombe*, ed. Malcolm Moos (Baltimore: Johns Hopkins University Press, 1996), 262; Mencken, "Three Years of Dr. Roosevelt," *American Mercury*, March 1936, 257; Charles A. Fecher, ed., *The Diary of H. L. Mencken* (New York: Knopf, 1989), 76; George Wolfskill and John Hudson, *All but the People: Franklin D. Roosevelt and His Critics, 1933–39* (New York: Macmillan, 1969), 28.

83 Rauch, *Roosevelt Reader*, 166.

84 "No Hasty Inflation," *New York Times*, May 9, 1933, 16; Leuchtenburg, *FDR Years*, 312; Lenthall, *Radio's America*, 126, 141.

85 Christopher Duggan, *The Force of Destiny: A History of Italy since 1796* (London: Allen Lane, 2007), 477; Alex Ross, *The Rest Is Noise: Listening to the Twentieth Century* (New York: Farrar, Straus and Giroux, 2007), 238. Ross here speaks of Hitler and Stalin, but the phrase is equally applicable to Il Duce.

CHAPTER TWO: SUCH A HAPPY LITTLE FACE!

1 The story of Shirley's weekly bleachings appeared in Lloyd Pantages, "I Cover Hollywood," *Los Angeles Examiner*, October 16, 1935, Clippings File—Shirley Temple, Margaret Herrick Library, Academy of Motion Picture Arts and Sciences, Beverly Hills, CA (hereafter MHL); see also Shirley Temple Black, *Child Star: An Autobiography* (New York: McGraw-Hill, 1988), 69. A brunette Shirley appears in *New Deal Rhythm* (1933).

2 Diana Serra Cary, *Hollywood's Children: An Inside Account of the Child Star Era* (Dallas: Southern Methodist University Press, 1997), 149.

3 Black, *Child Star*, 12–14.

4 Black, *Child Star*, 14.

5 Anne Edwards says that Shirley Temple's earnings from her films before *Stand Up and Cheer!* were $1,135. Edwards, *Shirley Temple: American Princess* (New York: William Morrow, 1988), 49. Shirley Temple Black says her earnings on the Educational Films shorts and her early bit parts amounted to $702.50. Black, *Child Star*, 31.

6 Tom Goldrup and Jim Goldrup, *Growing Up on the Set: Interviews with 39 Former Child Actors of Classic Film and Television* (Jefferson, NC: McFarland, 2002), 21, 334.

7 Black, *Child Star*, 15–16.

8 Black, *Child Star*, 14.

9 Black, *Child Star*, 20–21.

10 Black, *Child Star*, 21–23, 25–27, 19.

11 Edwards, *Shirley Temple*, 70.

12 Gertrude Temple, "Bringing Up Shirley," *American Magazine*, February 1935, 92; [Max Trell], "My Life and Times: The Autobiography of Shirley Temple, Part I," *Pictorial Review*, August 1935, 40. A *Time* magazine cover story echoed this assertion: "Her work entails no effort. She plays at acting as other small girls play at dolls." "Peewee's Progress," *Time*, April 27, 1936, 42.

13 For example, the mother of the silent film star "Baby Peggy" Montgom-

ery told reporters, "She [Peggy] works—if you would call it work—four hours a day, never at night and never on Sundays. She considers her work play and nothing is ever done or said to let her feel otherwise." The former child star found this comment bitterly amusing. Cary, *Hollywood's Children*, 92.

14 Viviana A. Zelizer, *Pricing the Priceless Child: The Changing Social Value of Children* (Princeton, NJ: Princeton University Press, 1994), 95.

15 Susan Rae Applebaum, "*The Little Princess* Onstage in 1903: Its Historical Significance," *Theatre History Studies* 18 (1998): 71–72. In New York City, applications to the mayor's office for licenses for juvenile actors, which had been fewer than two hundred in 1896, spiked to over four thousand in 1903. Benjamin McArthur, "'Forbid Them Not': Child Actor Labor Laws and Political Activism in the Theatre," *Theatre Survey* 36, no. 2 (1995): 63–80.

16 A particularly formidable critic was Elbridge Gerry, longtime head of the New York Society for the Prevention of Cruelty to Children. See McArthur, "'Forbid Them Not,'" 66–67.

17 National Alliance for the Protection of Stage Children, *Stage Children of America* (New York: Times Building, [1911]), 5, 16, 8, 22.

18 I. A. Taylor, "The Show-Child: A Protest," *Living Age* 9 (1896): 113, 116; see also F. Zeta Youmans, "Childhood, Inc.," *Survey* 52 (1924): 464.

19 Educational Films continued until 1939.

20 The song may also have had roots in Yiddish theater. See Howard Pollack, *George Gershwin: His Life and Work* (Berkeley and Los Angeles: University of California Press, 2006), 44.

21 Rob Kapilow, interview by Susan Stamberg, "A Depression-Era Anthem for Our Times," National Public Radio, broadcast November 15, 2008.

22 Gary Giddins, *Bing Crosby: A Pocketful of Dreams* (Boston: Little, Brown, 2001), 305.

23 Film dialogue throughout this book is my own transcriptions.

24 Black, *Child Star*, 232–33; David Emblidge, ed., *My Day: The Best of Eleanor Roosevelt's Acclaimed Newspaper Columns, 1936–1962* (New York: Da Capo

Press, 2001), 27. Black notes that originally the bill made no exceptions with respect to age for children in films. She mistakenly says Roosevelt signed the bill on the day of her visit, June 24, 1938. So ludicrous did the idea of Shirley Temple as a child laborer seem in the mid-1930s that it was the subject of a humorous imaginary interview between the child star and Secretary of Labor Frances Perkins, in which Shirley says, "I don't work. I dance and sing and make faces." Corey Ford with illustration by Miguel Covarrubias, "Impossible Interview: Frances Perkins vs. Shirley Temple," *Vanity Fair*, September 1935, 33.

25 In this context, FDR has been frequently quoted by Shirley Temple Black and others as paying tribute to her cheering smile, saying, "When the spirit of the people is lower than at any other time during this Depression, it is a splendid thing that for just 15 cents, an American can go to a movie and look at the smiling face of a baby and forget his troubles." Lester David and Irene David, *The Shirley Temple Story* (New York: Putnam, 1983),16; Black, *Child Star*, 59; George F. Custen, *Twentieth Century's Fox: Darryl F. Zanuck and the Culture of Hollywood* (New York: Basic Books, 1997), 199. I have been unable to verify the quotation, however, and suspect that it is apocryphal.

26 The character of Cromwell was loosely modeled on Florenz Ziegfeld. In the script's earliest conception, Will Rogers was to play the secretary of laughter. Rian James, "Fox Follies, Rough First Draft," 3, n.d. [c. July 1, 1933], Twentieth Century–Fox Scripts Collection, Cinema Arts Library, University of Southern California, Los Angeles (hereafter USC). On restrictions of Roosevelt's likeness in films, see Ronald Brownstein, *The Power and the Glitter: The Hollywood-Washington Connection* (New York: Pantheon Books, 1990), 76–77. Later, FDR broke this policy for *Yankee Doodle Dandy* (Warner Bros., 1942), in which Roosevelt's voice is used and an actor impersonates him. Melvyn Douglas, "Number One Movie Fan," *New Republic*, April 15, 1946, 543.

27 Shirley Temple earlier made a very brief appearance in another Hollywood homage to the NRA, Paramount's *New Deal Rhythm* (1933).

28 Mae Tinee, review of *Stand Up and Cheer!*, *Chicago Tribune*, May 2, 1934, 17; review of *Stand Up and Cheer!*, *Boston Globe*, May 4, 1934, 41; Boyd Martin, review of *Stand Up and Cheer!*, *Louisville Courier-Journal*, July 5, 1934, 8; George Shaffer, "Film Reporters See Stardom for Girl of 4," *Chicago Tribune*, May 30, 1934, 28.

29 "Shirley Temple a Sensation; 'Little Miss Marker' Cashes," *Hollywood Reporter*, May 29, 1934, 7; review of *Stand Up and Cheer!*, *Time*, April 30, 1934, 28.

30 Steven J. Ross, "How Hollywood Became Hollywood: Money, Politics, and Movies," in *Metropolis in the Making: Los Angeles in the 1920s*, ed. Tom Sitton and William Deverell (Berkeley and Los Angeles: University of California Press, 2001), 258–64.

31 Douglas Gomery, *The Hollywood Studio System: A History*, rev. ed. (London: BFI, 2005), 74.

32 Gomery, *Hollywood Studio System*, 76; Gomery, *The Hollywood Studio System* (New York: St. Martin's Press, 1986), 84–85.

33 See the cinema attendance surveys in Hadley Cantril and Mildred Strunk, eds., *Public Opinion, 1935–1946* (Princeton, NJ: Princeton University Press, 1951), 486.

34 Kerry Segrave, *American Films Abroad: Hollywood's Domination of the World's Movie Screens from the 1890s to the Present* (Jefferson, NC: McFarland, 1997), 115; Thomas M. Pryor, "More on Foreign Quotas," *New York Times*, October 24, 1937, 168; Ruth Vasey, *The World According to Hollywood, 1918–1939* (Madison: University of Wisconsin Press, 1997), 145.

35 Tino Balio, *Grand Design: Hollywood as a Modern Business Enterprise, 1930–1939* (New York: Scribner's, 1993), 13–18; Robert Sklar, *Movie-Made America: A Social History of American Movies* (New York: Random House, 1975), 161; Douglas Gomery, *The Coming of Sound: A History* (New York: Routledge, 2005), 37–45, 115–16. Lary May calculates that "in six major cities, theaters failed at an average of 36 percent from 1930 to 1933." Lary May with the assistance of Stephen Lassonde, "Making the American

Way: Moderne Theatres, Audiences, and the Film Industry, 1929–1945," *Prospects* 12 (1987): 121 n. 8.

36 Daniel A. Lord, *Played by Ear: The Autobiography of Daniel A. Lord, S. J.* (Chicago: Loyola University Press, 1956), 295. The Payne Fund investigators were especially concerned that of those attending the movies on a given week on the eve of the Depression, nearly 36 percent were under twenty-one, and roughly half of these were fourteen or younger. Henry James Forman, "Movie Madness," *McCall's*, October 1932, 14–15, 28, 30. Among the many books and articles on the coming of the Hollywood Production Code, see especially Richard Maltby, "The Production Code and the Hays Office," in Balio, *Grand Design*, 37–72.

37 Maltby, "Production Code and the Hays Office," 37–72.

38 "Good Cheer Wanted," *Moving Picture World*, February 20, 1909, 196; Ian Jarvie and Robert L. Macmillan, "John Grierson on Hollywood's Success, 1927," *Historical Journal of Film, Radio and Television* 9, no. 3 (1989): 315–16.

39 Vasey, *World According to Hollywood*, 204–5.

40 Martin Quigley, *Motion Picture Herald*, February 22, 1936, as quoted in Vasey, *World According to Hollywood*, 205; Martin Quigley, "Radicalism—an Industry Peril," *Motion Picture Herald*, December 11, 1937, 18.

41 Cantril and Strunk, *Public Opinion*, 485.

42 John Trumpbour, *Selling Hollywood to the World: U.S. And European Struggles for Mastery of the Global Film Industry, 1920–1950* (Cambridge: Cambridge University Press, 2002), 227.

43 Margaret Farrand Thorp, *America at the Movies* (New Haven: Yale University Press, 1939), 2–3.

44 Lary May, *The Big Tomorrow: Hollywood and the Politics of the American Way* (Chicago: University of Chicago Press, 2000), 122.

45 May, *Big Tomorrow*, 122–24, 130–31; Kevin Corbett, "Bad Sound and Sticky Floors: An Ethnographic Look at the Symbolic Value of Historic Small-Town Movie Theaters," in *Hollywood in the Neighborhood: Histori-*

cal Case Studies of Local Moviegoing, ed. Kathryn Fuller-Seeley (Berkeley and Los Angeles: University of California Press, 2008), 241–44. Thorp noted that movie theaters specifically catering to African Americans amounted to only one for every twenty thousand people. Thorp, *America at the Movies*, 9.

46 Trumpbour, *Selling Hollywood to the World*, 73; Mirra Komarovsky, *The Unemployed Man and His Family: The Effect of Unemployment upon the Status of the Man in Fifty-Nine Families* (New York: Dryden Press, for the Institute of Social Research, 1940), 124, 127.

47 May, *Big Tomorrow*, 110–21, 127–28.

48 Black, *Child Star*, 33, 39, 330.

49 Black, *Child Star*, 80–81.

50 "Just Pretending Nets Shirley Temple $1,250 a Week," *Newsweek*, July 28, 1934, 24; Miguel Covarrubias, "Miss Shirley Temple Signs a New Contract," *Vanity Fair*, November 1934, 33.

51 Runyon's short story first appeared in *Collier's*, March 26, 1932, 7–9, 40, 43, 44. In an earlier dialogue script (February 24, 1934, pp. A17–19), Marthy's father speaks more like a racehorse tout. Cf. later dialogue in script of May 9, 1934, Paramount Pictures Scripts, Special Collections, MHL.

52 See Gary S. Cross, *The Cute and the Cool: Wondrous Innocence and Modern American Children's Culture* (New York: Oxford University Press, 2004).

53 Komarovsky, *Unemployed Man and His Family*, 27, 28.

54 Komarovsky, *Unemployed Man and His Family*, 41, 45.

55 Richard Lowitt and Maurine Hoffman Beasley, eds., *One Third of a Nation: Lorena Hickok Reports on the Great Depression* (Urbana: University of Illinois Press, 1981), 206–7.

56 On the success of *Baby Take a Bow*, see Douglas W. Churchill, "Taking a Look at the Record," *New York Times*, November 25, 1934, X5. Shirley Temple ranked eighth in the *Motion Picture Herald*'s 1934 annual survey of "The Ten Biggest Money Making Stars" in the period beginning September 1, 1933, and ending September 1, 1934, even though her first

major film, *Stand Up and Cheer!*, did not open until April 1934. See *1935–36 Motion Picture Almanac* (New York: Quigley Publishing, n.d.), 94.

57 "Shirley Temple Wins," *New York Times*, March 23, 1938, 18; Janet Shprintz, "Tarnishing Temple's Image," *Variety*, January 27, 2006, A7; Black, *Child Star*, 184–85. For more recent criticism in this vein, see Robert M. Polhemus, *Lot's Daughters: Sex, Redemption, and Women's Quest for Authority* (Stanford, CA: Stanford University Press, 2005), 253–80; Geraldine Pauling, "The Psychohistorical Significance of Shirley Temple Films: Images of the Sexualized Female Child in Relation to Depression Era Group Fantasy," *Journal of Psychohistory* 30, no. 3 (2003): 306–9; Ara Osterweil, "Reconstructing Shirley: Pedophilia and Interracial Romance in Hollywood's Age of Innocence," *Camera Obscura* 24, no. 3 72 (2009): 1–39. On the larger shift in attitudes and behavior, see Ian Hacking, "The Making and Molding of Child Abuse," *Critical Inquiry* 17, no. 2 (Winter 1991): 253–88.

58 Robert Eichberg, "Lines to a Little Lady," *Modern Screen*, February 1935, 48.

59 Review of *Bright Eyes*, *Motion Picture Daily*, November 23, 1934, 10.

60 From 1935 to 1940 Withers was one of Twentieth Century–Fox's top five most lucrative actors. Geoff Gehman, *Down but Not Quite Out in Hollowweird: A Documentary in Letters of Eric Knight* (Lanham, MD: Scarecrow Press, 1998), 25 n. 4.

61 See Mae Tinee, review of *Bright Eyes*, *Chicago Tribune*, December 23, 1934, pt. 7, 5; review of *Bright Eyes*, *Motion Picture Herald*, February 16, 1935, 69.

62 "Peewee's Progress," 40; Edward Foote Gardner, *Popular Songs of the Twentieth Century: A Charted History*, vol. 1, *Chart Detail & Encyclopedia, 1900–1949* (St. Paul, MN: Paragon House, 2000), 25, 216.

63 *Motion Picture Herald*, February 16, 1935, 69.

64 *Motion Picture Herald*, November 30, 1935, 85; December 19, 1936, 81; December 31, 1938, 60; December 30, 1939, 58.

65 On this scene and the larger issue of the affirmative role of commer-

cial culture, see Lawrence W. Levine, "The Folklore of Industrial Society: Popular Culture and Its Audiences," *American Historical Review* 97 (1992): 1369–99; T. J. Jackson Lears, "Making Fun of Popular Culture," ibid., 1417–26; Levine, "Levine Responds," ibid., 1427–30; and Joel Pfister, "Complicity Critiques," *American Literary History* 12, no. 3 (Fall 2000): 610–32.

CHAPTER THREE: DANCING ALONG THE COLOR LINE

1 "Cinema: Academy Awards," *Time*, March 11, 1935, 52.

2 Robinson also appeared in *Rebecca of Sunnybrook Farm* (1938) and *Just around the Corner* (1938). He devised the choreography but did not perform in *Dimples* (1936).

3 Among the many books on this topic, see esp. M. M. Manring, *Slave in a Box: The Strange Career of Aunt Jemima* (Charlottesville: University Press of Virginia, 1998); Grace Elizabeth Hale, *Making Whiteness: The Culture of Segregation in the South, 1890–1940* (New York: Pantheon, 1998); Ralph Ellison in conversation with Robert O'Meally, Robert G. O'Meally, "Checking Our Balances: Ellison on Armstrong's Humor," *boundary* 2 30, no. 2 (2003): 120.

4 Harvard Sitkoff, *A New Deal for Blacks: The Emergence of Civil Rights as a National Issue: The Depression Decade*, 30th anniv. ed. (New York: Oxford University Press, 2009), 44.

5 Sitkoff, *New Deal for Blacks*, 27–28, 42, 31, 71.

6 "Players Aid Roosevelt," *New York Times*, October 24, 1930, 15; Nanette Kutner, "Hollywood Friendship No. 1," *Modern Screen*, November 1936, 91; Bernice Patton, "The Sepia Side of Hollywood," *Pittsburgh Courier*, November 30, 1935, A6.

7 James Haskins and N. R. Mitgang, *Mr. Bojangles: The Biography of Bill Robinson* (New York: William Morrow, 1988), 106.

8 Haskins and Mitgang, *Mr. Bojangles*, 26–28, 42–44, 50–53.

9 Bushrod Barnum, "Bojangles," *Cue*, August 14, 1937, 35. In one of Rob-

inson's versions of the story, the soup was oyster stew, and an oyster went wriggling down the customer's neck. S. J. Woolf, "Bill Robinson, 60, Taps Out the Joy of Living," *New York Times*, May 22, 1938, 117. For the contention that Marty Forkins concocted the story, see Haskins and Mitgang, *Mr. Bojangles*, 95–96.

10 Haskins and Mitgang, *Mr. Bojangles*, 212.

11 Robinson first appeared in the short *Hello, Bill* (1929) and performed a specialty number in RKO's feature-length *Dixiana* (1930).

12 Robinson was voted "best dressed" man as well as favorite tap-dancer in a 1935 Harlem poll. Ted Yates, "This Is New York: Popularity Poll," *Afro-American*, May 11, 1935, 8. A white journalist noted with patronizing wonder Robinson's "primitive taste for fine feathers" and jewelry (Barnum, "Bojangles," 7).

13 The honorary title was conferred in 1934 by the New York League of Locality Mayors, an unofficial philanthropic and boosters organization. Richard Strouse, "At 70, Still Head Hoofer," *New York Times*, May 23, 1948, sec. SM, 17. The title was adopted by African American newspapers. See, for example, "Bill Robinson Is Mayor of Harlem, Hero of Broadway," *Chicago Defender*, July 6, 1935, 9.

14 Tommye Berry, "Kansas City Likes the Film, 'Hooray for Love,'" *Chicago Defender*, August 17, 1935, 8. Despite black moviegoers' approval, within the context of the storyline of *Hooray for Love*, "Living in a Great Big Way" is being performed for the entertainment of whites. The number is supposedly being rehearsed as part of the revue that the lead character, Doug Tyler (played by Gene Raymond) hopes to produce. The number begins with a parting of the theater curtains, and a quick shot in the middle of the number and a second at its conclusion furnish the approving seal of the white director and producer, a synecdoche for white approval in general.

15 Marshall Winslow Stearns and Jean Stearns, *Jazz Dance: The Story of American Vernacular Dance* (New York: Macmillan, 1968), 187. For rem-

iniscences of Robinson and his distinctive qualities as a dancer, see Rusty E. Frank, *Tap! The Greatest Tap Dance Stars and Their Stories, 1900– 1955* (New York: William Morrow, 1990), esp. 66, 72–73, 97–98, 180–82.

16 Bernice Patton, "Bill Robinson Overcame Two Broken Legs to Become Greatest Tap Dancer," *New Journal and Guide*, February 22, 1936, 18; Barnum, "Bojangles," 7; Woolf, "Bill Robinson," 117.

17 In Shirley Temple's 1936 film *Dimples*, to which Robinson contributed choreography, Frank Morgan's character blacks up as Uncle Tom to elude pursuers. The movie ends in a full-scale black minstrel number, with Stepin Fetchit as Mr. Bones. Will Rogers sparked protests from African Americans when on January 21, 1934, in a radio broadcast he repeatedly used the phrase "nigger spiritual," instead of "Negro spiritual" and "spiritual," the words he had prepared in his notes. The National Broadcasting Company (NBC), which carried Rogers's program, was immediately deluged with telegrams and telephone calls protesting the racial epithet. Roy Wilkins complained on behalf of the National Association for the Advancement of Colored People. Rogers defended his good intentions, saying, "If the colored race has a more sympathetic friend than I have always been, I don't know who it is." Steven K. Gragert and M. Jane Johansson, eds., *The Papers of Will Rogers*, vol. 5, *The Final Years* (Norman: University of Oklahoma Press, 2006), esp. 455–56, 460 n. 2, 461, quotation normalized from telegram style. Tali Mendelberg, *The Race Card: Campaign Strategy, Implicit Messages, and the Norm of Equality* (Princeton, NJ: Princeton University Press, 2001), 69; see also Taylor Branch, *Parting the Waters: America in the King Years, 1954–63* (New York: Simon & Schuster, 1988), 51.

18 Andre Sennwald, review of *The Littlest Rebel*, *New York Times*, December 20, 1935, 30.

19 "You Ain't Seen Nuthin Yet, Says Papa of Staircase Dance," *Pittsburgh Courier*, December 29, 1934, sec. A, 8; Woolf, "Bill Robinson," 117; James Haskins, *Black Dance in America: A History through Its People* (New York:

Crowell, 1990), 54; Constance Valis Hill, *Tap Dancing America: A Cultural History* (New York: Oxford University Press, 2010), 63–64. Cf. Robinson's staircase dance in *Harlem Is Heaven* (1932).

20 Here I adapt a phrase from Jacqui Malone, "Jazz Music in Motion: Dancers and Big Bands," in Robert G. O'Meally, ed., *The Jazz Cadence of American Culture* (New York: Columbia University Press, 1998), 284.

21 Shirley Temple Black, *Child Star: An Autobiography* (New York: McGraw-Hill, 1988), 91–93; Kutner, "Hollywood Friendship No. 1," 91; "Bill Sorry He Couldn't See Shirley," *Chicago Defender*, April 29, 1939, 21; Karen Chilton, *Hazel Scott: The Pioneering Journey of a Jazz Pianist from Café Society to Hollywood to HUAC* (Ann Arbor: University of Michigan Press, 2008), 73.

22 Haskins and Mitgang, *Mr. Bojangles*, 225–26; Black, *Child Star*, 92.

23 This scene was Fox Film's first venture into Technicolor. Douglas Gomery, *The Hollywood Studio System* (New York: St. Martin's Press, 1986), 95.

24 Andre Sennwald, review of *The Little Colonel*, *New York Times*, March 22, 1935, 26; *Motion Picture Herald*, May 4, 1935, 64; June 1, 1935, 69; July 6, 1935, 87; October 5, 1935, 59.

25 Sennwald, review of *Littlest Rebel*, 30.

26 Edward Peple, foreword to *The Littlest Rebel* (New York: Grosset and Dunlap, 1914); Edward Peple, *The Littlest Rebel: A Play in Four Acts* (London: Samuel French, 1911), 9.

27 Andre Sennwald, review of *So Red the Rose*, *New York Times*, November 28, 1935, 39.

28 Review of *The Littlest Rebel*, *Variety*, December 25, 1935, 15. Like *The Little Colonel* and Shirley Temple's film *Dimples*, *The Littlest Rebel* was notably popular in white southern theaters, such as those in Birmingham, Alabama. It was also the most profitable of Twentieth Century–Fox's films for the 1935–36 season. Gomery, *Hollywood Studio System*, 1986 ed., 93; Gomery, *The Hollywood Studio System: A History*, rev. ed. (London: BFI, 2005), 72.

29 Advertisement for Florence Mills Theatre, *Los Angeles Sentinel*, April 1936, as quoted in Karen Orr Vered, "White and Black in Black and White: Management of Race and Sexuality in the Coupling of Child-Star Shirley Temple and Bill Robinson," *Velvet Light Trap* No. 39 (1997): 52–65; Richard Lacayo and Sue Carswell, "Mocking Black Stereotypes, a Black Artist makes Waves," *People*, May 22, 1989, 151.

30 December 25, 1935, 15; *Littlest Rebel* script, September 6, 1935, 14, Lilly Library, Indiana University, Bloomington.

31 The role was conceived with Stepin Fetchit in mind. See "first draft screen play" by Edwin Burke, 19, August 6, 1935, Lilly Library.

32 Hill, *Tap Dancing America*, 122–23.

33 Review of *The Littlest Rebel*, *Atlanta Constitution*, January 26, 1936, sec. E, 7; "Shirley Goes Harlem—Learns to Truck," *Chicago Defender*, January 11, 1936, 8. The 26th edition of the Cotton Club Parade, produced by Ted Koehler and opening in July 1935, featured a "Truckin'" number. Robinson performed such a number at the Cocoanut Grove in Hollywood later that year. "Bill Robinson at 'Cocoanut Grove,'" *Chicago Defender*, December 14, 1935, 8.

34 *Littlest Rebel* script, September 6, 1935, 122, Lilly Library.

35 *Littlest Rebel* script, "first draft screen play" by Edwin Burke, August 6, 1935, Lilly Library; Raymond Griffith to Darryl Zanuck, August 8, 1935, 1, Zanuck Manuscript Collection, Lilly Library.

36 Woolf, "Bill Robinson," 116; Barnum, "Bojangles," 35.

37 Alain Locke, *The Negro and His Music* (1936; rpt. New York: Arno Press, 1969), 134, 135.

38 "'Bojangles' in a Fit of Temper as Hecklers Heckle 'Uncle Tom' Jokes," *Chicago Defender*, November 1, 1941, 6. See also "Boston Patron Blasts 'Bojangles,'" *Afro-American*, January 16, 1926, 4.

39 Ralph Matthews, "The Negro Theatre—a Dodo Bird," in *Negro: An Anthology*, ed. Nancy Cunard and Hugh D. Ford (1970; rpt. New York: Continuum, 1996), 196; Ralph Matthews, "Dixie Prejudice Still Dominates the Movies but Not the Stage," *Afro-American*, February 8, 1936, 8; Renzi B.

Lemus, "Uncle Tom Roles for Stars on Screen Beat a Blank, Points out Lemus," *Afro-American*, February 22, 1936, 11.

40 Earl J. Morris, "Morris Interviews 'Bojangles'; Learns He Is Real Race Man," *Pittsburgh Courier*, July 31, 1937, 21.

41 Paul Laurence Dunbar, "We Wear the Mask," in *Majors and Minors: Poems* (Toledo, OH: Hadley and Hadley, 1895), 21; Haskins and Mitgang, *Mr. Bojangles*, 28, 44; Stearns and Stearns, *Jazz Dance*, 184–85.

42 For an instance of Robinson's temper onstage, see the account of an incident in which Bill Robinson rebuked a party of white southern hecklers as he performed his dance, "Bill Robinson Gets 'Em Told," *Chicago Defender*, September 29, 1928, 6. Later, Robinson responded to young black hecklers of his "Uncle Tom" jokes. "'Bojangles' in a Fit of Temper," 6. For offstage altercations, see "Bojangles Stops 'Black Hitler' in Dispute," *Chicago Defender*, November 17, 1934, 4; "Bill Robinson Freed on Assault," *New York Times*, September 21, 1938, 26. On Robinson's Hollywood disagreements, see "Bojangles Sore about Way His Film Is Cut," *Afro-American*, May 18, 1935, 8. Later, he reportedly pulled a gun on Benny Carter, the musical director of the film *Stormy Weather*. James Gavin, *Stormy Weather: The Life of Lena Horne* (New York: Atria Books, 2009), 131.

43 St. Clair McKelway, "Bojangles," *The New Yorker*, October 6, 1934, 26–27, and October 13, 1934, 30; Calgary newspaper clipping as quoted in Haskins and Mitgang, *Mr. Bojangles*, 130.

44 Haskins and Mitgang, *Mr. Bojangles*, 130, 290.

45 Haskins and Mitgang, *Mr. Bojangles*, 222.

46 "Celebrities and 8 Miles of Crowds Pay Tribute to Bill Robinson," *New York Times*, November 29, 1949, 1, 25.

47 "Gives Bojangles Left-Handed Slap," *New York Amsterdam News*, December 3, 1949, 18; Christopher C. De Santis, ed., *Langston Hughes and the "Chicago Defender": Essays on Race, Politics, and Culture, 1942–62* (Urbana: University of Illinois Press, 1995), 207. See also Hughes's essay "Curtain Time," unpublished during his lifetime, in Christopher C. De Santis, ed.,

Essays on Art, Race, Politics, and World Affairs, vol. 9 of *The Collected Works of Langston Hughes* (Columbia: University of Missouri Press, 2002), esp. 296.

CHAPTER FOUR: THE MOST ADORED CHILD IN THE WORLD

1 Lyn Tornabene, "Here's Oprah," *Woman's Day*, October 1, 1986, 56.

2 Samantha Barbas, *Movie Crazy: Fans, Stars, and the Cult of Celebrity* (New York: Palgrave, 2001), 113; Shirley Temple and the editors of *Look*, *My Young Life* (Garden City, NY: Garden City Publishing, 1945), 9; Lin Yutang, "China and the Film Business," *New York Times*, November 8, 1936, X4; *Simplicissimus*, February 11, 1940, 72; Frank Kerr, "Shirley Temple," *Cavalcade* (New York: Film Daily, 1939), 292.

3 "Prime Minister Returns," *Nambour Chronicle*, August 23, 1935, 2; "Japanese Envoy's Tot Visits Shirley Temple," *Citizen News*, May 2, 1936, Clippings File–Shirley Temple, MHL; "Chilean Navy," *Los Angeles Herald*, March 13, 1936, Clippings File–Shirley Temple, MHL; "Russian Polar Flyers Meet Shirley Temple," *New York Times*, July 18, 1937, sec. N, 2; Shirley Temple Black, *Child Star: An Autobiography* (New York: McGraw-Hill, 1988), 134–35, 207–8; H. G. Wells quoted in Kirtley Baskette, "The Amazing Temple Family," *Photoplay*, April 1936, 16.

4 Black, *Child Star*, 87, 74, 206.

5 Dika Newlin, ed., *Schoenberg Remembered: Diaries and Recollections, 1938–76* (New York, Pendragon Press, 1980), 42.

6 "Movie Survey Shows Shirley Temple as Fans' Big Favorite," *Arkansas Gazette*, December 13, 1935, 24.

7 "Quarterly Survey IX," *Fortune* (July 1937), 103–4.

8 John Trumpbour, *Selling Hollywood to the World: U.S. and European Struggles for Mastery of the Global Film Industry, 1920–1950* (Cambridge: Cambridge University Press, 2002), 226; "Gabriel Washington [Pseud. for Gabriel Meyers]," interview by Charles A. Von Ohsen, February 22, 1939, and John and Lizzie Pierce, interview by I.L.M., September 23, 1938, *American Life Histories: Manuscripts from the Federal Writers' Proj-*

ect, 1936–1940, Library of Congress, Manuscript Division, WPA Federal Writers' Project Collection, Washington, DC.

9 Data compiled from U.S. government Social Security Administration website, http://www.ssa.gov/OACT/babynames/.

10 On women and movie culture and stars' personalities, see Barbas, *Movie Crazy*, 36–37, 61–65.

11 Barbas, *Movie Crazy*, 98; see also Margaret Farrand Thorp, *America at the Movies* (New Haven: Yale University Press, 1939), 86; Joshua Gamson, *Claims to Fame: Celebrity in Contemporary America* (Berkeley and Los Angeles: University of California Press, 1994), 11, 21.

12 "Shirley Entertains," *Los Angeles Times*, April 20, 1934, sec. 1, 13; "Eiga no Oujo" (The Princess of the Theater), *Yomiuri Shimbun*, Tokyo, September 23, 1934, special ed., 1.

13 Advertisement, *Atlanta Constitution*, April 21, 1936, 6; advertisement for Ideal Shirley Temple dolls, *Playthings*, March 1935, 3; Gary S. Cross, *Kids' Stuff: Toys and the Changing World of American Childhood* (Cambridge, MA: Harvard University Press, 1997), 117; "Greeting to Shirley," *Variety*, April 29, 1936, 21. For Shirley Temple birthday events at department stores, see E. Evalyn Grumbine, *Reaching Juvenile Markets* (New York: McGraw-Hill, 1938), 341, 387–88; Black, *Child Star*, 138–39.

14 "Shirley Observes 7th Natal Day by Taking Pony Ride," *Citizen News*, April 23, 1936, 36, Clippings File—Shirley Temple, MHL; unidentified newspaper clipping, possibly from *Los Angeles Herald*, January (?) 1936, Clippings File – Shirley Temple, MHL.

15 Even in spring 1933 during the depths of the Great Depression, newsstand sales of the leading fan magazines were impressive: *Modern Screen* 556,421; *Silver Screen* 471,806; *Photoplay* 461,842; *Motion Picture* 456,002; *Picture Play* 341,218; *Movie Classic* 326,852; *Screen Book* 267,573; *Screenland* 262,611; *Screen Play* 211,132; *Hollywood* 181,694; *Screen Romances* 137,141; plus three Tower movie magazines sold at Woolworth's with a combined estimated sales of 1,360,669. "Big Fan Magazine Drop," *Hollywood Reporter*, May 25, 1933, 1, 7; see also Frank Pope, "Trade Views," *Holly-*

wood Reporter, August 15, 1934, 1, 3; " '35 Space Grab in Fan Mags," *Variety*, January 1, 1936, 6; Anthony Slide, *Inside the Hollywood Fan Magazine: A History of Star Makers, Fabricators, and Gossip Mongers* (Jackson: University Press of Mississippi, 2010), 73–92, 122–43; Barbas, *Movie Crazy*, 89, 98–99.

16 Fox Film advertisement, *Motion Picture Herald*, May 19, 1934, 81. See also similar ads on 73, 75, 77, 79, and 83; Helen Hunt, "Is Hollywood Spoiling Shirley Temple?" *Movie Mirror*, October 1934, 10.

17 Frank H. Ricketson Jr., *The Management of Motion Picture Theatres* (New York: McGraw-Hill, 1938), esp. 23, 214.

18 "Baby Photos," *Variety*, August 7, 1934, 17; "Temple Doubles," *Variety*, May 1, 1935, 19; Alan Davies, *Sydney Exposures: Through the Eyes of Sam Hood and His Studio, 1925–1950* (Sydney: State Library of New South Wales, 1991), 21; see, e.g., advertisement for "Shirley Temple Competition," *Bombay Chronicle*, November 7, 1936, 5.

19 Juan de La Habana, "Las Shirley Temple Cubanas" (The Cuban Shirley Temples), *Carteles*, April 5, 1935, 38–39, 73; see also Louis A. Perez Jr., *On Becoming Cuban: Identity, Nationality, and Culture* (Chapel Hill: University of North Carolina Press, 2007), 300–301.

20 "Shirley Temple of France Here," *New York Times*, May 7, 1936, 25; "Paris 'Shirley' Snubs U.S. One," *Salt Lake Tribune*, May 15, 1936, 19.

21 "Nihon no Temupuru" (I'm Shirley Temple), *Asahi Shimbun*, Tokyo, January 24, 1936, morning ed., 11; "Kodomo wo Tane ni Sagi" (Child Actor Scam), *Asahi Shimbun*, Tokyo, June 18, 1937, morning ed., 13; "Tenpuruchan Ijouda" (More Popular than Temple), *Yomiuri Shimbun*, Tokyo, June 18, 1937, morning ed., 77.

22 "Shirley Temple Contest Engineered by Ed Hart," *Motion Picture Herald*, August 11, 1934, 60; on "personality development" in the 1930s, see Celia B. Stendler, "Psychologic Aspects of Pediatrics: Sixty Years of Child Training Practice: Revolution in the Nursery," *Journal of Pediatrics* 36 (1950):122–35, as cited in Daniel Thomas Cook, *The Commodification of Childhood: The Children's Clothing Industry and the Rise of the Child Con-*

sumer (Durham, NC: Duke University Press, 2004), 89; "Shirley Temple Gift Contest," *Silver Screen*, December 1936, 51.

23 Henry James Forman, *Our Movie Made Children* (New York: Macmillan, 1933), 141; Herbert Blumer, *Movies and Conduct* (New York: Macmillan, 1933), 17.

24 Frank, *Taps!*, 175.

25 A. J. Liebling, *The Telephone Booth Indian* (New York: Broadway Books, 2004), 63.

26 Eileen Bennetto, "Carefree," in *When I Was Ten: Memories of Childhood, 1905–1985*, ed. Len Fox and Hilarie Lindsay (New South Wales: Fellowship of Australian Writers, 1993), 216.

27 Ruth Kligman, *Love Affair* (New York: William Morrow, 1974), 165.

28 Kligman, *Love Affair*, 140–41.

29 Kligman, *Love Affair*, 141–42.

30 Dorothy Weil, *The River Home: A Memoir* (Athens: Ohio University Press, 2002), 44–45.

31 Kathy Plotkin, *The Pearson Girls: A Family Memoir of the Dakota Plains* (Fargo, ND: Institute for Regional Studies, 1998), 196.

32 Roddy Doyle, *Rory & Ita* (New York: Viking Press, 2002), 137–39. Cf. the longing to escape her father's sexual abuse, to become Shirley Temple, and the nun's condemnation, circa 1956, in Catherine McCall, *When the Piano Stops: A Memoir of Healing from Sexual Abuse* (Berkeley: Seal Press, 2009), 27–28.

33 Beatrice Muchman, *Never to Be Forgotten: A Young Girl's Holocaust Memoir* (Hoboken, NJ: KTAV Publishing House, 1997), 14, 65, 79.

34 Diary of Anne Frank, July 11, 1942, quoted in Hans Westra, *Inside Anne Frank's House: An Illustrated Journey through Anne's World* (Woodstock, NY: Overlook Duckworth, 2004), 72–73, 130 ; Stacey Morris, "Ghosts of Prinsengracht: A Tour of the Anne Frank House," *Jewish Daily Forward*, April 13, 2007, http://forward.com/articles/10481/ghosts-of-prinsen gracht/; see also Carol Ann Lee, *Roses from the Earth: The Biography of Anne Frank* (London: Viking, 1999), 76.

35 Barbas, *Movie Crazy*, 38–39, 52–53.

36 Diana Serra Cary, *Jackie Coogan: The World's Boy King: A Biography of Hollywood's Legendary Child Star* (Lanham, MD: Scarecrow Press, 2003), 62, 86–87.

37 Grumbine, *Reaching Juvenile Markets*, 6; on the transformation of marketing to children in this period, see Cook, *Commodification of Childhood*, esp. 66.

38 Lisa Jacobson, *Raising Consumers: Children and the American Mass Market in the Early Twentieth Century* (New York: Columbia University Press, 2004), 46; Grumbine, *Reaching Juvenile Markets*, 288–90, 21–22, 32–53.

39 Grumbine, *Reaching Juvenile Markets*, 17, 28, 21.

40 Albert Darver, *Children's and Infants' Wear*, May 1937, as quoted in Grumbine, *Reaching Juvenile Markets*, 354–55.

41 Grumbine, *Reaching Juvenile Markets*, 387–88, 357.

42 Grumbine, *Reaching Juvenile Markets*, 342–44, 346, 351, 109, 6–7.

43 Grumbine, *Reaching Juvenile Markets*, 6–7; Quaker Oats advertisement, *Ladies' Home Journal*, April 1937, 119. For an example of a Quaker Oats advertisement directed to the mother's point of view, see the October 1937 advertisement "Suppose Shirley Temple were your little girl . . ." reproduced in Grumbine, *Reaching Juvenile Markets*, 290.

44 Grumbine, *Reaching Juvenile Markets*, 26; *Ladies' Home Journal*, September 1936, Clippings File—Shirley Temple, MHL; advertisement, *Parents Magazine*, April 1936, author's collection.

45 Grumbine, *Reaching Juvenile Markets*, 387–88.

46 "Conference with Mr. Zanuck [on Temporary Script of Jan. 19, 1938]," January 24, 1938, *Little Miss Broadway*, Twentieth Century–Fox Scripts Collection, Cinema Arts Library, USC.

47 *Pictorial Review*, June 1935, 20, as quoted in Cook, *Commodification of Childhood*, 92.

48 Boris Emmet and John E. Jeuck, *Catalogues and Counters: A History of Sears, Roebuck and Company* (Chicago: University of Chicago Press, 1950),

5; see also Sanford M. Jacoby, *Modern Manors: Welfare Capitalism since the New Deal* (Princeton: Princeton University Press, 1997), 99–101; Sears, Roebuck catalog, Fall/Winter 1935, 75; on the Sears catalog as a wish book, see Harry Crews, *A Childhood: The Biography of a Place* (New York: Harper & Row, 1978), 54.

49 "Morris Michtom, 68, Toy Manufacturer," *New York Times*, July 22, 1938, 17; Flossie Flirt doll advertisement, Sears, Roebuck catalog, Fall/Winter 1926–27, 652.

50 *Playthings*, October 1934, 6; *Playthings*, November 1934, 3.

51 Tonya Bervaldi-Camaratta, *The Complete Guide to Shirley Temple Dolls and Collectibles* (Paducah, KY: Collector Books, 2007), 6–7; Ian Fleming, *Powerplay: Toys as Popular Culture* (Manchester, UK: Manchester University Press, 1996), 40.

52 *Playthings*, April 1935, 13; Bervaldi-Camaratta, *Complete Guide to Shirley Temple Dolls*, 20, 25.

53 Bervaldi-Camaratta, *Complete Guide to Shirley Temple Dolls*, 92.

54 Ann Reebok, transcript 36, September 15, 1987, 7, 8; Joanne Wasenske, transcript 47, September 29, 1987, 24, 3; Lois Green-Stone, transcript 53, October 12, 1987, 16; Esther Zannie, transcript 35, September 14, 1987, 3, 4, Doll Oral History Project, Brian Sutton-Smith Library and Archives of Play, The Strong, Rochester, NY.

55 "200 Letters Show Shirley Temple's Grip on Children," *Motion Picture Herald*, February 16, 1935, 54. For an instance of a contest in which children colored a drawing, see "Concursa Shirley Temple" (Shirley Temple Competition), *Bohemia*, [Havana, Cuba], August 4, 1935, 27.

56 Robert Cohen, ed., *"Dear Mrs. Roosevelt": Letters from Children of the Great Depression* (Chapel Hill: University of North Carolina Press, 2002), 187–88.

57 Cohen, *"Dear Mrs. Roosevelt,"* 188–90.

58 See D. W. Winnicott, *Playing and Reality* (London: Routledge, 1971). Lisa Jacobson speaks of consumer envy in *Raising Consumers*, 7.

59 Bervaldi-Camaratta, *Complete Guide to Shirley Temple Dolls*, 78.

60 Bervaldi-Camaratta, *Complete Guide to Shirley Temple Dolls*, 60; Black, *Child Star*, 85.

61 Frank Dillon, "Shirley Temple, Saver of Lives," *Modern Screen*, December 1935, 26–27, 78–79.

CHAPTER FIVE: KEEPING SHIRLEY'S STAR ALOFT

1 This phrase was popularized by Hortense Powdermaker, *Hollywood, the Dream Factory: An Anthropologist Looks at the Movie-Makers* (Boston: Little, Brown, 1950).

2 "Amicable Settlement," *Time*, July 29, 1935, 46.

3 "All Fox Producers Fighting for Shirley," *Variety*, October 22, 1934, 3; Aubrey Solomon, *Twentieth Century–Fox: A Corporate and Financial History* (Metuchen, NJ: Scarecrow Press, 1988), 217.

4 Shirley Temple Black, *Child Star: An Autobiography* (New York: McGraw-Hill, 1988), 36; "Amicable Settlement," 46; Geoff Gehman, ed., *Down but Not Quite Out in Hollow-weird: A Documentary in Letters of Eric Knight* (Lanham, MD: Scarecrow Press, 1998), 11, 21.

5 Alva Johnston, "The Wahoo Boy," *The New Yorker*, November 10, 1934, 24–25; George F. Custen, *Twentieth Century's Fox: Darryl F. Zanuck and the Culture of Hollywood* (New York: Basic Books, 1997), 10–11, 173. I have drawn on Johnston's two-part profile (November 10 and 17, 1934) and Custen's book for much of the following material on Zanuck.

6 Quoted in Johnston, "Wahoo Boy," November 17, 1934, 27.

7 Johnston, "Wahoo Boy," November 17, 1934, 25; Custen, *Twentieth Century's Fox*, 251.

8 Custen estimates the costs as between $200,000 and $400,000 (*Twentieth Century's Fox*, 207). Aubrey Solomon agrees with the larger point, although his estimates of costs are between $400,000 and $700,000 (*Twentieth Century–Fox*, 29).

9 Custen, *Twentieth Century's Fox*, 211.

10 Cartoon, *The New Yorker*, April 13, 1935, 29. For criticisms of the subject

matter of *Little Miss Marker* and *Baby Take a Bow*, see "What the Picture Did for Me," *Motion Picture Herald*, September 8, 1934, 50; September 22, 1934, 49; October 13, 1934, 82; October 20, 1934, 65; October 27, 1934, 69; November 10, 1934, 63; November 17, 1934, 67; December 8, 1934, 75; December 15, 1934, 60; "Reich Bans 'Baby Take a Bow,'" *New York Times*, September 13, 1934, 26.

11 See Gary S. Cross, *The Cute and the Cool: Wondrous Innocence and Modern American Children's Culture* (New York: Oxford University Press, 2004); Lori Merish, "Cuteness and Commodity Aesthetics: Tom Thumb and Shirley Temple," in *Freakery: Cultural Spectacles of the Extraordinary Body*, ed. Rosemarie Garland Thomson (New York: New York University Press, 1996), 185–203.

12 Cross, *Cute and the Cool*, 60–61, 69–70.

13 Konrad Lorenz, "Part and Parcel in Animal and Human Societies," in *Studies in Animal and Human Behaviour* (Cambridge, MA: Harvard University Press, 1970), 2:154; Michael C. LaBarbera, "The Biology of B-Movie Monsters," 2003, *Fathom Archive*, http://fathom.lib.uchicago.edu/2/21701757/; Merish, "Cuteness and Commodity Aesthetics," 187.

14 Tino Balio, *Grand Design: Hollywood as a Modern Business Enterprise, 1930–1939* (New York: Scribner's, 1993), 97.

15 Black, *Child Star*, 116, 211.

16 Black, *Child Star*, 20; "While Shirley Plays in Her Sandbox," *Motion Picture Herald*, July 21, 1934, 18; "[Shirley] Temple's Physical Condition," *Screen Guide*, undated article [1938], Shirley Temple scrapbook, vol. 1, Constance McCormick Collection, USC; "*Life* Goes to Shirley Temple's Birthday Party," *Life*, May 15, 1944, 116–18, 121.

17 The first three Shirley Temple films in which Treacher appeared, in each case playing a butler or valet, were *Curly Top*, *Stowaway*, and *Heidi*.

18 Around 1936 an English newspaper reported that Shirley Temple was a thirty-year-old "midget" with two children. Shirley Temple Black, "Tomorrow I'll Be Thirty," *Good Housekeeping*, November 1957, 134; "Peewee's Progress," *Time*, April 27, 1936, 37. In 1937 Silvio Masante, a Sac-

ramento pastor and special correspondent for the Vatican newspaper *Osservatore Romano*, interviewing Shirley Temple and her mother, told them, "In Italy as in other countries in Europe there is the persistent rumor that Shirley Temple is no child at all; but that she is a midget." He thought that the rumor "was so vigorously spread, because many of the common people are unable to understand how such a child could do as many different things as Shirley does in her pictures." George Shaffer, "Shirley Temple Interviewed by Papal Journal," *Chicago Daily Tribune*, March 2, 1937, 14; see also Edith Lindeman, "The Real Miss Temple," *Richmond Times-Dispatch*, October 31, 1937, Sunday magazine sec., 7; and Michael Jackson, "Protecting the Future of the Greatest Little Star," *Photoplay*, March 1937, 27.

19 A. H. Saxon, *P. T. Barnum: The Legend and the Man* (New York: Columbia University Press, 1989), 124–30; P. T. Barnum, *The Life of P. T. Barnum, Written by Himself* (New York: Redfield, 1855), 263. The link between Shirley Temple and the exhibition of people with dwarfism is insightfully developed in Merish, "Cuteness and Commodity Aesthetics." The comic confusion between Shirley and a diminutive adult was made explicit in *Little Miss Broadway* (1938), in which a detective confuses her character with that of Olive Brasno, an actress with proportional dwarfism.

20 Review of *Baby Take a Bow*, *New York Times*, June 30, 1934, 17.

21 "*Dimples* conference with Mr. Zanuck," December 9, 1935, 8, Twentieth Century–Fox Scripts Collection, USC.

22 On her dimples, see Black, *Child Star*, 141.

23 Black, *Child Star*, 141, 142.

24 Review of *Dimples*, *Time*, October 19, 1936, 80–82; Frank S. Nugent, review of *Dimples*, *New York Times*, October 10, 1936, 21.

25 Nugent, review of *Dimples*, 21.

26 Review of *Dimples*, *Variety*, October 14, 1936, 15.

27 "What the Picture Did for Me," *Motion Picture Herald*, December 5, 1936, 6; January 2, 1937, 92.

28 "Conference with Mr. Zanuck on Treatment of July 25, 1936," and Zanuck's

notes on treatment outline of *Wee Willie Winkie* by Howard Ellis Smith, July 30, 1936, Twentieth Century–Fox Scripts Collection, USC.

29 Mel Gussow, *Don't Say Yes until I Finish Talking: A Biography of Darryl F. Zanuck* (Garden City, NY: Doubleday, 1970), 70.

30 Black, *Child Star*, 169–77, 179–80.

31 Review of *Wee Willie Winkie*, *Time*, July 19, 1937, 44; Howard Barnes, review of *Wee Willie Winkie*, *New York Herald Tribune*, July 24, 1937, 4.

32 "What the Picture Did for Me," *Motion Picture Herald*, November 27, 1937, 74; September 25, 1937, 64; December 25, 1937, 50.

33 "What the Picture Did for Me," *Motion Picture Herald*, December 4, 1937, 66; November 13, 1937, 74; January 15, 1938, 59; August 20, 1938, 60; October 23, 1937, 79; February 5, 1938, 73.

34 Peter Bogdanovich, *Allan Dwan: The Last Pioneer* (New York: Praeger, 1971), 108.

35 Howard Barnes, review of *Heidi*, *New York Herald Tribune*, November 6, 1937, 8.

36 "What the Picture Did for Me," *Motion Picture Herald*, February 12, 1938, January 1, 1938, 45.

37 "Conference with Mr. Zanuck," June 24, 1937; "Conference with Mr. Zanuck," July 7, 1937, *Rebecca of Sunnybrook Farm*, Twentieth Century–Fox Scripts Collection, USC.

38 Alexander Kahn, "Shirley Temple's Coiffure Taxes Filmdom's Brains," *Washington Post*, December 5, 1937, sec. TS, 1.

39 Review of *Rebecca of Sunnybrook Farm*, *Variety*, March 9, 1938, 14; Frank S. Nugent, review of *Rebecca of Sunnybrook Farm*, *New York Times*, March 26, 1938, 12.

40 Review of *Rebecca of Sunnybrook Farm*, *Motion Picture Daily*, March 9, 1938, 4.

41 W.R.W. [William R. Weaver], review of *Rebecca of Sunnybrook Farm*, *Motion Picture Herald*, March 12, 1938, 36–39.

42 Review of *Rebecca of Sunnybrook Farm*, *Time*, March 21, 1938, 42.

43 Ed Sullivan, "Looking at Hollywood: Zanuck in Person," *Chicago Daily*

Tribune, November 12, 1937, 19; "Conference with Mr. Zanuck," January 24, 1938, *Little Miss Broadway*, Twentieth Century–Fox Scripts Collection, USC.

44 William R. Weaver, review of *Little Miss Broadway*, *Motion Picture Herald*, July 9, 1938, 2, 8.

45 "What the Picture Did for Me," *Motion Picture Herald*, October 15, 1938, 47.

46 "What the Picture Did for Me," *Motion Picture Herald*, November 12, 1938, 58.

47 "What the Picture Did for Me," *Motion Picture Herald*, October 22, 1938, 55; August 13, 1938, 8.

48 Solomon, *Twentieth Century–Fox*, 218.

49 *Just around the Corner*, Twentieth Century–Fox Scripts Collection, USC. The phrase "just around the corner" achieved still greater currency after Irving Berlin incorporated it into his famous song "Let's Have Another Cup of Coffee" (1932).

50 William R. Weaver, review of *Just around the Corner*, *Motion Picture Herald*, November 5, 1938, 36, 38.

51 Frank S. Nugent, review of *Just around the Corner*, *New York Times*, December 3, 1938, 11.

52 Howard Barnes, review of *Just around the Corner*, *New York Herald Tribune*, December 3, 1938, 8.

53 "What the Picture Did for Me," *Motion Picture Herald*, January 7, 1939, 46.

54 Black, *Child Star*, 221.

55 Black, *Child Star*, 255.

56 Darryl F. Zanuck, signed advertisement, *New York Times*, March 9, 1939, 19. Film costs are notoriously difficult to calculate accurately, especially in this period. Shirley Temple Black reports the cost of *The Little Princess* as $1.3 million, six times the budget of her early movies for Fox. Black, *Child Star*, 252. Aubrey Solomon reports the cost of *Stowaway* at

$500,000, *Heidi* at $600,000, *The Little Princess* at $700,000, and *The Blue Bird* at $1,000,000. Solomon, *Twentieth Century–Fox*, 240.

57 Nelson Bell, review of *The Little Princess*, *Washington Post*, March 24, 1939, 12; Mae Tinee, review of *The Little Princess*, *Chicago Daily Tribune*, March 22, 1939, 15.

58 Black, *Child Star*, 263.

59 Review of *Susannah of the Mounties*, *Time*, July 3, 1939, 37; review of *Susannah of the Mounties*, *Variety*, June 21, 1939, 16; Frank S. Nugent, review of *Susannah of the Mounties*, *New York Times*, June 24, 1939, 20.

60 What the Picture Did for Me," *Motion Picture Herald*, August 26, 1939, 78; September 9, 1939, 67; September 23, 1939, 62.

61 Black, *Child Star*, 274, 277.

62 Hubbard Keavy, "Shirley Temple at Crucial Stage in Her Career," [Baltimore] *Sun*, July 30, 1939, sec. SM, 6; "Studio Pays $200,000 for New Movie Stories to Put Shirley over Age Barrier (She's 10!)," *Atlanta Constitution*, July 30, 1939, 12.

63 Keavy, "Shirley Temple at Crucial Stage," 6.

64 Black, *Child Star*, 274–75. Black quotes Zanuck's remark that "specialists never last long" but omits his additional remark that she was "the exception to the rule."

65 "20th Outbids Disney for Bluebird," *Variety*, April 26, 1939, 5; Maurice Maeterlinck, *The Blue Bird: A Fairy Play in Five Acts*, trans. Alexander Teixeira de Mattos (London: Methuen, 1910).

66 Black, *Child Star*, 288 (ellipses in original).

67 Black, *Child Star*, 289–90.

68 Black, *Child Star*, 291.

69 Black, *Child Star*, 289.

70 "'Blue Bird' Lures Industry's Top Executives to Premiere," *Motion Picture Daily*, January 20, 1940, 1, 9; Black, *Child Star*, 292.

71 Edwin Schallert, review of *The Blue Bird*, *Los Angeles Times*, January 20, 1940, sec. A, 7.

72 Review of *The Blue Bird, Motion Picture Herald*, January 27, 1940, 50.

73 Howard Barnes, review of *The Blue Bird, New York Herald Tribune*, January 20, 1940, 6; Schallert, review of *The Blue Bird*, 7.

74 Frank S. Nugent, review of *The Blue Bird, New York Times*, January 20, 1940, 15; Nugent, review of *The Wizard of Oz, New York Times*, August 18, 1939, 16.

75 "What the Picture Did for Me," *Motion Picture Herald*, April 20, 1940, 51; April 27, 1940, 71; May 25, 1940, 59 ; August 24, 1940, 74.

76 Rudy Behlmer, ed., *Memo from Darryl F. Zanuck: The Golden Years at Twentieth Century–Fox* (New York: Grove Press, 1993), 36

77 Behlmer, *Memo from Darryl F. Zanuck*, 36–37.

78 Black, *Child Star*, 298–99.

79 Grant Hayter-Menzies, *Charlotte Greenwood* (Jefferson, NC: Macfarland, 2007), 8.

80 "Shirley Temple Leaving Screen, Mother States," *New York Times*, May 12, 1940, 47; "Shirley Temple, 11, Leaves Film Stage," *New York Times*, May 13, 1940, 16.

81 Howard Barnes, review of *Young People, New York Herald Tribune*, August 24, 1940, 6; Richard L. Coe, review of *Young People, Washington Post*, August 31, 1940, 14.

82 Bosley Crowther, review of *Young People, New York Times*, August 24, 1940, 16.

83 "What the Picture Did for Me," *Motion Picture Herald*, October 19, 1940, 61; November 23, 1940, 58.

CHAPTER SIX: WHAT'S A PRIVATE LIFE?

1 Julia Grant, *Raising Baby by the Book: The Education of American Mothers* (New Haven: Yale University Press, 1998), esp. 115, 153.

2 Amy Gajda, "What if Samuel D. Warren Hadn't Married a Senator's Daughter? Uncovering the Press Coverage That Led to 'The Right to Privacy,'" *Michigan State Law Review*, Spring 2008, 36–60.

3 Samuel Warren and Louis Brandeis, "The Right to Privacy," *Harvard Law Review* 4 (December 15, 1890): 195, 196, 206.

4 Warren I. Susman, "Personality and the Making of Twentieth-Century Culture," in *Culture as History: The Transformation of American Society in the Twentieth Century* (New York: Pantheon, 1984), esp. 277, 280, 282–84.

5 Ida Zeitlin, "The Private Life of Shirley Temple," *Modern Screen*, June 1939, 34.

6 Samantha Barbas, *Movie Crazy: Fans, Stars, and the Cult of Celebrity* (New York: Palgrave, 2001), 19–20. The quotations are from an IMP advertisement in *Moving Picture World*, as quoted in Barbas, 19; and "Ovation for Film Star at Union Station," *St. Louis Times*, March 26, 1910, 3.

7 Barbas, *Movie Crazy*, 169; Alexander Woollcott, "The Strenuous Honeymoon," *Everybody's Magazine*, November 1920, 36.

8 "Crowd Surges at Theater," *Los Angeles Times*, January 27, 1923, II1.

9 Barbas, *Movie Crazy*, 169–70; "Many Injured in Crush to View Valentino Bier," [Baltimore] *Sun*, August 25, 1926, 1; "Thousands in Riot at Valentino Bier, More than 100 Hurt," *New York Times*, August 25, 1926, 1, 3.

10 Harold Hefferman, "Hollywood Today: Shirley Temple Hidden by Thoughtless Stars," *Atlanta Constitution*, July 5, 1937, 11.

11 Marsha Oregeron, *Hollywood Ambitions: Celebrity in the Movie Age* (Middletown, CT: Wesleyan University Press, 2008), 102; Barbas, *Movie Crazy*, 31, 138.

12 Gertrude Temple, "Bringing Up Shirley," *American Magazine*, February 1935, 92; Shirley Temple Black, *Child Star: An Autobiography* (New York: McGraw-Hill, 1988), 51. On fan letters and the movies, see Barbas, *Movie Crazy*, passim; on letters from radio listeners expressing personal bonds with radio personalities, see Bruce Lenthall, *Radio's America: The Great Depression and the Rise of Modern Mass Culture* (Chicago: University of Chicago Press, 2007), 68–76.

13 Robert Eichberg, "Lines to a Little Lady," *Modern Screen*, February 1935,

48, 74ff.; "Deluge of Mail Surprises Tiny Shirley Temple," *Washington Post*, December 16, 1934, MB2.

14 Temple, "Bringing Up Shirley," 92; Thornton Sargent, "New Slant on Shirley!" *Screenland*, March 1935, 82.

15 "Crowds End Vacation of Film Child," *Los Angeles Times*, August 25, 1934, A1.

16 Sargent, "New Slant on Shirley!" 81; Rod MacLean, "Letters," *Time*, August 20, 1934, 6; "Shirley Temple Draws to 2 Kinds of Windows," *Variety*, July 24, 1934, 1.

17 Black, *Child Star*, 59, 51; Sargent, "New Slant on Shirley!" 82; Dorothy Calhoun, "Shirley Temple—One Year Later," *Movie Classic*, July 1935, 66.

18 David Gebhard and Robert Winter, *A Guide to Architecture in Los Angeles & Southern California* (Santa Barbara, CA: Peregrine Smith, 1977, 104; Black, *Child Star*, 120; "Shirley Temple Home Listed for $1.75 Million," *Los Angeles Times*, April 23, 1983, L1.

19 Anne Edwards, *Shirley Temple: American Princess* (New York: William Morrow, 1988), 87.

20 Black, *Child Star*, 121, 115–16.

21 Stanley Hamilton, *Machine Gun Kelly's Last Stand* (Lawrence: University Press of Kansas, 2003), 9–11; Black, *Child Star*, 121, 115–16, 80, 116–18.

22 Paula Fass, *Kidnapped: Child Abduction in America* (New York: Oxford University Press, 1997), 119–21, 125–26.

23 Fass, *Kidnapped*, 99; interview with Maurice Sendak, *NOW with Bill Moyers*, March 12, 2004, http://billmoyers.com/content/author-and-illustrator-maurice-sendak/; "Maurice Sendak, Author of Splendid Nightmares, Dies at 83," *New York Times*, May 9, 2012, A1. Among the many books on the Lindbergh case, see esp. Lloyd C. Gardner, *The Case That Never Dies: The Lindbergh Kidnapping* (New Brunswick, NJ: Rutgers University Press, 2004).

24 On this point, see Fass, *Kidnapped*, 6–8, 51–56, 127–29, and passim. The phrase "public property" appears on p. 51. On ransom kidnapping in the 1920s and 1930s, see Ernest Kahlar Alix, *Ransom Kidnapping in America*,

1874–1974: The Creation of a Capital Crime (Carbondale: Southern Illinois University Press, 1978), 38–124.

25 Kathleen Norris, "Novelist Sketches the Trial Scene," *New York Times*, January 3, 1935, late city ed., 4; see also Fass, *Kidnapped*, 126.

26 Although released in 1936, *Poor Little Rich Girl* had its first prepared treatment in October 1934. Kidnapping was an element from early on. See *Poor Little Rich Girl*, Twentieth Century–Fox Script Files, USC.

27 For threats to Withers and Bartholomew, see, for example, "Reveal Freddie Bartholomew Is Threat Target," *Chicago Daily Tribune*, November 28, 1936, 1; "Jane Withers Threatened in $50,000 Demand," *Chicago Daily Tribune*, December 31, 1936, 3

28 "$25,000 Demand on Child Star's Father Admitted," *Illinois Daily News*, August 1, 1936, Clippings File—Shirley Temple, MHL; "Arrested in Threat to Shirley Temple," *New York Times*, August 1, 1936, 30; "Shirley Temple Threatened in Plea of Guilty," [Hollywood?] *Citizen* [*News?*], August 3, 1936, Clippings File—Shirley Temple, MHL; "Youth Free under Bond in Shirley Temple Plot," *Los Angeles Times*, August 2, 1936, Clippings File—Shirley Temple, MHL; "Boy Pleads Guilty in Temple Threat," [Baltimore] *Sun*, August 2, 1936, 6.

29 "Boy Admits Threats to Shirley Temple," *New York Times*, September 16, 1936, 52; "Youth Blames Movie for Shirley Threat," unidentified clipping, September 16, 1936, Clippings File—Shirley Temple, MHL; Black, *Child Star*, 148–49. The film that inspired the plot was apparently *Thirteen Hours by Air* (Paramount, 1936).

30 Black, *Child Star*, 148–49.

31 "Shirley Temple in Peril," *New York Times*, August 12, 1935, 10; Black, *Child Star*, 109–13.

32 "Surging Crowd Greets Shirley Temple Here," *Boston Globe*, August 4, 1938, 1, 8; Black, *Child Star*, 244–47.

33 Black, *Child Star*, 293–95.

34 "The Story behind Shirley Temple's Amazing Career," *Screen Book*, August 1934, 42, 63, 67; Edith Lindeman, "The Real Miss Temple," *Richmond*

Times-Dispatch, October 31, 1937, Sunday magazine sec., 6–7; Dorothy Spensley, "The Life and Loves of Shirley Temple," *Motion Picture*, July 1936, 34–35, 78; Zeitlin, "Private Life of Shirley Temple." See also Berta A. de Martínez Márquez, "Esta es la historia de Shirley Temple," *Bohemia* [Havana, Cuba], May 12, 1935, 8, 9, 66, 80.

35 "Child Actors and the Law," *New York Times*, December 23, 1934, X4; Edwards, *Shirley Temple*, 77–78; "Peewee's Progress," 88.

36 Lester David and Irene David, *The Shirley Temple Story* (New York: Putnam, 1983, 97–98; "Acting Points Given Cooper by Shirley Temple," *Los Angeles Times*, September 1, 1934, 5; George Hurrell and Whitney Stine, *The Hurrell Style: 50 Years of Photographing Hollywood* (New York: John Day, 1976), 126.

37 "Biography of Shirley Temple," Fox Film, March 1935, Clippings File— Shirley Temple, MHL. On the legend of Lana Turner's discovery, see Jib Fowles, *Starstruck: Celebrity Performers and the American Public* (Washington, DC: Smithsonian Institution Press, 1992), 60.

38 "The Story behind Shirley Temple's Amazing Career," *Screen Book*, August 1934, 42, 63, 67; Gladys Hall, telegram to Lester Grady, May 20, 1936, Gladys Hall Papers, MHL.

39 Rosalind Shaffer, "The Private Life of Shirley Temple, Wonder Child of the Screen," *Chicago Daily Tribune*, September 9, 1934, G1ff.; Black, *Child Star*, 55–57. On breaches of requisite rest and instructional periods for child film actors, see Diana Serra Cary, *Hollywood's Children: An Inside Account of the Child Star Era* (Dallas: Southern Methodist University Press, 1997), 224.

40 Ida Zeitlin, "A Day on the Set with Shirley," *Screenland*, September 1936, 78; Thornton Martin, "Miracle Moppet," *Ladies' Home Journal*, February 1938, 22.

41 "More Fun," *Modern Screen*, May 1935, 51; "Summer's the Time for Fun," *Modern Screen*, July 1936, 8; "From Eight to Eight with Shirley," *Modern Screen*, March 1936, 42–43; "[Shirley] Temple's Physical Condition,"

Screen Guide, n.d. 1938, in Shirley Temple scrapbook, vol. 1, Constance McCormick Collection, USC.

42 Joshua Gamson, *Claims to Fame: Celebrity in Contemporary America* (Berkeley: University of California Press, 1994), 28–32.

43 See, for example, Temple, "Bringing Up Shirley," 22–27, 92–94; Gertrude Temple, as told to Mary Sharon, *How I Raised Shirley Temple* (Akron, OH: Saalfield, 1935, first pub. in *Silver Screen*); Gertrude Temple, "Shirley Temple" (excerpted version of "How I Raised Shirley Temple" trans. into Spanish), *Bohemia* [Havana, Cuba], March 3, 1935, 6, 7, 59, 60, 64; Constance J. Foster, "Mrs. Temple on Bringing Up Shirley," *Parents Magazine*, October 1938, 22–23. In one national survey in the early 1930s, 91 percent of mothers and 65 percent of fathers from professional classes reported reading child-rearing advice in newspapers and magazines. Lisa Jacobson, *Raising Consumers: Children and the American Mass Market in the Early Twentieth Century* (New York: Columbia University Press, 2004), 174.

44 Helen Hunt, "Is Hollywood Spoiling Shirley Temple?" *Movie Mirror*, October 1934, 94; Temple, "Bringing Up Shirley," 92; Dixie Wilson, "The Answer to Shirley Temple's Future," *Photoplay*, November 1937, 26.

45 Dorothy Cocks, "Beauty Secrets of a Star," *Pictorial Review*, May 1936, 65; Lindeman, "Real Miss Temple," 6.

46 Black, *Child Star*, 145.

47 David and David, *Shirley Temple Story*, 100–101; Black, *Child Star*, 48. Black says that Hall tried to trick her into thinking that her mother was truly gone.

48 Black, *Child Star*, 517, 7; Robert Windeler, *The Films of Shirley Temple* (Secaucus, NJ: Citadel Press, 1978), 38.

49 Hunt, "Is Hollywood Spoiling Shirley Temple?" 11.

50 Benzion Liber, *The Child and the Home: Essays on the Rational Bringing-up of Children*, 2nd ed. (New York: Rational Living, 1923), 74; Temple, "Bringing Up Shirley," 22–27, 92–94; Temple, *How I Raised Shirley Temple*, 14;

Foster, "Mrs. Temple on Bringing Up Shirley," 22; "Peewee's Progress," cover (*Time*), 37. For Shirley's memory of her first spanking by her mother, see Black, *Child Star*, 58. Only several years later did Gertrude Temple profess not to remember ever spanking her daughter. On theories and practices of punishing children in this period, see Grant, *Raising Baby by the Book*, 150–52.

51 Hurrell and Stine, *Hurrell Style*, 127.

52 Zeitlin, "Day on the Set with Shirley," 78; Joseph F. Dinneen, "Shirley Acclaimed by Boston," *Boston Globe*, July 30, 1938, 1. For similar views, see, for example, Ruth Biery, "We Disagree with Shirley's Mother," *Modern Screen*, September 1935, 26–27ff.; Michael Jackson, "Protecting the Future of the Greatest Little Star," *Photoplay*, March 1937, 26–27, 99–100.

53 Norman J. Zierold, *The Child Stars* (New York: Coward-McCann, 1965), 23.

54 David Emblidge, ed., *My Day: The Best of Eleanor Roosevelt's Acclaimed Newspaper Columns, 1936–1962* (New York: Da Capo Press, 2001), 27–28; Black, *Child Star*, 236–37 (emphasis in original).

55 Theodore Taylor, *Jule: The Story of Composer Jule Styne* (New York: Random House, 1979), 67, 69, 71.

56 "George F. Temple, Father and Manager of Shirley Temple," *Washington Post*, October 2, 1980, C4; Black, *Child Star*, 83.

57 Black, *Child Star*, 156–57.

58 Black, *Child Star*, 52; Cary, *Hollywood's Children*, 142. "You Are the Ideal of My Dreams" was written by Herbert Ingraham and published in 1910. Oliver Hardy popularized it in Laurel and Hardy's 1931 film *Beau Hunks*.

59 Cary, *Hollywood's Children*, 134.

60 Wilson, "Answer to Shirley Temple's Future," 69.

61 Foster, "Mrs. Temple on Bringing Up Shirley," 23.

62 Viviana Zelizer, *Pricing the Priceless Child: The Changing Social Value of Children* (Princeton: Princeton University Press, 1994), 97–112; Jacobson, *Raising Consumers*, esp. 56–92.

63 Cary, *Hollywood's Children*, 242–43.

64 "Coogan a 'Bad Boy,' His Mother Testifies," *New York Times*, April 19,

1938, 24; "Cinema: Kid," *Time*, May 2, 1938, 41; "Coogan Says Stepfather Bet $100 as He Risked $2," *New York Herald Tribune*, April 13, 1938, 16.

65 Black, *Child Star*, 80–83; Ben Maddox, "What Insiders Know about Shirley," *Screenland*, August 1939, 91. For reassurances of George Temple's careful stewardship of Shirley's earnings, see, e.g., Temple, "Bringing Up Shirley," 93–94; Temple, *How I Raised Shirley Temple*, 30; Sargent, "New Slant on Shirley," 82; "Peewee's Progress," 44; "Hedda Hopper's Hollywood," *Los Angeles Times*, April 25, 1940, 12. Jackie Coogan's father had made similar assurances as early as 1923. Diana Serra Cary, *Jackie Coogan: The World's Boy King: A Biography of Hollywood's Legendary Child Star* (Lanham, MD: Scarecrow Press, 2003), 99.

66 Gladys Hall, "Is Shirley Temple Going to Leave Us?" *Movie Mirror*, May 1940, 83.

57 Arlie Russell Hochschild, *The Managed Heart: Commercialization of Human Feeling* (Berkeley and Los Angeles: University of California Press, 1983), 7; Hochschild, *Managed Heart*, 20th anniv. ed. (Berkeley and Los Angeles: University of California Press, 2003), 199–207.

68 Milton Berle with Haskel Frankel, *Milton Berle: An Autobiography* (New York: Delacorte, 1974), 44, 67; Tom Goldrup and Jim Goldrup, *Growing Up on the Set: Interviews with 39 Former Child Actors of Classic Film and Television* (Jefferson, NC: McFarland, 2002), 65.

EPILOGUE: SHIRLEY VISITS ANOTHER PRESIDENT

1 Shirley Temple Black, *Child Star: An Autobiography* (New York: McGraw-Hill, 1988), 324–26, 340, 347–50; Gladys Hall, "Mrs. Temple Tells What Shirley Will Do," *Movie Mirror*, October 1940, 48.

2 During production of *Since You Went Away* in 1943, for example, David Selznick wrote, "I'm anxious to get the accent off this as a Temple vehicle and start hammering away at its tremendous cast." Rudy Behlmer, ed., *Memo from David O. Selznick* (New York: Viking, 1972), 327.

3 T.S. [Theodore Strauss], review of *Miss Annie Rooney*, *New York Times*, June 8, 1942, 11.

4 Bosley Crowther, review of *Kiss and Tell, New York Times*, October 26, 1945, 16; Crowther, review of *"Honeymoon, New York Times*, May 19, 1947, 27; Crowther, review of *That Hagen Girl, New York Times,* October 25, 1947, 13. Reagan testified before the committee on October 23, 1947. Cooper also testified on October 23, and Menjou on October 21, 1947.

5 Bosley Crowther, review of *Adventure in Baltimore, New York Times*, April 29, 1949, 27.

6 Black, *Child Star,* 377–79, 381, 383–84.

7 "And They Lived Happily," *Newsweek*, October 1, 1945, 32; Black, *Child Star*, 382, 385, 446; Dan Ford, *Pappy: The Life of John Ford* (Englewood Cliffs, NJ: Prentice-Hall, 1979), 217.

8 "Remembering Charles Alton Black," *Stanford Magazine*, November–December 2005, http://www.stanfordalumni.org/news/magazine/2005/novdec/classnotes/black.html; Black, *Child Star*, 449, 458–60, 475.

9 Black, *Child Star,* 479–87.

10 Black, *Child Star,* 486.

11 "Shirley Temple Pays a Call on President," *New York Times*, May 15, 1953, 19; Black, *Child Star,* 514; John Updike, "How to Love America and Leave It at the Same Time," in *Problems and Other Stories* (New York: Knopf, 1979), 44. The story first appeared in the August 19, 1972, issue of *The New Yorker*. Among the many books on postwar mass consumption, see esp. Lizabeth Cohen, *A Consumers' Republic: The Politics of Mass Consumption in Postwar America* (New York: Knopf, 2003). Philip Rieff, review of *The Organization Man,* by William H. Whyte Jr., *Partisan Review,* Spring 1957, 305.

INDEX

Page numbers in *italics* refer to illustrations.